D0909366

STATUTORY INTERPRETATION

By

SIR RUPERT CROSS, D.C.L., F.B.A.

Solicitor; Vinerian Professor of English Law in the University of Oxford and Fellow of All Souls College, Oxford

LONDON

BUTTERWORTHS

1976

England London — Butterworth & Co (Publishers) Ltd, 88 Kingsway, WC2B 6AB

Australia Sydney — Butterworths Pty Ltd, 271-273 Lane Cove Road, North Ryde, NSW 2113
Also at Melbourne, Brisbane, Adelaide and Perth

Canada Toronto — Butterworth & Co (Canada) Ltd, 2265 Midland Avenue, Scarborough, M1P 4S1

New Zealand Wellington — Butterworths of New Zealand Ltd, 33-35 Cumberland Place

South Africa Durban — Butterworth & Co (South Africa) (Pty) Ltd, 152-154 Gale Street

USA Boston — Butterworth (Publishers) Inc, 10 Tower Office Park, Woburn, Mass. 01801

Reprinted 1978
Reprinted 1981

ISBN 0 406 57016 7

Printed by Mansell (Bookbinders) Limited, Witham, Essex

To the memory of Lord Reid, one of the great judges of the twentieth century, to whose views on statutory interpretation this book owes so much

Preface

When reading for a law degree at Oxford in the early 1930s, I studied jurisprudence, a subject which, then as now, was commonly assumed to include statutory interpretation. I was told to write an essay criticising the English rules and I dutifully said my piece about the literalism of the Courts, their failure to implement the purpose of the statutes with which they dealt and, worst of all, their intransigent refusal to consult *travaux preparatoires*. All the time I was experiencing a malaise which, I am bound to confess, was not wholly set at rest by my tutor, with regard to the nature of the English rules of interpretation. What were they? Where were they stated? I then practised the law for a decade and it was as much as I could do to make sense of the day-to-day operation of the legislation that came my way. The mystery of the precise nature of the general rules of statutory interpretation remained unsolved.

When teaching law at Oxford in the 1950s and 1960s I treated my pupils as I had been treated and told them to write essays criticising the English rules governing the subject. By that time Willis's landmark article mentioned on p. 169 of this book had appeared in the Canadian Bar Review. Each and every pupil told me that there were three rules—the literal rule, the golden rule and the mischief rule, and that the Courts invoke whichever of them is believed to do justice in the particular case. I had, and still have, my doubts, but what was most disconcerting was the fact that whatever question I put to pupils or examinees elicited the same reply. Even if the question was What is meant by "the intention of parliament"? or What are the principal extrinsic aids to interpretation? back came the answers as of yore: "There are three rules of interpretation—the literal rule, the golden rule and the mischief rule." I was as much in the dark as I had been in my student days about the way in which the English rules should be formulated.

This book, an enlargement on lectures given from time to time at

Oxford, has been composed in order to clarify my own mind as much as anyone else's. It is intended for law students, but I hope that it may be found to be sufficiently brief to constitute spare time reading for any practitioner who likes to devote part of his spare time to the contemplation of the law.

Criticism from any source will be welcome, and it is not by way of anticipation of criticism that I say the following three things: there seemed to be no point in including a table of statutes; the selection of cases for citation in a book of this sort is a very subjective matter; and I have filled the book up with an inordinately large number of quotations. I doubt whether this shortcoming is adequately excused by the fact that it is shared with every book on statutory interpretation that I have come across. I must therefore apologise to, as well as thank, Mrs. Bryant, who then worked in the office of the Oxford Law Faculty, for having produced an admirable typescript from my dictation on to tapes. I tremble to think of the number of occasions on which the words "Colon, indented quotation" must have reverberated in her ears. The publishers have, as always, been very tolerant of my dilatoriness.

RUPERT CROSS
May 1976

Table of Contents

Page

Preface v
Table of Cases ix

INTRODUCTION 1

CHAPTER I— HISTORICAL 8

CHAPTER II—JURISPRUDENTIAL 17

A. Blackstone 17
B. Bentham 20
C. Austin 23
D. Gray 25
E. The Canons of Interpretation 27
F. The Intention of Parliament 34
G. The Meaning of Interpretation 40

CHAPTER III—THE BASIC RULES STATED 42
A. Context 44
B. Evidence 52
C. The Different Kinds of Meaning 56

CHAPTER IV—THE BASIC RULES ILLUSTRATED .. 61
A. Choice Between Ordinary Meanings in the Context .. 61
B Choice Between an Ordinary and a Technical Meaning 64
C. Fringe Meaning and the Extent of General Words .. 67
D. Choice Between Primary and Secondary Meaning .. 74
E. Reading Words In and Out of a Statute 84

CHAPTER V—INTERNAL AIDS TO CONSTRUCTION 99
A. Enacting Parts of the Same Statute 99
B. Other Parts of the Same Statute 107
C. Rules of Language 115

CHAPTER VI—EXTERNAL AIDS TO CONSTRUCTION 122
A. Miscellaneous 122
B. Legislative History 129

CHAPTER VII—PRESUMPTIONS 142
A. Presumptions Generally 142
B. Presumptions against Unclear Changes in the Law .. 145
C. Presumptions against Retrospective Operations .. 153

CHAPTER VIII—LEGISLATIVE PROPOSALS AND CONCLUDING QUESTIONS 156
A. Legislative Proposals 156
B. Concluding Questions 164

INDEX 173

Table of Cases

A *Page*

Abley *v.* Dale (1851), 11 C.B. 378 170
Abrahams *v.* Cavey, [1968] 1 Q.B. 479; [1967] 3 All E.R. 179 61
Adler *v.* George, [1964] 2 Q.B. 7; [1964] 1 All E.R. 628 .. .. 32, 52, 84
Alexander *v.* Tredegar Iron and Coal Co., Ltd., [1944] K.B. 390 117
Allen *v.* Emmerson, [1944] 1 K.B. 362; [1944] 1 All E.R. 344 116, 117, 119
Allen *v.* Thorn Electrical Industries, Ltd., [1968] 1 Q.B. 487; [1967] 2 All E.R. 1137, C.A. 148, 149, 153
Alleson *v.* Marsh (1690), 2 Vent. 181 127
Altrincham Electric Supply, Ltd. *v.* Sale Urban District Council (1936), 154 L.T. 379, H.L. 82, 95, 97, 98
Applin *v.* Race Relations Board, [1975] A.C. 259; [1974] 2 All E.R. 73, H.L. 73
Ashbury Railway Carriage and Iron Co. *v.* Riche (1875), L.R. 7 H.L. 653, H.L 117
Assam Railways and Trading Co., Ltd. *v.* Inland Revenue Comrs., [1935] A.C. 445, H.L. 136,138
Athlumney, *Re*, [1898] 2 Q.B. 547 153
A.-G. *v.* Beauchamp, [1920] 1 K.B. 650 86
A.-G. *v.* Edison Telephone Co. (1880), 6 Q.B.D. 244 45
A.-G. *v.* Lockwood (1842), 9 M.W. 378 30
A.-G. *v.* Prince Ernest Augustus of Hanover, [1957] A.C. 436, H.L. .. 42, 47, 51, 109, 128, 130
A.-G. *v.* Sillem (1864), 2 H. & C. 431 10
A.-G. for Ontario *v.* A.-G. for Canada, [1947] A.C. 127, P.C. 46

B

Ball *v.* Richard Thomas and Baldwins, Ltd., [1968] 1 All E.R. 389, C.A. 69
Bank of England *v.* Vagliano Brothers, [1891] A.C. 107 5
Bank of Toronto *v.* Lambe (1887), 12 App. Cas. 575, P.C. 125
Barnard *v.* Gorman, [1941] A.C. 378, H.L. 77, 79, 82, 84
Barras *v.* Aberdeen Fishing and Steam Trawling Co., Ltd., [1933] A.C. 402, H.L. 147
Bassett *v.* Bassett (1744), 3 Atk. 203 125
Becke *v.* Smith (1836), 2 M. & W. 191 15
Bennett *v.* Chappell, [1966] Ch. 391; [1965] 3 All E.R. 130, C.A. 146
Beswick *v.* Beswick, [1968] A.C. 58, H.L. 130, 131, 135
Bidie, *Re*, [1948] 2 All E.R. 995, C.A. 44, 58, 84
Black-Clawson International, Ltd. *v.* Papierwerke Waldhof-Aschaffenburg A.G., [1975] 1 All E.R. 810, H.L. .. 39, 130, 131, 132, 133, 136, 137, 138, 145
Blackburn *v.* Flavelle (1881), 6 App. Cas. 628, P.C. 120
Blyth *v.* Blyth, [1966] A.C. 643, H.L. 155, 162

Page
Boaler, *Re*, [1915] 1 K.B. 21, C.A. 112
Bourne *v.* Norwich Crematorium, Ltd., [1967] 2 All E.R. 576 64, 118, 164
Bowers *v.* Gloucester Corpn., [1963] 1 Q.B. 881 52
Bracey *v.* Read, [1963] Ch. 88; [1962] 3 All E.R. 472 100
Brett *v.* Brett (1826), 3 Add. 210 .. .. 48, 111
Brown (R. F.) & Co., Ltd. *v.* T. and J. Harrison (1927), 43 T.L.R. 394 .. 89
Brutus *v.* Cozens, [1973] A.C. 854; [1972] 2 All E.R. 1297, H.L. 52
Bulmer (H. P.), Ltd. *v.* J. Bollinger S.A., [1974] 2 All E.R. 1226, C.A. .. 171

C

Callady *v.* Pilkington (1694), 12 Mod. 513 9
Camden (Marquess) *v.* Inland Revenue Comrs., [1914] 1 K.B. 641, C.A. .. 53
Campbell College, Belfast (Governors) *v.* Valuation Comrs. for Northern Ireland, [1964] 2 All E.R. 705, H.L. 127
Candy Maid Confections, Ltd. *v.* Customs and Excise Comrs., [1969] 1 Ch. 611; [1968] 3 All E.R. 773 68
Carson *v.* Carson, [1964] 1 All E.R. 681 .. .. 154, 155
Carter *v.* Bradbeer, [1975] 3 All E.R. 158, H.L. 55, 104, 165, 168
Cartledge *v.* E. Joppling and Sons, Ltd., [1963] A.C. 758; [1963] 1 All E.R. 341 .. .. 93, 94
Castioni, *Re*, [1891] 1 Q.B. 149 .. .. 60, 125
Cathcart, *Re*, *Ex parte* Campbell (1869), 5 Ch. App. 603 146
Central Press Photos, Ltd. *v.* Department of Employment and Productivity, [1970] 3 All E.R. 775, C.A. 54
Chandler *v.* Director of Public Prosecutions, [1964] A.C. 763, H.L. .. 113, 123
Charter *v.* Race Relations Board, [1973] A.C. 868; [1973] 1 All E.R. 512, H.L. 72, 73
Cheng *v.* Governor of Pentonville Prison, [1973] A.C. 931, H.L. 56
Chorlton *v.* Lings (1869), L.R. 4 C.P. 373 68
Christopherson *v.* Lotinga (1864), 15 C.B.N.S. 809 15
Claydon *v.* Green (1868), L.R. 3 C.P. 511 127
Colchester (Lord) *v.* Kewney (1867), L.R. 1 Ex. Ch. 368 66
Coleridge-Taylor *v.* Novello & Co., Ltd., [1938] Ch. 608; [1938] 2 All E.R. 318 3
Corkery *v.* Carpenter, [1951] 1 K.B. 102; [1950] 2 All E.R. 745 68
Cory and Sons, Ltd. *v.* Inland Revenue Comrs., [1965] A.C. 1088, H.L. .. 152
Cow *v.* Casey, [1949] 1 K.B. 474; [1949] 1 All E.R. 197, C.A. 145
Coward *v.* Motor Insurers' Bureau, [1963] 1 Q.B. 259; [1962] 1 All E.R. 531, C.A. 100
Customs and Excise Comrs. *v.* Savoy Hotel, Ltd., [1966] 2 All E.R. 299 .. 68
Customs and Excise Comrs. *v.* Thorn Electrical Industries, Ltd., [1975] 3 All E.R. 881, H.L... .. .. 154, 155
Cutler *v.* Wandsworth Stadium, Ltd., [1949] A.C. 398, C.A. 163

D

D.M.L., *Re*, [1965] Ch. 1113 100
Daly *v.* Cannon, [1954] 1 All E.R. 315 68
Dapueto *v.* James and Wyllie & Co. (1874), L.R. 5 P.C. 482 6
Dean *v.* Wiesengrund, [1955] 2 Q.B. 120, C.A. 121
Devonshire (Duke) *v.* O'Connor (1890), 24 Q.B.D. 468, C.A.. 114
Dilworth *v.* Stamps Comr., [1899] A.C. 99 103
Director of Public Prosecutions *v.* Hester, [1973] A.C. 296 .. .. 60, 85
Director of Public Prosecutions *v.* Ottewell, [1970] A.C. 642, H.L. 77, 132, 150
Director of Public Prosecutions *v.* Schildcamp, [1971] A.C. 1, H.L. .. 49, 108, 112, 114, 158

Page

Dockers' Labour Club and Institute, Ltd. *v.* Race Relations Board, [1974] 3 All E.R. 592, H.L. 27, 73, 160
Draper (C. E. B.) & Sons, Ltd. *v.* Edward Turner and Sons, Ltd., [1964] 3 All E.R. 148, C.A. 4
Dyson Holdings, Ltd. *v.* Fox, [1975] 3 All E.R. 1030, C.A. 46

E

Ealing London Borough *v.* Race Relations Board, [1972] A.C. 342, H.L. 35, 62
Eastman Photographic Materials Co., Ltd. *v.* Comptroller General of Patents, [1898] A.C. 571 .. .. 136, 137
Eddis *v.* Chichester Constable, [1969] 2 Ch. 345; [1969] 2 All E.R. 912, C.A. 32, 86, 95
Ellerman Lines *v.* Murray, [1931] A.C. 126, H.L. .. 139, 140, 141, 144, 159
Engineering Industry Training Board *v.* Samuel Talbot (Engineers), Ltd., [1969] 2 Q.B. 270, C.A. 49
Escoigne Properties, Ltd. *v.* Inland Revenue Comrs., [1958] A.C. 549, H.L. 56, 122
Eton College *v.* Minister of Agriculture, [1964] Ch. 274; [1962] 3 All E.R. 290 4
Eyston *v.* Studd (1574), 2 Plowd. 459 24

F

Farrell *v.* Alexander, [1975] 3 W.L.R. 642 150
Federal Steam Navigation Co., Ltd. *v.* Department of Trade and Industry, [1974] 2 All E.R. 97, H.L. 43, 89, 90, 94, 167
Fisher *v.* Bell, [1961] 1 Q.B. 394; [1960] 3 All E.R. 731 .. 11, 65, 151, 164, 167, 168
Fisher *v.* Raven, [1964] A.C. 210; [1963] 2 All E.R. 389, H.L. .. 111, 112

G

Gammans *v.* Ekins, [1950] 2 K.B. 328; [1950] 2 All E.R. 140, C.A. .. 46
Gelberg *v.* Miller, [1961] 1 All E.R. 291, H.L. 101
Gibson and Johnson *v.* Minet and Fector (1791), H. Bl. 569 31
Great Western Rail. Co. *v.* S.S. Mostyn (owners), [1928] A.C. 57, H.L. .. 83
Greenberg *v.* Inland Revenue Comrs., [1972] A.C. 109, H.L. 152
Gregory *v.* Fearn, [1953] 2 All E.R. 559, C.A. 116
Grey *v.* Pearson (1857), 6 H.L. Cas. 61 .. .. 15, 74

H

Hardwick Game Farm *v.* Suffolk Agricultural and Poultry Producers Association, Ltd., [1966] 1 All E.R. 309, C.A. 125
Harris *v.* Quine (1869), L.R. 4 Q.B. 653 137
Hebbert *v.* Purchas (1871), L.R. 3 P.C. 605 127
Heydon's Case (1584), 3 Co. Rep. 7a 9, 10, 11, 13, 16, 19, 50
Hill *v.* East and West India Dock Co. (1884), 9 App. Cas. 448, H.L. .. 88

I

Income Tax Special Purposes Comr. *v.* Pemsel, [1891] A.C. 531, H.L. .. 96
Inland Revenue Comrs. *v.* Ayrshire Employers' Mutual Insurance Association, Ltd., [1946] 1 All E.R. 637 .. .. 92, 93
Inland Revenue Comrs. *v.* Hinchy, [1960] A.C. 748, H.L. .. 75, 76, 99, 114
Inland Revenue Comrs. *v.* Ross and Coulter, [1948] 1 All E.R. 616 .. 152

Page

J

Jamieson *v.* Inland Revenue Comrs., [1964] A.C. 1445, H.L. 152
Jenkins *v.* Inland Revenue Comrs., [1944] 2 All E.R. 491, C.A. 125
Jenner *v.* Allen West & Co., Ltd., [1959] 2 All E.R. 115, C.A. 65
Jennings *v.* Kelley, [1940] A.C. 206, H.L. 106
Jones *v.* Director of Public Prosecutions, [1962] A.C. 635, H.L. 29
Jones *v.* Smart (1784), 1 Term. Rep. 44 10

K

Kensington Borough Council *v.* Walters, [1960] 1 Q.B. 361; [1959] 3 All E.R. 652 83
Kirkness *v.* John Hudson & Co., Ltd., [1955] A.C. 696, H.L. 77
Kruhlak *v.* Kruhlak, [1958] 2 Q.B. 32 70

L

Leach *v.* R., [1912] A.C. 305, H.L. 146
Lee *v.* Showmen's Guild of Great Britain, [1952] 2 Q.B. 329, C.A. .. 125, 148
Letang *v.* Cooper, [1965] 1 Q.B. 232; [1964] 2 All E.R. 929, C.A. .. 119
Lindsay *v.* Cundy (1876), 1 Q.B.D. 348 104
Lockwood, *Re*, [1958] Ch. 231; [1957] 3 All E.R. 520 .. .. 90, 91, 95, 166
London and India Docks *v.* Thames Steam and Lighterage Co., Ltd., [1909] A.C. 7, H.L. 123
London and North Eastern Rail Co. *v.* Berriman, [1946] A.C. 278; [1946] 1 All E.R. 255, H.L. 55, 63, 151
London County Council *v.* Central Land Board, [1958] 3 All E.R. 676 .. 126
London County Council *v.* Cutts, [1961] 1 All E.R. 600 66
London Transport Executive *v.* Betts, [1959] A.C. 231, H.L. 33
Longford, The (1889), 14 P.D. 34 45
Luby *v.* Newcastle-upon-Tyne Corpn., [1965] 1 Q.B. 214; [1964] 3 All E.R. 169, C.A. 115
Luke *v.* Inland Revenue Comrs., [1963] A.C. 557, H.L. 31, 79, 82, 165, 170

M

MacManaway, *Re*, [1951] A.C. 161, H.L. 129
McMillan *v.* Crouch, [1972] 3 All E.R. 61, H.L. 160
Magor and St. Mellons Rural District Council *v.* Newport Corpn., [1952] A.C. 189; [1951] 2 All E.R. 839, H.L. .. 23, 33, 37, 39, 86, 167, 171
Maunsell *v.* Olins, [1975] A.C. 373, H.L. 29, 43, 51, 66, 74, 145
Metropolitan Film Studios, Ltd. *v.* Twickenham Film Studios, Ltd., [1962] 3 All E.R. 508 148
Midland Rail Co. and Kettering, Thrapston and Huntingdon Rail Co. *v.* Robinson (1890), 15 App. Cas. 19 124
Miller *v.* Taylor (1769), 4 Burr. 2303 134
Mills *v.* Cooper, [1967] 2 Q.B. 459; [1967] 2 All E.R. 100 62
Mitchell *v.* Torrup (1766), Park. 227 14
Muir *v.* Keay (1875), L.R. 10 Q.B. 594 118

N

Nairn *v.* St. Andrews University, [1909] A.C. 147, H.L. 68
Newberry *v.* Simmonds, [1961] 2 Q.B. 345; [1961] 2 All E.R. 318 67
Nisbet *v.* Rayne and Burn, [1910] 2 K.B. 689, C.A. 58, 62
Nokes *v.* Doncaster Amalgamated Collieries, Ltd., [1940] A.C. 1014; [1940] 3 All E.R. 549, H.L. 69

Page

No-Nail Cases Proprietary, Ltd. *v.* No-Nail Boxes, Ltd., [1944] 1 K.B. 629 105
Norwhale, The, [1975] Q.B. 589; [1975] 2 All E.R. 501 110
Nuth *v.* Tamplin (1881), 8 Q.B.D. 247, C.A. 82

P

Palmer *v.* Snow, [1900] 1 Q.B. 725 116
Pengelley *v.* Bell Punch Co., Ltd., [1964] 2 All E.R. 945, C.A. .. 118, 119
Phillips *v.* Pamaby, [1934] 2 K.B. 299 128
Pinner *v.* Everett, [1969] 3 All E.R. 257, H.L. .. 29, 71, 72, 74, 168; 170
Platt *v.* Sheriffs of London (1550), 1 Plowd. 35 25
Pratt, *Re Ex parte* Pratt (1884), 12 Q.B.D. 334 45
Prophet *v.* Platt Brothers & Co., Ltd., [1961] 2 All E.R. 644, C.A. .. 54, 65
Pugh *v.* Pugh, [1951] P. 482; [1951] 2 All E.R. 680 4
Pyx Granite Co., Ltd. *v.* Minister of Housing and Local Government, [1960] A.C. 260; [1959] 3 All E.R. 1, H.L. 147

R

R. *v.* Allen (1872), L.R. 1 C.C.R. 367 100
R. *v.* Anderson, [1972] 1 Q.B. 304; [1971] 3 All E.R. 1152, C.A. .. 54
R. *v.* Bates, [1952] 2 All E.R. 842, C.C.A. 109, 112
R. *v.* Bishop of Oxford (1879) 4 Q.B.D. 525, H.L. 134
R. *v.* Bow Road Justices (Domestic Proceedings Court), *Ex parte* Adedibva, [1968] 2 Q.B. 572, C.A. 146, 147
R. *v.* Brixton Prison Governor, *Ex parte* Naranjansingh, [1962] 1 Q.B. 211; [1961] 2 All E.R. 565 114
R. *v.* Calder and Boyars, Ltd., [1969] 1 Q.B. 151; [1968] 3 All E.R. 644, C.A. 54
R. *v.* Caledonian Railway (1850), 16 Q.B. 19 120
R. *v.* Casement, [1917] 1 K.B. 98, C.C.A. 126
R. *v.* Chapman, [1931] 2 K.B. 606 150
R. *v.* City of London Court Judge, [1892] 1 Q.B. 273 .. .. .. 30, 43, 82
R. *v.* Cleworth (1864), 4 B. & S. 927 116
R. *v.* Collingwood and Tomkins (1848), 12 Q.B. 681 70
R. *v.* Ettridge, [1909] 2 K.B. 24, C.C.A... 97
R. *v.* Forest Justices, *Ex parte* Dallaire, [1962] 2 Q.B. 629; [1961] 3 All E.R. 1138 101
R. *v.* Gould, [1968] 2 Q.B. 65; [1968] 1 All E.R. 849, C.A. 107
R. *v.* Governor of Leeds Prison, *Ex parte* Stafford, [1964] 2 Q.B. 625; [1964] 1 All E.R. 610 106
R. *v.* Governor of Pentonville Prison, *Ex parte* Cheng, [1973] A.C. 931; [1973] 2 All E.R. 204, H.L. 123
R. *v.* Hare, [1934] 1 K.B. 354, C.C.A. 112
R. *v.* Harris (1836), 7 C. & P. 416 .. .. 10, 151
R. *v.* Hertford College, Oxford (1878), 3 Q.B.D. 693 134
R. *v.* Liggetts-Finlay Drug Stores, Ltd., [1919] 3 W.W.R. 1025 60
R. *v.* Loxdale [1758], 1 Burr. 445.. 128
R. *v.* Luffe (1807), 8 East 193 70
R. *v.* Munks, [1964] 1 Q.B. 304; [1963] 3 All E.R. 757, C.C.A. .. 10, 52, 151
R. *v.* Oakes, [1959] 2 Q.B. 350, C.C.A. 90, 94
R. *v.* Peters (1886), 16 Q.B.D. 636 .. .. 54, 124
R. *v.* Prince (1875), L.R. 2 C.C.R. 154 102
R. *v.* St. Mary, Whitechapel (1848), 12 Q.B. 120 .. .. .. 153, 154
R. *v.* Sedgley Inhabitants (1831), 2 B. & Ad. 65 120
R. *v.* Stamford, [1972] 2 Q.B. 391; [1972] 2 All E.R. 430, C.A. .. 54
R. *v.* Stocks, [1921] 2 K.B. 119, C.C.A. 106, 107
R. *v.* Titterton, [1895] 2 Q.B. 61 128
R. *v.* Tolson (1889), 23 Q.B.D. 168 .. .. 106, 107, 143
R. *v.* Vasey and Lapley, [1905] 2 K.B. 748 96

Page

R. *v.* Webb, [1964] 1 Q.B. 357; [1963] 3 All E.R. 177, C.C.A. 85
R. *v.* Westminster Betting Licensing Committee, *Ex parte* Peabody Donation Fund, [1963] 2 Q.B. 750; [1963] 2 All E.R. 544 129
R. *v.* Wheat, [1921] 2 K.B. 119, C.C.A. 106, 107
Rhondda's (Viscountess) Claim, [1922] 2 A.C. 339, H.L. 68
Richard Thomas and Baldwins, Ltd. *v.* Cummings, [1955] A.C. 321, H.L. 80, 81, 82, 170
River Wear Comrs. *v.* Adamson (1877), 2 App. Cas. 743 .. .. 82, 84
Royal Crown Derby Porcelain, Ltd. *v.* Raymond Russell, [1949] 2 K.B. 417, C.A. 147

S

Sagnata Investments, Ltd. *v.* Norwich Corpn., [1971] 2 Q.B. 614, C.A. .. 135
Sakhuja *v.* Allen, [1973] A.C. 152; [1972] 2 All E.R. 311, H.L. 72
Sales-matic, Ltd. *v.* Hinchliffe, [1959] 3 All E.R. 401 150
Salmon *v.* Duncombe (1886), 11 App. Cas. 627, P.C. 90, 95, 96, 166
Saloman *v.* Saloman & Co., Ltd., [1897] A.C. 22, H.L. 36
Salomon *v.* Customs and Excise Comrs., [1967] 2 Q.B. 116 140
Sandiman *v.* Breach (1827), 5 L.J.O.S. K.B. 298 116
Santos *v.* Santos, [1972] Fam. 247; [1972] 2 All E.R. 246, C.A. 160
Savoy Hotel Co. *v.* London County Council, [1900] 1 Q.B. 665 104
Seaford Court Estates, Ltd. *v.* Asher, [1949] 2 K.B. 481 .. .. 27, 33, 38
Seward *v.* Vera Cruz (1884), 10 App. Cas. 59 3
Sigsworth, *Re*, [1935] Ch. 89 .. .. 28, 143
Skinner *v.* Shew, [1893] 1 Ch. 413 117
Smart *v.* Allan, [1963] 1 Q.B. 291; [1962] 3 All E.R. 893, C.A. 67
Smith *v.* East Elloe, [1956] A.C. 736; [1956] 1 All E.R. 855, H.L. 143
South Eastern Rail. Co. *v.* Railway Comrs. (1881), 50 L.J. Q.B. 201 134
Stephens *v.* Cuckfield Rural District Council, [1960] 2 Q.B. 373, C.A. .. 113
Stockport Ragged Industrial and Reformatory Schools, *Re*, [1898] 2 Ch. 687, C.A. 116
Stowell *v.* Lord Zouch (1569), 1 Plowd. 369 13
Stradling *v.* Morgan (1560), 1 Plowd. 199 .. .. .. 8, 9, 11, 50, 68
Summers (E. G.) *v.* Salford Corpn., [1943] A.C. 283, H.L. 165
Sussex Peerage Claim (1884), 11 Cl. & Fin. 85 .. .. 4, 13, 16, 44, 51, 132
Sutherland Publishing Co., Ltd. *v.* Caxton Publishing Co., Ltd., [1938] Ch. 174 88
Swart and Nicol *v.* De Kock 1951, 3 S.A. 589 42

T

Thompson *v.* Dibdin, [1912] A.C. 533, H.L. 105
Thompson *v.* Goold & Co., [1910] A.C. 409, H.L. 16
Thompson *v.* Thompson, [1956] P. 414; [1956] 1 All E.R. 603 .. 80, 82
Trim Joint District School Board of Management *v.* Kelly, [1914] A.C. 637, H.L. 58, 62
Tuck and Sons *v.* Priester (1887), 19 Q.B.D. 629, C.A. 150

U

United Dominions Trust, Ltd. *v.* Kirkwood, [1966] 2 Q.B. 431, C.A. .. 126
United Society *v.* Eagle Bank (1829), 7 Conn. 457 128
United States *v.* American Trucking Association, 310 U.S. 534 132
Unwin *v.* Hanson, [1891] 2 Q.B. 115, C.A. 53, 65

Page

V

Vacher and Sons, Ltd. *v.* London Society of Compositors, [1913] A.C. 107, H.L. 112
Vera Cruz, The (1884), 10 App. Cas. 59, H.L. 69
Vickers, Sons, and Maxim, Ltd. *v.* Evans, [1910] A.C. 444, H.L. 16

W

Wainwright, *Re* (1843), 1 Ph. 258 .. .. 86, 95, 167, 168
Walton, *Ex parte* (1881), 17 Ch. D. 746, C.A. 87, 95
Ward *v.* Holman, [1964] 2 Q.B. 580: [1964] 2 All E.R. 729 .. 109, 110, 157
Warner *v.* Metropolitan Police Comr., [1969] 2 A.C. 256, H.L. 135
West Derby Union *v.* Metropolitan Life Assurance Society, [1897] A.C. 647, H.L. 106
West Ham Church Wardens and Overseers *v.* Fourth City Mutual Building Society, [1892] 1 Q.B. 654 3
Whiteley *v.* Chappell (1868), L.R. 4 Q.B. 147 .. .. .. 151, 164, 165
Whitton *v.* Garner, [1965] 1 All E.R. 70.. 70
Wiltshire *v.* Barrett, [1966] 1 Q.B. 312, C.A. 78, 79, 84
Workington Harbour and Dock Board *v.* S.S. Towerfield (Owners), [1951] A.C. 112, H.L... .. .. 83, 143

Z

Zimmerman *v.* Grossman, [1972] 1 Q.B. 167, C.A. 147

Introduction

This book is concerned with the major contemporary canons of statutory interpretation, but the subject is best approached through history and jurisprudence, matters which are dealt with in the first two chapters. The basic rules are set out and illustrated in Chapters III and IV which enlarge on some points made in Chapters I and II. The essential rule is that words should generally be given the meaning which the normal speaker of the English language would understand them to bear in their context at the time when they were used. It would be difficult to over-estimate the importance of this rule because the vast majority of statutes never come before the courts for interpretation. If it were not a known fact that, in the ordinary case in which the normal user of the English language would have no doubt about the meaning of the statutory words, the courts will give those words their ordinary meaning, it would be impossible for lawyers and other experts to act and advise on the statute in question with confidence. The reference to lawyers and other experts is made advisedly because we would be deceiving ourselves if we were to imagine that some form of expertise is not necessary for the comprehension of most statutes; indeed, the ordinary meaning rule is qualified so as to allow for the application of a technical meaning when the words in question are used in a statute dealing with a particular trade or business. The regulation of most of the affairs with which they deal is such a complex matter that it is unlikely that it will ever be possible to draft Acts of Parliament in such a way that a significant number of them will be comprehensible to the ordinary layman; but this unfortunate fact should not be allowed to depreciate the importance of the ordinary meaning rule. Some criticism of the canons of statutory interpretation are couched in terms which suggest that their authors do not realise that it is only a very small proportion of the statute book that ever comes before the courts.

Even when full allowance has been made for the context, there will inevitably be a number of occasions on which doubt may legitimately be entertained on the question of the ordinary meaning of certain statutory provisions. Drafting is not always as clear as it might be and, owing to the lack of human prescience, there will always be cases for which inadequate provision is made by the statute. Valuable assistance may often be derived from various aids to interpretation which are discussed in Chapters V and VI. Over the years the courts have acted on certain presumptions which sometimes help in doubtful cases. For example, when it is unclear whether the conduct of the accused comes within a criminal statute, there is a presumption in favour of a narrow construction which would result in an acquittal; or, where one interpretation would produce an unjust or inconvenient result and another would not have these effects, there is a presumption in favour of the latter. These presumptions are only guides, and two of them may point in different directions in the same case, but they certainly have their uses; the more important of them are discussed in Chapter VII.

The emphasis which has been placed upon the merits of the plain meaning rule must not be taken to suggest that anything in the nature of an attitude of complacency with regard to the contemporary canons of statutory interpretation is justified. They form the subject of a Law Commission paper[1] containing legislative proposals which are discussed in Chapter VIII. Statutory drafting is, and almost always has been, under attack (much of which is unjustified). It is the principle subject of a report entitled The Preparation of Legislation, produced by a committee chaired by Sir David Renton;[2] some of its proposals are also considered in Chapter VIII. Over and above the specific points touched on in the proposals of these two official publications, a number of more general questions are raised in Chapter VIII. Do the courts interpret statutes too narrowly without adequate regard to the social purpose of the legislation? Are they unduly timorous when confronted with an obvious mistake or omission in a particular statute? Is their approach to interpretation of statutes designed to affect social change too conservative? These questions lose none of their interest even if it is the case, as it probably is, that any deficiencies which their discussion may reveal can hardly be remedied by legislation. One of the problems of the day is how to convey messages to judges otherwise than by statute. Lord WILBERFORCE may well have been right when he doubted whether law reform can really grapple with statutory interpretation. He said "it is a matter of educating the judges and practitioners and hoping that the work is better done".[3] The author must at once disclaim any intention of attempting

[1] The Interpretation of Statutes (Law Comm. 21, Scott. Law Comm. 11).
[2] Cmnd. 6953 1975. [3] 277 H.L. Deb. Ser. 5, col. 1254, 6th November 1966.

to do any such thing in this little book which is intended more for the student than for the practitioner.

Although the book is only seriously concerned with the major contemporary canons of statutory interpretation, there are certain other matters which are generally mentioned in works of this nature. They relate to the operation of statutes and the different kinds of statute. The rest of this introduction is devoted to a very brief and very elementary discussion of them. The matters to be considered under the head of the operation of statutes relate to their coming into force, repeal and territorial extent.

At common law statutes came into effect on the first day of the parliamentary session in which they were enacted unless there was a provision to the contrary. This was the outcome of a fiction according to which all business was done on the first day of the session. It could produce grossly unjust results because a statute passed on the last day of a session was legally deemed to have been passed on the first day and therefore had retrospective effect in fact. The common law rule was abolished by the Acts of Parliament (Commencement) Act 1793 under which statutes come into force on the day on which they receive the Royal assent in the absence of a provision to the contrary. The endorsement by the Clerk of the Parliaments on the Act, immediately after its title, of the date of the Royal assent forms part of the Act. Express provisions in the Act with regard to the date of coming into force of the whole or any part of it are very common. When the two differ, the words "after the passing of this Act" refer to the date endorsed by the clerk to the Parliament and not to the date on which the Act comes into force.[4] There is no doctrine of desuetude in English law, so a statute never ceases to be in force merely because it is obsolete. Normally there must be an express repeal, but the whole or part of an enactment may be impliedly repealed by a later statute.

> "The test of whether there has been a repeal by implication by subsequent legislation is this: are the provisions of a later Act so inconsistent with, or repugnant to, the provisions of an earlier Act that the two cannot stand together."[5]

The fact that two provisions overlap is therefore not enough, and general words in a later enactment do not repeal earlier statutes dealing with a special subject. Accordingly it was held in *Seward* v. *Vera Cruz* that the Admiralty Court Act 1861 which conferred jurisdiction *in rem* over claims for damage done by any ship did not confer jurisdic-

---

[4] *Coleridge-Taylor* v. *Novello & Co., Ltd.*, [1938] Ch. 608; [1938] 2 All E.R. 318.

[5] *West Ham Church Wardens and Overseers* v. *Fourth City Mutual Building Society*, [1892] 1 Q.B. 654, at p. 658, *per* A. L. SMITH, J.

tion on the Court of Admiralty over claims under the Fatal Accidents Act 1846.[6] The common law rule was that where an Act was repealed and the repealing Act was in its turn repealed, the first Act was revived unless the repealing Act manifested an intention to the contrary; but where an Act passed after 1850 repeals a repealing enactment, "it shall not be construed as reviving any enactment previously repealed, unless words are added reviving that enactment".[7]

The general rule with regard to territorial extent is "that an Act of Parliament only applies to transactions within the United Kingdom and not to transactions outside".[8] This is, however, no more than a general rule for, although statutes are almost always equally binding on British subjects and foreigners resident in England, there are many cases in which they have been held to bind British subjects or British domiciliaries abroad. Notable instances are the Royal Marriage Act 1772[9] and the Age of Marriage Act 1929. Under this statute marriages between two persons either of whom is under 16 are void. In *Pugh* v. *Pugh*[10] it was held, in accordance with the general principles of English private international law, that a marriage in Austria between a British subject, domiciled in England, and a Hungarian girl of fifteen, domiciled in Austria, was void although it was valid by Austrian and Hungarian law. In general the jurisdiction of the English criminal courts is confined to crimes committed in this country, but there are exceptions applicable to British subjects, murder[11] and bigamy,[12] for example. It is a commonplace for statutes to provide that they shall not extend to Scotland or Northern Ireland, but complaints are sometimes made that too much is left to implication in a case, for instance, where an Act must be treated as confined to England and Wales because it amends an Act which was similarly restricted.[13]

A distinction is drawn between public and private Acts. A public Act relates to some matter of public policy, while a private Act relates to the affairs of some individual or body in a matter which is not of public concern. The only clear practical importance of the distinction relates to the law of evidence and even that is minimal nowadays. Someone who wishes to rely on the provisions of a public Act does not have to produce any special kind of copy whereas private Acts

---

[6] (1884), 10 App. Cas. 59.

[7] Interpretation Act 1889, s. 11 (1). For an example of the common law rule, see *Eton College* v. *Minister of Agriculture*, [1964] Ch. 274; [1962] 3 All E.R. 290.

[8] *C. E. B. Draper & Sons, Ltd.* v. *Edward Turner & Sons, Ltd.*, [1964] 3 All E.R. 148, at p. 159, *per* LORD DENNING, M.R.

[9] *Sussex Peerage Claim* (1884), 11 Cl. & Fin. 85.

[10] [1951] P. 482; [1951] 2 All E.R. 680.

[11] Offences Against the Person Act 1861, s. 9.

[12] *Ibid.*, s. 57.

[13] Preparation of Legislation 6.11.

must be proved by production of a Queen's Printer's copy or, if they have not been printed, by an examined or certified copy of the original. Section 9 of the Interpretation Act 1889 provides that every Act passed after 1850 shall be a public Act and judicially noticed as such unless the contrary is expressly provided by the Act. Some of the older cases show a tendency to construe private Acts more strictly than public Acts,[14] but the distinction is of no importance in relation to the general law of interpretation.

A distinction of greater importance in this field is that between consolidating and codifying statutes. A consolidating statute is one which collects the statutory provisions relating to a particular topic, and embodies them in a single Act of Parliament, making only minor amendments and improvements. A codifying statute is one which purports to state exhaustively the whole of the law on a particular subject (the common law as well as previous statutory provisions).[15] An example of a consolidating statute is the Matrimonial Causes Act 1973, while the Bills of Exchange Act 1882 is one of the comparatively few instances of a codifying statute. The importance of the distinction lies in the courts' treatment of the previous case law, the existence of special procedural provisions with regard to consolidating statutes and the existence of a presumption that they do not change the law.

The authorities on previous statutory provisions consolidated in a later enactment retain their force as precedents, whereas recourse should only be had to the previous authorities on a codifying statute in cases in which the construction is doubtful or in order to settle a dispute about the state of the previous law.[16] There would not be much point in codifying the common law if previous cases could be invoked to cast doubt on the clear words of the code.

The Consolidation of Enactments (Procedure) Act 1949 lays down a special procedure, allowing only for minor amendments in the consolidated provisions of the relevant statutes. Since 1965 there has existed a procedure whereby consolidation effected by the Law Commissions, which may contain amendments that are not merely minor, can be placed before the relevant joint committee of both Houses of Parliament with a view to prompt enactment. It follows that the presumption that consolidating statutes do not change the law loses some of its force in the case of recent consolidations.

In a sense the distinction between remedial and other statutes is of greater importance from the point of view of the law of interpretation than either of the distinctions previously mentioned; but it is not

---

[14] Maxwell, *On the Interpretation of Statutes*, 12th ed., pp. 262–3.
[15] For a full discussion, see Maxwell, *op. cit.*, pp. 202–7.
[16] *Bank of England* v. *Vagliano Brothers*, [1891] A.C. 107.

one which it is possible to draw with precision. The essence of a remedial statute is that it was passed to remedy some defect in the common law and the cases suggest that such a statute should be broadly construed. A commonly cited example is the case law relating to s. 9 of the Admiralty Court Act 1861. The statute provided that the court should have jurisdiction over any claim by the owner or consignee of "any goods carried into England or Wales", for damage done to the goods by the negligence, misconduct or breach of contract of the owner, master or crew of the ship. The courts refused to restrict the operation of the section to cases in which goods were carried into English or Welsh ports for the purpose of delivery. Accordingly the court had jurisdiction over claims by the registered owners of goods consigned to foreign ports which were carried into our ports when the master of the ship simply required orders from the shipowners concerning the particular foreign port to which he should proceed.

> "The statute, being remedial of a grievance, by amplifying the jurisdiction of the English Court of Admiralty, ought, according to the general rule applicable to such statutes, to be construed liberally, so as to afford the utmost relief which the fair meaning of its language will allow."[17]

Finally it is necessary to mention interpretation acts. Many statutes contain definition clauses relating to some of their key words, but an interpretation act provides that, subject to any provision to the contrary, all statutes shall be construed as indicated; for example, so that the singular shall include the plural, the masculine the feminine and vice versa. The current English Interpretation Act is that of 1889. There was an earlier one of 1850, hence the references to that year in the citations from the 1889 Act made above. There is no doubt that this Act needs to be up-dated. Some of its provisions are still useful, but there are far too many obsolete provisions relating, for example, to various defunct poor law institutions and the British Government of India. Some countries have more ambitious interpretation acts. For instance s. 5 (j) of the Acts Interpretation Act 1924 of New Zealand reads as follows:

> "Every Act, and every provision or enactment thereof, shall be deemed remedial, whether its immediate purport is to direct the doing of anything Parliament deems to be for the public good, or to prevent or punish the doing of anything it deems contrary to the public good, and shall accordingly receive such fair, large and liberal construction and interpretation as will best ensure the attainment of the object of the Act and of such provision or enactment according to its true intent, meaning and spirit."

Whether we should gain by having some such enactment in this country is a question to be considered elsewhere in this book.

---

[17] *Dapueto* v. *James & Wyllie & Co.* (1874), L.R. 5 P.C. 482, at p. 492, *per* Sir Montague SMITH.

It only remains to add that what is said about interpretation in the following chapters applies, where relevant, to subordinate legislation. Its construction is sometimes particularly affected by that of the parent statute and, in the case of subordinate legislation, there is the general question of *ultra vires* with which we shall have no concern.

I

Historical[1]

The most frequent complaint concerning the contemporary approach of the courts to statutory interpretation is that it is excessively literal. All too frequently, it is urged, is the object of the legislature frustrated by an undue insistence on the part of the courts on applying the statutory words to the particular case in a strictly literal sense. The merits of such complaints are considered in Chapter VIII, but it is important to realise at the outset that the approach of the courts of the 16th century was anything but literal.

To establish this point it is only necessary to quote Plowden's report of *Stradling* v. *Morgan*,[2] the case in which a statute of Edward VI's reign referring to receivers and treasurers without any qualifying words was held to be confined to such officials appointed by the King and not to extend to receivers and treasurers acting on behalf of private persons. Various authorities were cited

> "from which cases it appears that the sages of the law heretofore have construed statutes quite contrary to the letter in some appearance, and those statutes which comprehend all things in the letter they have expounded to extend but to some things, and those which generally prohibit all from doing such an act they have interpreted to permit some people to do it, and those which include every person in the letter they have adjudged to reach some persons only, which expositions have always been founded on the intent of the legislature which they have collected sometimes by considering the calls and necessity of making the Act, sometimes by comparing one part of the Act with another, and sometimes by foreign circumstances. So that they have ever been guided by the intent of the legislature, which they have always taken according to the necessity of the matter, and according to that which is consonant to reason and good discretion."

[1] I am heavily indebted to an article by J. A. Corry entitled "Administrative Law and the Interpretation of Statutes" in 1 Toronto Law Journal 286 (1936). It is reprinted with new introductory paragraphs in appendix 1 of E. A. Driedger's *The Construction of Statutes* (Butterworths Canada 1974), a work to which this book owes a very great deal.

[2] (1560), 1 Plowd. 199, at p. 204.

In modern terms *Stradling* v. *Morgan* was an example of restrictive interpretation; the broad effect of general words was held to be limited by the context which was mainly concerned with royal revenue. *Heydon's* case,[3] on the other hand, could be said to have been an instance of extensive interpretation because a grant of copyholds for life at the will of the lord was held to create "an estate and interest for lives" within the meaning of the statute of Henry VIII in spite of decisions to the effect that the words in question were, when used in other statutes, confined to freeholds; but its real importance lies in the resolutions of the Barons of the Exchequer which contain the classic statement of the "mischief rule" upon which reliance is often placed by the courts of today.

> "And it was resolved by them that for the sure and true interpretation of all statutes in general (be they penal or beneficial, restrictive or enlarging of the common law), four things are to be discerned and considered:
>
> 1st. What was the common law before the making of the Act,
> 2nd. What was the mischief and defect for which the common law did not provide,
> 3rd. What remedy the Parliament hath resolved and appointed to cure the disease of the Commonwealth, and
> 4th. The true reason of the remedy;
>
> and then the office of all the judges is always to make such construction as shall suppress the mischief, and advance the remedy, and to suppress subtle inventions and evasions for continuance of the mischief, and *pro privato commodo*, and to add force and life to the cure and remedy, according to the true intent of the makers of the Act, *pro bono publico*."

Heydon's case was decided in 1584 and the spirit which animated the Barons of the Exchequer tended in the main to animate the judges of the 17th century. In fact it has never been extinguished for no modern lawyer would deny the relevance of the object of a statute to its interpretation; but the resolutions of 1584 were, like Plowden's observations in *Stradling* v. *Morgan*, the typical product of the period preceding the complete establishment of the sovereignty of Parliament. As late as 1701 HOLT, C.J., felt able to say "Let an Act of Parliament be ever so charitable, yet if it give away the property of a subject it ought not to be countenanced".[4]

A more literal approach is to be discerned in the decisions of the 18th and 19th centuries. This was the outcome of the attitude towards government engendered by Locke and the revolution of 1688. No doubt the words of HOLT, C.J., were specious, but any Parliamentary change in the existing state of affairs must, if it were to be enforced by the courts, be cast in the clearest possible terms. Examples of this

---

[3] (1584), 3 Co. Rep. 7a.
[4] *Callady* v. *Pilkington* (1694), 12 Mod. 513.

approach are provided by decisions placing a strikingly strict interpretation on criminal statutes, and by the courts' complacent attitude towards the *casus omissus*—the inexplicable and probably inadvertent failure of the draftsman to use words entirely apt to cover the instant case.

It is open to question whether the Barons of the Exchequer had criminal statutes in mind when, in *Heydon's* case, they declared their resolutions to be applicable to all statutes in general "be they penal or beneficial".[5] However that may be, it is certain that the 18th century witnessed the growth of a presumption in favour of a strict construction of criminal statutes which persists to this day. In *R.* v. *Harris*[6] it was held that an accused who bit off the end of his victim's nose was not guilty of wounding within the meaning of a statute of George IV which punished anyone "who shall unlawfully and maliciously stab, cut, or wound any person". The court took the view that the intention of Parliament was, according to the words of the statute, that an instrument should have been used, a conclusion strengthened by an earlier reference to shooting. The decision is rendered nugatory so far as the construction of the contemporary statutory equivalent is concerned by the inclusion in the prohibition of wounding or inflicting grievous bodily harm by s. 20 of the Offences Against the Person Act 1861 of the words "either with or without any weapon or instrument".

Jones v. *Smart*[7] may be taken as an illustration of the attitude of an 18th-century court to the *casus omissus*. The question was whether a doctor of physic was qualified to kill game under a statute of Charles II which disqualified those who lacked various property qualifications "other than the son and heir apparent of an esquire, or other person of higher degree". It was not disputed that he was of higher degree than an esquire or the son and heir apparent of an esquire, but the majority of the court held that the words "son and heir apparent" governed "other persons of higher degree", although the *casus omissus* could easily have been provided for by confining them to esquires.

It must not be thought that what to many may appear to be an excessively strict construction of a criminal statute or what some critics may consider timidity in the face of a *casus omissus* are things of the past. In *R.* v. *Munks*,[8] for example, a husband who was minded to give his wife an electric shock attached electric wires to the light and windows of a room. He was held not guilty of setting or placing "an *engine* calculated to destroy human life or inflict grievous bodily harm"

---

[5] See *A.-G.* v. *Sillem* (1864), 2 H. & C. 431, at p. 509.
[6] (1836), 7 C. & P. 416.
[7] (1784), 1 Term Rep. 44.
[8] [1964] 1 Q.B. 304; [1963] 3 All E.R. 757.

contrary to s. 31 of the Offences Against the Person Act 1861. An "engine", it was said, may mean either a product of human ingenuity or else a mechanical contrivance and the Divisional Court adopted the latter narrower meaning for the purposes of the section.

In *Fisher* v. *Bell*[9] a shopkeeper was charged with offering a flick-knife for sale contrary to s. 1 (1) of the Restriction of Offensive Weapons Act 1959 according to which "any person who manufactures, sells or *offers for sale* or hire or lends or hires to any other person any knife sometimes known as a flick-knife" is guilty of an offence. The defendant had placed a flick-knife in his shop window, but the Divisional Court held that he had not offered it for sale because Parliament must be taken to have legislated with reference to the general law of contract according to which the placing of goods in a shop window constitutes an invitation to treat and not an offer. Lord PARKER, C.J., said:

> "At first sight it seems absurd that knives of this sort cannot be manufactured, sold, hired, lent or given, but apparently they can be displayed in shop windows; but even if this—and I am by no means saying that it is—is a *casus omissus* it is not for this court to supply the omission."

It is difficult to escape the conclusion that the draftsman inadvertently omitted some such words as "exposes for sale" or "has in his possession for the purpose of sale", and the Restriction of Offensive Weapons Act 1961 provides for the insertion in s. 1 (1) of the Act of 1959, after the words "offers for sale or hire", the words "or exposes or has in his possession for the purpose of sale or hire". It is unlikely that any court of the 20th century would have read these words into the 1959 Act, but the draftsman's omission, if there was one, could have been remedied by a refusal to apply the technicalities of the law of contract to a criminal case for, in their non-technical sense, the words "offers for sale" might well be thought to apply to a shopkeeper who places goods in his shop window.

We shall see that there is something to be said on both sides with regard to the merits of decisions such as *Fisher* v. *Bell*. The important point for present purposes is that they are apt to produce a parliamentary reaction. This has been the baneful effect of the literal approach to statutory interpretation as contrasted with the approaches canvassed in *Stradling* v. *Morgan* and *Heydon's* case.[10] At times a state of war appears to exist between the courts and the parliamentary draftsman. The courts decline to come to the rescue when a *casus omissus* is revealed, so words appropriate to cover the *casus omissus* are added to the statute. More frequently the draftsman gets in first and,

---

[9] [1961] 1 Q.B. 394; [1960] 3 All E.R. 731.
[10] Pp. 8–9 *supra*.

anticipating a strict construction by the courts coupled with a total lack of sympathy if there should happen to be a *casus omissus*, he produces a statute which is nothing less than horrific in its detail. One of the most notorious examples is provided by s. 1 of the Wills Act Amendment Act 1852. It was passed in order to resolve doubts concerning the requirement of the Wills Act 1837 that the will must be signed "at the foot or end thereof" and it reads:

> Where by an Act passed in the First Year of the Reign of Her Majesty Queen Victoria, intituled An Act for the Amendment of the Laws with respect to Wills, it is enacted, that no Will shall be valid unless it shall be signed at the Foot or End thereof by the Testator, or by some other Person in his Presence, and by his Direction: Every Will shall, so far only as regards the Position of the Signature of the Testator, or of the Person signing for him as aforesaid, be deemed to be valid within the said Enactment, as explained by this Act, if the Signature shall be so placed at or after, or following, or under, or beside, or opposite to the End of the Will, that it shall be apparent on the Face of the Will that the Testator intended to give Effect by such his Signature to the Writing signed as his Will, and that no such Will shall be affected by the Circumstance that the Signature shall not follow or be immediately after the Foot or End of the Will, or by the Circumstance that a blank Space shall intervene between the concluding Word of the Will and the Signature, or by the Circumstance that the Signature shall be placed among the Words of the Testimonium Clause or of the Clause of Attestation, or shall follow or be after or under the Clause of Attestation, either with or without a blank Space intervening, or shall follow or be after, or under, or beside the Names or One of the Names of the subscribing Witnesses, or by the Circumstance that the Signature shall be on a Side or Page or other Portion of the Paper or Papers containing the Will whereon no Clause or Paragraph or disposing Part of the Will shall be written above the Signature, or by the Circumstance that there shall appear to be sufficient Space on or at the Bottom of the preceding Side or Page or other Portion of the same Paper on which the Will is written to contain the Signature; and the Enumeration of the above Circumstances shall not restrict the Generality of the above Enactment; but no Signature under the said Act or this Act shall be operative to give Effect to any Disposition or Direction which is underneath or which follows it, nor shall it give Effect to any Disposition or Direction inserted after the Signature shall be made.

This book is not concerned with statutory drafting, an insufficiently appreciated art,[11] but it is important to appreciate the mutual dependence of the draftsman and the courts when the latter are engaged in statutory interpretation. It is the courts' duty to give effect to the intention of Parliament[12] but their main source of information on this matter is the wording of the statute; if this is not clear there is obviously a risk that the courts will be unable to do their work properly.

---

[11] Useful books are E. A. Driedger, *The Composition of Legislation* (Ottawa 1957), Reed Dickerson, *The Fundamentals of Legal Drafting* (Boston 1965) and G. C. Thornton, *Legislative Drafting* (Butterworths 1971). [12] P. 34 *infra*.

On the other hand the draftsman will find it difficult to convey the parliamentary intent to the court unless he knows that they will attach the same meaning to his words as that in which he employs them. Hence the need for a common standard of interpretation and there can hardly be a better standard that the ordinary, or, in appropriate cases, the technical, meaning of English words.

As legislation increased in quantity and as it came to deal more and more with matters unknown to the common law, the resolutions of *Heydon's* case became less and less satisfactory as the sole guide to interpretation. Primacy, though not total supremacy, had to be given to the words of the statute. The mischief rule came to be largely, though not entirely, superseded by the "literal" or, as it came to be called in America, the "plain meaning" rule. One of the most frequently quoted of the numerous statements of this latter rule is that of TINDAL, C.J., when advising the House of Lords on the *Sussex Peerage* claim:[13]

> "The only rule for the construction of Acts of Parliament, is that they should be construed according to the intent of the Parliament which passed the Act. If the words of the statute are in themselves precise and unambiguous, then no more can be necessary than to expound those words in that natural and ordinary sense. The words themselves alone do, in such a case, best declare the intention of the lawgiver. But if any doubt arises from the terms employed by the legislature, it has always been held a safe means of collecting the intention, to call in aid the ground and cause of making the statute, and to have recourse to the preamble, which, according to Chief Justice DYER,[14] is 'a key to open the minds of the makers of the Act, and the mischiefs which they intend to redress'."

This passage is of especial interest because it states the commonly accepted view concerning the relationship of the literal and mischief rules. *Heydon's* case is only applicable when the court finds that the statutory words are obscure or ambiguous. Whether the object of the statute is not something which may be taken into account at an earlier stage even though it may suggest that an otherwise clear and unambiguous meaning is not the right one is a point to be considered in Chapter III.

The principal question at the hearing of the *Sussex Peerage* case was whether the claimant's father had been validly married. He was a descendant of George II and his marriage was void for want of the requisite consent if the Royal Marriage Act 1772 applies to marriage ceremonies celebrated abroad. Section 1 reads as follows:

> "That no descendant of the body of His Late Majesty King George II, male or female, (other than the issue of princesses who have married or

[13] (1844), 11 Cl. & Fin. 85, at p. 143.
[14] *Stowell* v. *Lord Zouch* (1569), 1 Plowd. 369.

may marry into foreign families) shall be capable of contracting matrimony, without the previous consent of His Majesty, his heirs or successors, signified under the great seal, and declared in council (which consent, to preserve the memory thereof, is hereby directed to be set out in the licence and register of marriage, and to be entered in the books of the Privy Council); and that every marriage or matrimonial contract of any such descendant, without such consent first had and obtained, shall be null and void to all intents and purposes whatsoever."

It was held that the claimant's marriage was void because the words of the Act applied in their ordinary sense to any marriage of a descendant of George II wherever it might be celebrated, subject of course to the exception mentioned in the first set of brackets. This exception was thought to strengthen the case against the validity of the claimant's father's marriage for it would have been of dubious necessity if the Act were confined to marriages celebrated within the realm. TINDAL, C.J., also found support for the conclusion that the marriage was invalid from the second section of the Act of 1772 which validates marriages of descendants of the body of George II above the age of 25, even though the consent required by s. 1 was not obtained, provided the year's notice is given and no objection is raised by Parliament. These points are worth mentioning because it seems that TINDAL, C.J., recognised that, before deciding whether the words are "in themselves precise and unambiguous" the court must have regard to the whole of the enacting part of the statute. The proper application of the literal rule does not mean that the effect of a particular word or phrase, clause or section is to be determined in isolation from the rest of the statute in which it is contained.

This had been recognised by PARKER, C.B., in the middle of the 18th century; but his words may be thought to have contained the germs of a third rule which, in order that it may be distinguished from the mischief and literal rules, is commonly called the "golden" rule.[15] It allows for a departure from the literal rule when the application of the statutory words in the ordinary sense would be repugnant to or inconsistent with some other provision in the statute or even when it would lead to what the court considers to be an absurdity. The usual consequence of applying the golden rule is that words which are in the statute are ignored or words which are not there are read in. The scope of the golden rule is debatable, particularly so far as the meaning of an "absurdity" is concerned. This word was not used by PARKER, C.B. who said:[16]

"In expounding Acts of Parliament where words are express, plain and

---

[15] The literal rule, with or without the qualification mentioned in the text, is also often spoken of as the golden rule.

[16] *Mitchell* v. *Torrup* (1766), Park. 227.

clear, the words ought to be understood according to their plain and natural signification and import, unless by such exposition a contradiction or inconsistency would arise in the Act by reason of some subsequent clause from whence it might be inferred that the intent of Parliament was otherwise."

In *Becke* v. *Smith*[17] PARKE, B., said:

"It is a very useful rule, in the construction of a statute, to adhere to the ordinary meaning of the words used, and to the grammatical construction, unless that is at variance with the intention of the legislature, to be collected from the statute itself, or leads to any manifest absurdity or repugnance, in which case the language may be varied or modified, so as to avoid such inconvenience, but no further."

Neither PARKER, C.B., nor PARKE, B., found it necessary to modify the application of the literal rule in the judgments from which the above passages are taken. In *Becke* v. *Smith*, PARKE, B., may have used the word "absurdity" to mean no more than repugnant to other provisions in the statute;[18] but the same judge's statement of the golden rule in *Grey* v. *Pearson*,[19] a case concerned with the construction of a will, is less easily susceptible of that interpretation and this statement of the rule is probably the one which is most commonly cited today:

"I have been long and deeply impressed with the wisdom of the rule now, I believe, universally adopted, at least in the courts of law in Westminster Hall, that in construing wills and indeed, statutes, and all written instruments, the grammatical and ordinary sense of the words is to be adhered to, unless that would lead to some absurdity, or some repugnance or inconsistency with the rest of the instrument, in which case the grammatical and ordinary sense of the words may be modified, so as to avoid the absurdity and inconsistency, but no farther."

On occasions the golden rule simply serves as a guide to the court where there is doubt as to the true import of the statutory words in their ordinary sense. When there is a choice of meanings there is a presumption that one which produces an absurd, unjust or inconvenient result was not intended; but it should be emphasised that when the rule is used as a justification for ignoring or reading in words resort may only be made to it in the most unusual cases. This is borne out by two dicta in the same volume of Appeal Cases which also reveal the difference of opinion about the scope of the rule discernible in a number of judgments.

---

[17] (1836), 2 M. & W. 191, at p. 195.

[18] "I subscribe to every word of that, [the statement of PARKE, B., in *Becke* v. *Smith*] assuming the word 'absurdity' to mean no more than 'repugnance'." (*Per* WILLES, J., in *Christopherson* v. *Lotinga* (1864), 15 C.B.N.S. 809, at p. 813).

[19] (1857), 6 H.L.Cas. 61, at p. 106.

"It is a strong thing to read into an Act of Parliament words which are not there, and in the absence of clear necessity it is a wrong thing to do."[20]

"We are not entitled to read words into an Act of Parliament unless clear reason for it is to be found *within the four corners of the Act* itself."[1]

The mischief rule, the literal rule and the golden rule are the only canons of statutory interpretation which need to be placed in an historical perspective. It has been said that they have been fused so that we now have just one rule of interpretation, a modern version of the literal rule which requires the general context to be taken into consideration before any decision is reached concerning the ordinary meaning of the words. The mischief rule, it is urged, is now used to explain what was said by Parliament not to change it as at the time of *Heydon's* case; and it is argued that the object of the statute is relevant on all occasions, not only when the meaning is doubtful as was said in the *Sussex Peerage* case.[2] The final contention is that the golden rule can only be invoked where there is internal disharmony in the statute, not in cases in which a literal interpretation would produce results which are absurd or inconvenient for other reasons.[3] "First it was the spirit and not the letter, then the letter and not the spirit, and now the spirit and the letter."[4]

---

[20] Lord MERSEY in *Thompson* v. *Goold & Co.*, [1910] A.C. 409, at p. 420.

[1] Lord LOREBURN in *Vickers, Sons, and Maxim, Ltd.* v. *Evans*, [1910] A.C. 444, at p. 445 (italics supplied).

[2] P. 13 *supra*.

[3] E. A. Driedger, *The Construction of Statutes*, p. 2.

[4] *Ibid.*, pp. 63–4.

II

Jurisprudential

There is a great deal of juristic writing on the subject of statutory interpretation, but it will be sufficient to say something about the work of Blackstone, Bentham, Austin and Gray as a prelude to a discussion of the nature of the canons of interpretation, and the meaning of "the intention of Parliament". One curious feature which all four of the writers who have just been mentioned had in common is the absence of any discussion of this last subject. We are frequently told that it is necessary to ascertain what was "the intention" or "will" of the "legislator" or "legislature" and even that it is sometimes necessary for the judge to be empathetic to the extent of inquiring what the legislature would have done if he, she or it had contemplated the situation which confronts him. But it seems to make no difference whether the legislative organ is an individual or a collectivity. Yet the legislature with which Blackstone, Bentham and Austin were most directly concerned was the English Parliament, while, although Gray roams very much at large, he refers in the main to happenings in the United States. The intention of a collectivity is not the only problem; even if such a psychological oddity can be defined, further difficulties with regard to their "intentions" are presented by legislatures with a second chamber not to mention tripartite entities like the English Queen in Parliament whose legislation is formally that of the monarch acting "by and with the advice and consent of the lords spiritual and temporal, and commons, in this present Parliament assembled".

A. BLACKSTONE

Blackstone gives a brief account of "the interpretation of laws" at the end of the second section of the *Introduction to the Commentaries*.[1] Ten rules "to be observed with regard to the construction of statutes"

[1] First published in 1765.

are given at the end of the third section. The rules of construction are a motley assortment varying from the mischief rule to rules concerning the repeal and revival of statutory provisions. There is no explanation of the distinction between interpretation and construction, nor can it be inferred from the matters dealt with under each head. The distinction is drawn in some modern works, but it is not taken in this book because it lacks an agreed basis. Some writers treat interpretation as something which is only called for when there is a dispute about the meaning of statutory words, while speaking of construction as a process to which all statutes, like all other writings, are necessarily subject when read by anyone.[2] Others treat interpretation as something which is mainly concerned with the meaning of statutory words, while regarding construction as a process which mainly relates to the ascertainment of the intention of the legislature.[3]

Blackstone tells us that:[4]

> "The fairest and most rational method to interpret the will of the legislator, is by exploring his intentions at the time when the law was made, by *signs* the most natural and probable. And these signs are either the words, the context, the subject matter, the effects and consequence, or the spirit and reason of the law."

Words are generally to be understood "in their usual and most known signification", although terms of art "must be taken according to the acceptation of the learning in each art trade and science." "If words happen to be still dubious", we may establish their meaning from the context which includes the preamble to the statute and laws made by the same legislator *in pari materia*. Words are always to be understood as having regard to the subject matter of the legislation. The law of Edward III forbade all ecclesiastical persons to purchase *provisions* at Rome, "it might seem to prohibit the buying of grain and other victuals; but when we consider that the statute was made to redress the usurpations of the Papal See, and that the nominations to benefices by the Pope were called provisions, we shall see that the restraint is intended to be laid on such provisions only". As to the effects and consequences, the rule is that, where the words when literally construed have no meaning in the context or only a very absurd one, we must deviate a little from their received sense. A Bolognan law mentioned by Puffendorf enacted that "whoever drew blood in the streets should be punished with the utmost severity". It was held, after long debate, not to extend to a surgeon who opened the vein of someone who fell down in the street in a fit. "But lastly, the most

---

[2] E. A. Driedger, *The Construction of Statutes*, ix.
[3] R. W. M. Dias, *Jurisprudence*, 3rd Edn., p. 128.
[4] *Commentaries*, 1813 edition, vol. 1, p. 78.

universal and effectual way of discovering the true meaning of a law, when the words are dubious, is by considering the reason and spirit of it; or the cause which moved the legislator to enact it."

The most significant feature of this brief account of the rules of statutory interpretation is its approximation to the present law. First we have the literal rule, but it is stated in broad terms, full allowance being made for the context. It is true that there is the implication that the context is only relevant when there is doubt about the meaning of the statutory provision under consideration if its words are taken in isolation, but we shall see that it is debatable to this day whether recourse may be had to the preamble in the absence of such doubt. Then we have something which looks very like the golden rule, and this is followed by the mischief rule. It is true that here too the suggestion is that a narrow version of the literal rule confined to a particular statutory provision must prevail unless there is sufficient doubt about the meaning of its words to warrant recourse to the object of the legislation, but we shall see that it is often assumed that this is true today.

It is strange that, after allowing for the mischief rule at the end of this account of interpretation, Blackstone should have set that rule out more fully in terms substantially similar to those of *Heydon's* case[5] as the first of his rules of construction; but it seems to be recognised at the present day that the object of a statute may be considered by a judge at two stages of his deliberations, the stage at which he asks himself whether he has any doubt about the meaning of the provision under review, and the stage at which, having answered that question in the affirmative, he is assessing the pros and cons of a decision in favour of one of several doubtful meanings. This is a subtle, some might say over-subtle, distinction and it is not suggested that the distinction was present to Blackstone's mind when he was preparing the *Commentaries*.

The remaining rules of construction illustrate the similarity of Blackstone's treatment of the subject to that of modern English writers on jurisprudence, but they do not call for detailed consideration. The third rule is that penal statutes must be construed strictly, and it is illustrated by a statute of Edward VI according to which those who stole *horses* should not have the benefit of clergy. "The judges conceived that this did not extend to him that should steal but one *horse* and therefore procured a new Act for that purpose in the following year."[6] Reference is made in the fifth rule to the canon of construction *ut res magis valeat quam pereat*, a canon which is elevated to the status

[5] P. 9 supra.

[6] The point is now covered by s. 1 (1) (*b*) of the Interpretation Act 1889.

of a general principle in Maxwell's *Interpretation of Statutes*, the leading modern treatise on the subject.

B. BENTHAM

In *A Comment on the Commentaries* Bentham was no less critical of Blackstone on statutory interpretation and construction than of other portions of his work; but all the criticisms are pedantic and most of them are unjustified. Part of the trouble is that Bentham took Blackstone's paragraphs about interpretation to be addressed to the general reader of the statute, someone who is consulting the statute for himself with a view to taking or abstaining from a particular course of action, whereas it is tolerably clear that Blackstone conceived of himself as formulating, in an elementary way, rules on which a court should act in the event of a dispute concerning the meaning of statutory words coming before it. Speaking of Blackstone's statement that words are generally to be understood in "their usual and most known signification", Bentham concedes that no objection can be taken to its propriety, but he asks what use there can be "for making a rule to bid us do what by the supposition we should do without bidding".[7] No doubt it is true that the ordinary reader, pondering on the effect a statute may have on some action contemplated by him, could do little else than construe the words according to their ordinary sense, but it is of the utmost importance that the law student for whom Blackstone was writing should realise the primacy of the literal rule. The student was to be made to understand at the outset that, should a dispute about interpretation come before the courts, they would generally act on the usual meaning of the words (where no technical sense was involved) in preference to some secondary or less usual meaning. Bentham utterly fails to make allowance for the fact that three of the "signs" mentioned by Blackstone, "the context, ..., the effects, ... and reason of the law", are only to be followed if a case can be made for the displacement of the "usual and most known signification". The context is only to be considered if the words "happen still to be dubious", the effects only when, if literally understood, the words bear "either none or a very absurd signification", the reason only "when the words are still dubious".

Bentham's criticism of the third indication of legislative intent mentioned by Blackstone, the subject matter, is largely misconceived. He makes the point that the example of the statute of Edward III forbidding ecclesiastics to purchase provisions at Rome would equally well fit Blackstone's earlier rules concerning the technical meaning

[7] *A Comment on the Commentaries* (edited by C. W. Everett, Oxford 1928), p. 107. The manuscript was written in 1774–6 but it was not published in Bentham's lifetime.

of words and the context. We have seen that Blackstone says that terms of art must be taken according to the acceptation of the learned in each art, trade or science. Bentham rightly adds in parenthesis that "occupation" might have been included;[8] but how can anyone know whether a word such as "provisions" is used in a specialised sense in the absence of information concerning the subject matter of the statute? No doubt this is part of the context of a statutory word, and Blackstone could have combined what he said about the one with what he said about the other, but only at the cost of confusing his readers, for one of his points was that resort must always be had to the subject matter before any pronouncement can be made about the meaning of a statutory word, whereas such other contextual items as the preamble can only be considered in case of doubt. There is no reference to any kind of requirement that the meaning of the words should be dubious when Blackstone comes to mention the importance of the subject matter. Put at its highest, his sin was not dealing with this before the other contextual items.[9]

There is greater merit in Bentham's comments on Blackstone's examples of the application of the mischief rule and the presumption in favour of a strict construction of penal statutes. The first concerns the statute of Elizabeth I under which leases by ecclesiastical corporations for terms longer than 21 years or three lives were declared to be "utterly void and of none effect, to all intents, constructions, and purposes". The mischief at which the statute was aimed was the granting of excessively long leases to the detriment of the grantors' successors whose freedom of alienation would be restricted and who might have to be content with an unduly low rent. Blackstone refers to a construction under which leases for longer than the permitted terms, if made by a bishop, were not void during his life, or, if made by a dean and chapter, were not void during the dean's life. The basis of this construction was that the Act aimed at the protection of the lessor's successors and the mischief was sufficiently suppressed by avoiding the lease on the death of the lessor.[10] This is indeed the construction of the days when the mischief rule was used to supplant rather than to interpret a statute and it would be difficult for a modern lawyer to disagree with Bentham's comment: "This our author calls construction; this I call alteration. The judges did not like the remedy provided by the legislature, they therefore put another they liked better in its room."[11]

---

[8] *Ibid.*, p. 108.

[9] It must be conceded that Blackstone's example was not a good one because references to abbeys and priories accompany the word "provisions" in the body of the statute (see *A Comment on the Commentaries*, pp. 116–17).

[10] Blackstone's *Commentaries*, vol. 1, 104 (1813 edition.)

[11] *A Comment on the Commentaries*, p. 139.

When speaking of the illustration of the strict construction of the statute of Edward VI according to which the withdrawal of benefit of clergy from those who stole horses was held not to extend to someone who stole a single horse, Bentham said that he realised that it had been cited as an instance of scrupulousness carried to extreme, but he questioned the justice of this view because the value of the thing stolen might have been taken as the measure of guilt, "and it follows not, that because the legislature has thought fit to annexe a certain degree of punishment to a certain degree of guilt, it therefore should annexe the same to half that guilt".[12] All the same he recognised that the intention probably was to deny benefit of clergy to the thief of a single horse, and though he thought the safest decision was that taken by the judges, he commended them for seeking a further statute. That step pointed out to their successors "the true method of giving the public the benefit of their discernment without transgressing the limits of their authority".

In *Of Laws In General* Bentham distinguishes between strict and liberal interpretation.[13]

> "It may be styled strict where you attribute to the legislator that will which at the time of making the law, you suppose, he really entertained. It may be styled liberal where what you attribute to him is that which you suppose he failed of entertaining only through inadvertency: insomuch that had the individual case which calls for interpretation been present to his view, he would have entertained that will, which by the interpretation put upon his law you act up to, as though it had been his in reality."[14]

Liberal interpretation is subdivided into extensive and restrictive. An extensive interpretation applies a statutory provision to a case which does not fall within its words when literally construed; restrictive interpretation fails to apply a statutory provision to a case which does fall within its words when literally construed.

> "In either case thus to interpret a law is to alter it: *interpretation* being put by a sort of euphemism for *alteration*. Now to extend an old law is in fact to establish a new law: as on the other hand to qualify the old law is *pro tanto* to destroy it. The only circumstance that can serve to distinguish the alteration itself, when made in this way, from alteration at large is, that the alteration goes no farther from what it appears in the legislator's will to what, it is supposed, would have been his will had the case in question been present to his view: from his actual to his hypothetical will. If then there is a new law made, it is made however upon the pattern, and with some of the materials of the old, if there is part of the old law destroyed,

---

[12] *A Comment on the Commentaries*, p. 141.

[13] *Of Laws in General* (edited by H. L. A. Hart, 1970) p. 162. The book was substantially completed in 1782 but not published in Bentham's lifetime.

[14] *Ibid.*, p. 163. Words such as "strict", "liberal", "restrictive" and "extensive" are frequently used with less precision, roughly as synonyms for narrow and broad.

it is such part only as he himself it is supposed would have destroyed, had the particular case in question come before him."[15]

Bentham was not opposed to liberal interpretation. He spoke of it as "that delicate and important branch of judiciary power the concession of which is dangerous, the denial ruinous".[16] Consistently with the admiration he expressed in *A Comment on the Commentaries* for the judges who procured an amending statute to withdraw benefit of clergy from those who stole a single horse, he suggested in *Of Laws in General* that, whenever a statute was interpreted liberally, the judge should draw up a statement to be placed before the legislature indicating how the statute should be amended, the proposed amendment to have the force of law if not vetoed within a specified time.[17] No doubt the implementation of such a proposal would give rise to many difficulties. It is not easy to distinguish between cases in which an interpretation is liberal in Bentham's sense of attributing to the legislator an intention with regard to a particular case which he plainly did not entertain, and an interpretation which attributes to the legislator's words a restricted or extended meaning on account of an intention he was believed to have entertained. The constitutionality of judicial drafting of legislative amendments might well be questioned, but the merits of closer co-operation between Parliament and the judges in matters of statutory drafting and interpretation are undeniable. The problem of the *casus omissus* has, as we have seen, loomed large in relation to the statutory interpretation of the past, and no doubt it will prove equally troublesome in the future. A point in favour of Bentham's proposal is that it recognises that judges sometimes legislate, though in a comparatively minor way, when applying statute law, just as they sometimes legislate when applying the common law. Views may well vary concerning the occasions on which and the extent to which gaps left by the legislature should be filled in by the judges, but nothing is gained by pejorative references to the process as "a naked usurpation of the legislative power."[18]

C. AUSTIN

Austin really added nothing to Bentham's discussion of statutory interpretation, but his terminology and account of the rationale of liberal interpretation may be briefly mentioned. Liberal interpretation is spoken of as interpretation "*ex ratione legis*": "the judge extends

---

[15] *Ibid.*, p. 163.
[16] *Ibid.*, p. 239.
[17] *Ibid.*, p. 241.
[18] *Per* Lord SIMONDS in *Magor and St. Mellons Rural District Council* v. *Newport Corporation*, [1952] A.C. 189; [1951] 2 All E.R. 839.

the law to the omitted case, because the omitted case falls within the general design, although it is not embraced by the actual unequivocal provision".[19] Austin is careful to distinguish cases in which the object of a statute is used as a basis of liberal interpretation *ex ratione legis* from those in which it is used as a means of ascertaining the legislative intent. In the latter case the interpretation is genuine, designed to produce a result which the legislator had in mind, whereas interpretation *ex ratione legis* is 'spurious" although the perjorative undertones were probably unintended.

Austin's discussion of the subject occurs in a lecture on equity. The idea underlying extensive interpretation *ex ratione legis* is uniformity, the exclusion of the *casus omissus* would be unjust. The idea underlying restrictive interpretation *ex ratione legis* is consistency, failure to exclude the case that is in fact within the broad words of the statute would lead to an inconsistency with the decisions required by the narrower object of the statute. Austin seems to have been suspicious of restrictive interpretation *ex ratione legis*, but the principle of justice that unlike cases should be treated differently is in no way inferior to the principle of justice that like cases should be treated alike. We shall see that on the rare occasions when the modern English judges interpret a statute *ex ratione legis* in the Austinian sense they appear to be more at their ease when doing so restrictively than when their interpretation is extensive. To ignore statutory words looks less like legislating than to add to them.

It was in accordance with tradition for Austin to have chosen to discuss interpretation *ex ratione legis* in connection with equity, for the old way of describing such interpretation was to speak of it as being in accordance with the equity of the statute. In his note to *Eyston* v. *Studd*[20] Plowden spoke of equity as something which

> "enlarges or diminishes the letter according to its discretion ... experience shows us that no lawmakers can foresee all things which may happen, and therefore it is fit that if there be any defect in the law, it should be reformed by equity.... It is a good way, when you peruse a statute, to suppose that the lawmaker is present, and that you have asked him the question you want to know touching the equity, then you must give yourself such an answer as you imagine he would have done, if he had been present."

In Plowden's time the notion of the equity of a statute was used to justify decisions concerning the application of statutes which no modern judge would contemplate. The Prisoners for Debt Act 1377, forbidding the Warden of the Fleet to suffer his prisoners for judgment debts to go at large until they had satisfied their debts was held to

---

[19] Austin's *Jurisprudence* (Campbell edition 1885), p. 578; see also *ibid.*, pp. 989 *et seq.* Austin's lectures were delivered between 1828 and 1832.

[20] (1574), 2 Plowd. 459.

include all jailors,[1] and the statute or writ *circumspecte agatis*, directing the judges not to interfere with the Bishop of Norwich or his clergy in spiritual pursuits, was held to protect other bishops, because "the Bishop of Norwich is here put but for an example".[2] Although such drastic extensive interpretations would be out of the question today, it would be a mistake to suppose that the Courts never indulge in milder acts of rectification. Something of the sort happens whenever "and" is read as "or" or vice versa; but these milder acts of rectification are most exceptional.

D. GRAY

Gray's major contribution to the theory of statutory interpretation is reminiscent of Plowden's exhortation to the interpreter to give such an answer as he imagines the lawmaker would have done. According to Gray it is a mistake to suppose that the chief function of interpretation is to discover what the meaning of the legislature really was because it is only in the most exceptional cases that there can be any doubt what the intention of the legislature was with regard to a particular point when it really had such an intention.

> "The fact is that the difficulties of so called interpretation arise when the legislature has had no meaning at all; when the question which is raised on the statute never occurred to it; when what the judges have to do is, not to determine what the legislature did mean on a point which was present to its mind, but to guess what it would have intended on a point not present to its mind, if the point had been present."[3]

Interpretation is accordingly defined as "the process by which a judge (or indeed any person, lawyer or layman, who has occasion to search for the meaning of a statute) constructs from the words of a statute book a meaning which he either believes to be that of the legislature, or which he proposes to attribute to it".

Gray illustrates the process of attributing a meaning to the legislature by reference to the construction of a statute of Edward III granting an action of trespass to executors for trespasses to the goods of the testator committed in his lifetime. The Courts applied this to administrators, to actions for the misappropriation of goods and to an action for wrongful disposition by an executor. These were drastic instances of what Austin would have called extensive interpretation *ex ratione legis*. Gray's illustration of restrictive interpretation is less

---

[1] *Platt* v. *Sheriffs of London* (1550), 1 Plowd. 35.

[2] 2 Inst. 487.

[3] *The Nature and Sources of Law* (2nd Edn. 1921), p. 173. The book was first published in 1909.

felicitous. He takes the instance of a statute prohibiting arson and says that no court in a country where the common law prevails would so construe the statute as to include children under seven, "and yet the legislature has not excluded them, it never thought about them. The judge is clear that it would have excluded them had it thought about the matter, and so he attributes to it the actual intention to exclude them."[4] Surely the approach of a common law judge would be based on the presumption (sensible enough if placed in its proper perspective) that statutes are to be so construed as to make no more change in the common law than is necessary for giving effect to them. The draftsman must be taken to have been aware of this presumption and of the enormous weight to be attached to it when the question is whether a statute has abolished one of the general common law defences to a criminal charge. The legislature must be taken to have been aware of this presumption and, as there is nothing in the statutory wording to suggest even an implied rebuttal (assuming that to be possible in such a case), the presumption must prevail.

Gray points out that it has been said over and over again that the courts must not undertake to make the legislature say what it has not said; but he asks whether the true rule is not "that the judge should give to the words of a statute the meaning which they would have had, *if he had used them himself*, unless there be something in the circumstances which makes him believe that such was *not* the actual meaning of the legislature". There is a great deal of force in this suggestion for, whenever anyone is asked to say what he thinks someone else meant by certain words, all he can do is to state what he would have meant by those words in the circumstances known to him; but Gray should have revealed the essential, though inevitable, weakness of his proposed rule in its dependence on the circumstances known to the legislature. The judge has to ask himself what the words would have meant if he had used them *when* they were used for, to revert to Blackstone, "the fairest and most rational method to interpret the will of the legislator is by exploring his intentions at the time when the law was made".

Gray is open to criticism for having attached far too much importance to the *casus omissus*. The problems which commonly confront the courts are of a more subtle nature. They concern such matters as the applicability of general words to particular cases (is a bicycle a "carriage"? for instance), the meaning of phrases in a particular context (does "national origins" mean the same thing as nationality for the purposes of the Race Relations Act 1968?), or the effect of provisions which cannot have been intended to be construed in a

[4] *The Nature and Sources of Law* (2nd Edn. 1921), p. 179.

strictly literal sense. For example, s. 8 of the Road Traffic Act 1972 entitles a constable to require any person "driving or attempting to drive" a motor vehicle on a road to provide a specimen of his breath if the constable has reasonable cause to suspect him of having alcohol in his body. Obviously the word "driving" cannot be confined to cases in which the vehicle is in motion, but when does the driver who has stopped his car and got out of it cease to be a person "driving or attempting to drive" it? The question, the answer to which is not unaffected by other provisions of the Act, has proved to be one of the most difficult that has confronted the English courts in modern times.

Although the preparation of a statute and its passage through Parliament frequently involves a consideration of hypothetical cases, Gray's approach to the question of intent is too atomistic.[5] Much statutory drafting is done in terms of general principles. To ask whether the legislature had specific facts in mind is, whatever the question may mean, frequently quite unreal. Even when the possible application of a statute to particular situations has been considered, their number is necessarily limited. The chances against their coinciding in all relevant respects with the facts of a future case must be small indeed. Nonetheless, the fact that a particular situation has been considered by the legislature is of great significance for a court grappling with the interpretation of a statute, and there is something to be said for the suggestion that an opinion expressed by the promoter or the minister of the Crown responsible for a Bill concerning its application in certain contingencies should be the subject of express enactment.[6]

Gray's general approach does not lack judicial support. He would have approved of the following remark of DENNING, L.J.:[7]

> "A judge should ask himself how, if the makers of the Act had themselves come across this ruck in the texture of it, they would have straightened it out. He must then do as they would have done. A judge must not alter the material of which the Act is woven but he can and should iron out the creases."

E. THE CANONS OF INTERPRETATION

Ever since Professor R. M. Dworkin published a seminal article in the Chicago Law Review in 1967[8] it has become fashionable to divide the contents of a legal system into rules and principles. One of the

---

[5] Fuller, *The Morality of Law*, p. 85.

[6] *Per* Lord SIMON OF GLAISDALE in *Dockers' Labour Club and Institute Ltd.*, v. *Race Relations Board*, [1974] 3 All E.R. 592, at p. 601.

[7] *Seaford Court Estates, Ltd.* v. *Asher*, [1949] 2 K.B. 481, at p. 499.

[8] 35 University of Chicago Law Review 14, reprinted under the title "Is Law a System of Rules?" in *Essays in Legal Philosophy* (ed. Summers 1968) 25.

examples of a rule given by him is "the maximum legal speed on the turnpike is 60 miles per hour".

> "Rules are applicable in an all or nothing fashion. If the facts a rule stipulates are given, then either the rule is valid, in which case the answer it supplies must be accepted, or it is not, in which case it contributes nothing to the decision."[9]

One of Professor Dworkin's examples of a principle is "no man may profit from his own wrong". This is recognised by English law and has formed the basis of a number of decisions, but judges are not obliged to apply it in the sense in which they are obliged to apply a rule after making certain findings of fact. Our law sometimes permits a man to profit from his own wrong as when it protects the adverse possessor of property even against the owner. Once a principle has been applied in a case it frequently creates a rule to which effect must be given in similar situations in the future. For example, the principle that no man may profit from his own wrong has produced a rule of the English law that a murderer cannot benefit as a result of his victim's intestacy because it was held in *Re Sigsworth* that someone who murdered his mother could not succeed to her estate notwithstanding the mandatory wording of s. 46 of the Administration of Estates Act 1925 which ordains that "the residuary estate shall be distributed" in accordance with its provisions. "General words which might include cases obnoxious to the principle must be read and construed subject to it."[10] But this does not mean that general words in other statutes must necessarily be construed in the same way.

> "All that is meant when we say that a particular principle is a principle of our law is that the principle is one which officials must take into account, if it is relevant, as a consideration inclining in one direction or another."[11]

Principles, unlike rules, may conflict without detriment to the operation of the legal system as a whole, and, again unlike rules, they may vary in the degree of their persuasiveness. Of course rules can and do have exceptions, but if two rules are contradictory of each other there is something seriously wrong with the law. No-one has suggested that there is something seriously wrong with the canons of statutory interpretation because of the frequent conflict between the principles that statutes should be construed so as to alter the common law as little as possible, and that they should be construed so as to conform to international law.

If we apply Professor Dworkin's terminology to the canons of statu-

---

[9] *Essays in Legal Philosophy* 37.
[10] [1935] Ch. 89, at p. 92, per CLAUSON J.
[11] *Essays in Legal Philosophy* 39.

tory interpretation, there are two rules, one so general as to approximate to a principle, and the other subject to an ill-defined limitation. For the rest there is a congeries of principles capable of pointing in different directions and incapable of arrangement in any kind of systematic hierarchy according to their differing degrees of persuasiveness. This paucity of rules and confusion of principles amply justifies Lord WILBERFORCE's description of statutory interpretation as "what is nowadays popularly called a non-subject."[12] Lord WILBERFORCE was expressing doubts about its suitability for law reform, but the matters which have just been mentioned also render it extremely difficult to give a coherent account of the subject or to assess the merits of criticisms.

The following three passages from speeches of Lord REID in the House of Lords may be cited in support of the remarks made at the beginning of the last paragraph.

(i) "In determining the meaning of any word or phrase in a statute the first question to ask always is what is the natural or ordinary meaning of that word or phrase in its context in the statute. It is only when that meaning leads to some result which cannot reasonably be supposed to have been the intention of the legislature that it is proper to look for some other possible meaning of the word or phrase."[13]

(ii) "Then [in case of doubt] rules of construction are relied on. They are not rules in the ordinary sense of having some binding force. They are our servants, not our masters. They are aids to construction, presumptions or pointers. Not infrequently one 'rule' points in one direction, another in a different direction. In each case we must look at all relevant circumstances and decide as a matter of judgment what weight to attach to any particular 'rule'."[14]

(iii) "It is a cardinal principle applicable to all kinds of statutes that you may not for any reason attach to a statutory provision a meaning which the words of that provision cannot reasonably bear. If they are capable of more than one meaning, then you can choose between those meanings, but beyond that you must not go."[15]

The inverted commas round the word rule in the second quotation show that Lord REID was fully aware of the distinction between rules and principles taken by Professor Dworkin; but consistency with the terminology of the article in the Chicago Law Review requires the substitution of "rule" for "principle" in the third quotation.

The first quotation sets out a rule combining the literal and golden rules mentioned in the last chapter. It is plainly a rule in Professor Dworkin's sense of the word, the judge *must* ask himself what is the natural or ordinary meaning of the word or phrase in question and

[12] 274 H. L. Deb. Ser. 5, col. 1294, 16th November 1966.
[13] *Pinner* v. *Everett*, [1969] 3 All E.R. 257, at p. 258.
[14] *Maunsell* v. *Olins*, [1975] A.C. 373, at p. 382.
[15] *Jones* v. *Director of Public Prosecutions*, [1962] A.C. 635, at p. 668.

apply it to the facts of the case unless the result is something which cannot reasonably be supposed to have been intended by the legislature; but the rule is one which leaves a lot to the choice of the particular judge. In a great many cases it can plausibly be contended that there is more than one ordinary meaning in the context. In that event the judge may consider that there is sufficient doubt to bring the principles mentioned in the second quotation into play; but he may also conclude that there is no doubt that one of the meanings is the ordinary one. In cases which come before appellate tribunals it is by no means uncommon for different judges to express diametrically opposite views with regard to the ordinary meaning of a word or phrase, and the same is true when the question is whether the result of applying the ordinary meaning to the facts cannot reasonably be supposed to have been intended by the legislature. A decision on the interpretation of one statute generally cannot constitute a binding precedent with regard to the interpretation of another statute. The consequence is that the rule of interpretation, unlike most other common law rules, can never be rendered more specific by decisions on points of detail, it can only create other rules applicable to particular statutes. The rule is liable to be stated in a variety of ways. The reference to context is comparatively new. That word does not occur in any of the statements of the literal and golden rules in the previous chapter; nor does it occur in the statement of ALDERSON, B., in *A.-G.* v. *Lockwood*[16] which is frequently cited today:

> "The rule of law I take it upon the construction of all statutes is, whether they be penal or remedial, to construe them according to the plain literal and grammatical meaning of the words in which they are expressed unless that construction leads to a plain and clear contradiction of the apparent purpose of the Act or to some palpable and evident absurdity."

What is far more disconcerting is the fact that there are dicta flatly denying that the courts have any power to reject the natural or ordinary meaning of a word or phrase on the ground that it leads to some result which cannot reasonably be supposed to have been intended by the legislature. For example, in *R.* v. *City of London Court Judge*[17] Lord ESHER said:

> "If the words of an Act are clear, you must follow them, even though they lead to a manifest absurdity. The court has nothing to do with the question whether the legislature has committed an absurdity. In my opinion the rule has always been this—if the words of an Act admit of two interpretations, then they are not clear; and if one interpretation leads to an absurdity and the other does not, the court will conclude that the legislature did not intend to lead to an absurdity, and will adopt the other interpretation."

---

[16] (1842), 9 M. & W. 378, at p. 398.
[17] [1892] 1 Q.B. 273, at p. 290.

The contrast between this passage and the concluding portion of Lord REID's first quotation is striking enough, but its contrast with the following observation in another of Lord REID's speeches is even more striking:

> "It is only where the words are absolutely incapable of a construction which will accord with the apparent intention of the provision and will avoid a wholly unreasonable result, that the words of the enactment must prevail."[18]

This remark was part of the *ratio decidendi* of a tax case in which a majority of the House of Lords rejected the natural and ordinary meaning of statutory words in favour of a decidedly strained construction in order to avoid what was considered to be an absurd result which could not have been intended by the legislature. Remarks such as those of Lord ESHER and Lord REID cannot both be taken to represent the law and the preponderance of authority certainly favours Lord REID. The precise nature of the absurdity required to bring the golden rule into play will be considered in Chapter IV.

The second of the three quotations from Lord REID's speeches set out on page 29 comes from a case in which he entertained doubts about the meaning of the word "premises" in s. 18 (5) of the Rent Act 1968. Was the word in the particular context limited to premises which were dwelling houses? There was a wide choice of meanings and no question of avoiding an absurdity produced by the application of the literal meaning. Accordingly, when answering the question raised in the affirmative, Lord REID considered it was right to review the legislative history of the provision and to lean in favour of the construction involving the least interference with the common law. Although there is no fixed hierarchy of the rules of construction (or presumptions) to which Lord REID was referring, we shall see in Chapter VII that some are, in general, less compelling than others.

The third of the numbered quotations from Lord REID's speeches refers to a rule rather than a principle in the sense in which those words are used by Professor Dworkin. It is an absolute prohibition on going beyond certain limits; the words must not be given a meaning they cannot, by any stretch of imagination, bear. This point was neatly put by EYRE, C.B., in a case concerned with the construction of private documents.

> "All latitude of construction must submit to this restriction; namely that the words may bear the sense which, by construction, is put upon them. If we step beyond this line, we no longer construe men's deeds, but make deeds for them."[19]

---

[18] *Luke* v. *Inland Revenue Commissioners*, [1963] A.C. 557, at p. 577.
[19] *Gibson and Johnson* v. *Minet and Fector* (1791), H.Bl. 569, at p. 615.

The restriction marks the boundary between interpretation and amendment. It is said that the courts have no power to amend the statute although they may read in words which it can be inferred that the legislature meant to insert.

> "It is one thing to put in or take out words to express more clearly what the legislature did say, or must from its own words be presumed to have said by implication, it is quite another matter to amend a statute to make it say something it does not say, or to make it say what it is conjectured that the legislature could have said or would have said if a particular situation had been before it."[20]

But do the courts really confine their activities to putting in words which were already in the statute by implication? Section 3 of the Official Secrets Act 1920 provides that "no person shall *in the vicinity of* any prohibited place obstruct any member of Her Majesty's Forces..." In *Adler* v. *George*[1] the defendant, a member of the Committee of One Hundred, was actually on a Norfolk airfield (a prohibited place) when he obstructed a member of the Forces; nonetheless he was convicted because "in the vicinity of" could be taken to mean "in" as well as near. Lord PARKER, C.J., said he was quite satisfied that this was a case

> "where no violence is done to the language by reading the words 'in the vicinity of' as meaning 'in or in the vicinity of'. Here is a section in an Act of Parliament designed to prevent interference with members of Her Majesty's Forces among others engaged on guard, sentry, patrol or other similar duties in relation to a prohibited place. It would be extraordinary, I venture to think absurd, if an indictable offence were thereby created when the obstruction took place outside the precincts of the station, albeit in the vicinity, and no offençe at all was created if the obstruction occurred on the station itself. There may of course be many contexts in which 'vicinity' must be confined to its literal meaning of being near in place, but under this section I am quite clear that the context demands that the words should be construed in the way I have said."

Was this a case in which the ordinary meaning of the words was rejected under the golden rule in favour of an implied extended meaning which they were just capable of bearing or was it a case of rectification by the insertion of the intended, though inadvertently omitted, words "in or"? The point is a nice one and Lord PARKER evidently took the former view, but Lord DENNING was clearly canvassing rectification in *Eddis* v. *Chichester-Constable*.[2] The action was brought by the trustees of a settlement against the personal representatives of the tenant for life who had, in circumstances assumed to amount to concealed fraud, sold entailed heirlooms to a consortium, also a defen-

---

[20] E. A. Driedger, *The Construction of Statutes*, pp. 79–80.
[1] [1964] 2 Q.B. 7, [1964] 1 All E.R. 628
[2] [1969] 2 Ch. 345, [1969] 2 All E.R. 912.

dant. The claim was for damages for conversion committed more than six years before the action was brought. It was held that the action was not statute barred because the purchasers had notice of the fraud, but two members of the Court of Appeal considered what the position would have been if the purchasers had not had notice of the fraud. The answer to this question turned on the proviso to s. 26 of the Limitation Act 1939. After enacting that, where the right of action is concealed by the fraud of the defendant or anyone through whom he claims, the limitation period shall not run until the plaintiff has discovered the fraud or could have done so with reasonable diligence, the section continues:

> "provided that nothing in this section shall enable any action to be brought to recover or enforce any charge against or set aside any transaction affecting any property which in the case of fraud has been purchased for valuable consideration by a person who was not a party to the fraud and at the time of the purchase did not know or have reason to believe that fraud had been committed."

The absence of any reference to claims for damages or for the recovery of the value of the property means that the proviso does not in terms apply to a claim for conversion so that, even if they had not had notice of the fraud, the consortium would have been liable; but Lord DENNING, with the concurrence of FENTON ATKINSON, L.J., would add "or its value" after the word "property" in the proviso.

> "I know this means that we in this court are filling in a gap left by the legislature—a course which was frowned on some years ago. But I would rather the courts fill in a gap than wait for Parliament to do it. Goodness knows when they would get down to it. I would apply the principle which I stated in *Seaford Court Estates, Ltd* v. *Asher*,[3] 'a judge should ask himself this question: If the makers of the Act had themselves come across this ruck in the texture of it how would they have straightened it out? He must then do as they would have done. A judge must not alter the material of which it is woven, but he can and should iron out the creases.' "[4]

"Rectification" is the right word for this procedure because it is a word which at least implies some sort of intention on the part of Parliament with regard to the added words whereas an amendment could result in words the presence of which in the statute was neither intended nor ever would have been intended by the Parliament which passed it.

---

[3] P. 27 supra.

[4] [1969] 2 Ch. 345, at p. 358, Lord DENNING's remarks in the Seaford case were disapproved by Lord SIMONDS in *Magor and St. Mellons Rural District Council* v. *Newport Corporation* [1952] A.C. 189; [1951] 2 All E.R. 839 and Lord DENNING had later accepted the view that judges cannot fill in gaps (see *London Transport Executive* v. *Betts*, [1959] A.C. 231, at p. 247).

F. THE INTENTION OF PARLIAMENT

But what is meant by "the intention of Parliament"?[5] The phrase is frequently used by the judges although it is meaningless unless it is recognised for what it is, an expression used by analogy, but in no way synonymously, with the intention of an individual concerning the general and particular effects of a document he prepares and signs. A testator may, with perfect propriety, be said to have intended to dispose of all of his property, to have done so in accordance with a particular scheme (equality among his children, or with a preference for sons, for example) and to have intended that his will should have a certain effect in the situation before the Court (e.g. that X should or should not benefit under one of its provisions); but the word "intention" is used in a very different sense when it is said that, in passing the Race Relations Act 1968, Parliament did or did not intend the Act to apply to all racial discrimination, did or did not intend to distinguish between discrimination in the private and public sectors, and did or did not intend the Act to apply to clubs. Each of these statements can be used meaningfully although it is quite impossible to point to specific individuals, like the testator in the previous examples, who did or did not entertain the intentions in question.

The "intention of Parliament" with regard to a particular statute cannot mean the intention of all those who were members of either House when the royal assent was given, for many of them might have been out of the country at all material times and never have heard of the statute. Equally plainly the phrase cannot mean the intention of the majority who voted for the statute as this will almost certainly have been constituted by different persons at the different stages of the passage of the bill and, in any event, it would be rash to assume that all those who vote for it have the same intentions with regard to a particular piece of legislation. For example, it has been pointed out that, in a debate on what became the Statute of Westminster 1932, Mr. Winston Churchill and the Solicitor-General agreed that there was no obscurity in the provisions concerning the Irish Free State, although they took diametrically opposite views concerning their effect.[6]

Someone bent on identifying the intention of specific human beings as that to which reference is made when people speak of the intention of Parliament might resort to the notion of agency. It could be said

---

[5] See an article on Legislative Intent by G. A. MacCallum 75 Yale Law Journal 754 (reprinted in Summers, *Essays in Legal Philosophy*, 236.) Reference is made to most of the Anglo-American literature on the subject in this article, and the failure to mention other articles seriatim by the present author must not be taken to betoken any lack of appreciation of this literature.

[6] Geoffrey Marshall, *Constitutional Theory*, p. 76.

that the promoters of a bill must have some consequences in mind as its general and particular effects, but promoters, whoever they may be, are initiators who place proposals before Parliament rather than act as its agents; and many bills contain amendments which are not the work of the promoters. Nonetheless, if it were thought essential to regard the intention of Parliament as the same sort of thing as the intention of an individual legislator, or the intention of a number of individual legislators all of whom had in mind identical objects and effects of the statutes they jointly draft, the intention of the members of Parliament who promote parliamentary legislation would be the closest approximation. In modern times they give instructions to the draftsman and he can be regarded as their agent. To quote Lord SIMON OF GLAISDALE:[7]

> "it is the duty of a court so to interpret an Act of Parliament as to give effect to its intention. The court sometimes asks itself what the draftsman must have intended. This is reasonable enough: the draftsman knows what is the intention of the legislative initiator (nowadays almost always an organ of the executive); he knows what canons of construction the courts will apply; and he will express himself in such a way as accordingly to give effect to the legislative intention. Parliament, of course, in enacting legislation assumes responsibility for the language of the draftsman. But the reality is that only a minority of legislators will attend the debates on the legislation."

An analogy could be drawn with cases in which the intention of its officers is imputed to a corporation, but it would be a false analogy. Parliament is not a corporation and those who speak of the intention of Parliament do so in spite of the fact that they know that proof that members of Parliament, even those who were the legislative initiators, believed that a statute would produce certain results, is not a condition precedent to the proper use of the phrase. That use is the outcome of linguistic convention having nothing to do with such conclusions of law as the imputation of the intention of a particular individual to a corporation.

In the context of the interpretation of statutes there are three principal situations in which people in general and judges in particular speak of the intention of Parliament. In the first place, whenever the meaning of specific words is under consideration, the idea that a particular meaning is that which would or would not have been attached to a word or phrase by the average member of Parliament, sitting at the time when the statute was passed, may be expressed or refuted by some such statement as "that is (or is not) what Parliament intended by those words". Secondly, when the consequences of a particular construction are under consideration, the idea that a particu-

---

[7] *Ealing London Borough* v. *Race Relations Board*, [1972] A.C. 342, at p. 360.

lar consequence might well have been in the mind of the average member of Parliament is often expressed by some such statement as "that was likely (or unlikely) to have been the intention of Parliament". Finally, although it is impossible to identify the individual members whose purpose it was, it is common to speak of the purpose, aim or object of a statute as the intention of Parliament. The third situation is the most important if only because reflection upon it shows that those who feel uncomfortable about the use of the expression "the intention of Parliament" ought not to feel any more at ease if they abandon the phrase for some other one such as "the intention of the statute", "legislative purpose" or "the object of the statute". Only human beings can really have intentions, purposes or objects, but, in the situation under consideration, the intentions, purposes or objects are not those of identifiable human beings. The words are used by close analogy to the intentions of a single legislator. The analogy is more remote when the "intention of Parliament" is used as a synonym for what the average member of Parliament of a particular epoch would have meant by certain words or expected as the consequences of a statutory provision. All the analogies are so obvious that Blackstone, Bentham, Austin and Gray may well have been right not to worry about the meaning of the intention of Parliament. The expression is not so much a description as a linguistic convenience.

The major judicial statements with regard to the intention of Parliament have been made in cases in which the issue has been whether statutory wording could be ignored or the meaning of statutory language strained, in order to prevent an injustice, or supposed injustice, which, it was thought, could not have been contemplated by Parliament. The answer has almost always been in the negative, and the preponderant view seems to be that, when the question is whether Parliament did or did not intend a particular result, the "intention of Parliament" is what the statutory words mean to the normal speaker of English. The fact that a judge feels confident that, had the situation before him been put to them, the members of the Parliament in which the statute was passed would have voted for a different meaning or for additional words is immaterial.

In *Saloman* v. *Saloman & Co., Ltd.*[8] Lord WATSON said:

> "'The intention of the legislature' is a common but very slippery phrase, which, popularly understood, may signify anything from intention embodied in positive enactment to speculative opinion as to what the legislature probably would have meant, although there has been an omission to enact it. In a court of law or equity, what the legislature intended to

[8] [1897] A.C. 22, at p. 38.

be done or not to be done can only be legitimately ascertained from that which it has chosen to enact, either in express words or by reasonable and necessary implication."

The case, decided in days when the one-man company was a novelty, raised the question whether a debenture, issued by such a company to its one-man as part payment for the business he transferred to it, entitled him to priority over unsecured creditors in the winding-up. The argument which found favour with the Court of Appeal was that an affirmative answer would have been contrary to the intention of the Companies Act 1862 but it could not be supported by reference to any provision in the Act. This was the background of Lord WATSON's allusion to speculative opinion about what the legislature probably would have meant. The House of Lords unanimously decided that Saloman was, as a debenture holder, entitled to priority over the unsecured creditors of his company, and it is a reasonable inference from their speeches that the decision would have been the same even if every member of Parliament who participated in the debates preceding the 1862 Act had expressly stated that it did not permit the formation of such a company or the issue of such a debenture. The statutory words which clearly did permit these things were paramount.

The main importance of *Magor and St. Mellons Rural District Council* v. *Newport Corporation*[9] lies in the comments by Lord SIMONDS in the House of Lords on some observations of DENNING, L.J., in the Court of Appeal; but the factual background is not without significance. The Newport Extension Act 1934 provided for the transfer to Newport of some of the high rate-paying areas of the then separate rural districts of Magor and St. Mellons. Section 58 of the Act incorporated ss. 151–2 of the Local Government Act 1933 which provided for adjustment by arbitration, failing agreement, at the instance of a deprived local authority, "in respect of any increase of burden which, as a consequence of any alteration of boundaries, would properly be thrown on the rate-payers of the area of that local authority in meeting the costs incurred by that local authority in the discharge of any of their functions". The Newport Extension Act came into force on 1st April 1935, and it was common ground that, had nothing occurred to affect their separate existence, Magor and St. Mellons would each have incurred costs which could have been properly thrown on their rate-payers in consequence of the loss of the high rate-paying areas; but, on 1st April 1935, the minister made an order abolishing the separate rural districts and creating a new one of Magor and St. Mellons combined. The order came into force immediately after the Newport Extension Act; it provided for the transfer of the property of the

[9] [1952] A.C. 189, The case is fully reported in [1951] 2 All E.R. 839.

old rural district councils to the new one and it was not disputed that a right to adjustment came within the definition of "property" referentially included in the order from the Local Government Act 1888. In due course the Magor and St. Mellons R.D.C. went to arbitration against the Newport Corporation claiming adjustment under s. 58 of the Extension Act, and the arbitrator stated a case for the opinion of the High Court. PARKER J., the Court of Appeal by a majority of two to one, and the House of Lords by a majority of four to one, held that, although the new rural district council had acquired notional rights to adjustment under the Order, there was no claim which could go to arbitration because no costs had been incurred by the old authorities in consequence of the change of boundaries. The Magor and St. Mellons R.D.C. had no claim in its own right because it had not functioned at all before the change. The result was plainly unjust to the rate-payers of Magor and St. Mellons because the new rural district council had to increase its rates to meet costs incurred in consequence of the change of boundaries, and it is hard to believe that anyone responsible for the legislation before the court would not have striven to avoid the result had such a possibility been drawn to his attention.

DENNING, L.J., dissented in the Court of Appeal on the ground that, although the Order had changed the identity of the two Rural District Councils, the right to adjustment was a continuing right of the rate-payers which could be enforced by the new Council on proof that it had incurred costs in consequence of the change of boundaries. He said that this was so obviously the intention of the minister's Order that he had "no patience with an ultra-legalistic interpretation" which would deprive the rate-payers of their rights altogether. In words similar to those he had already used in *Seaford Court Estates, Ltd.* v. *Asher*,[10] he said:

> "We do not sit here to pull the language of Parliament to pieces and make nonsense of it. That is an easy thing to do and it is a thing to which lawyers are too often prone. We sit here to find out the intention of Parliament and of ministers and carry it out, and we do this better by filling in the gaps and making sense of the enactment than by opening it up to destructive analysis."

In the House of Lords, Lord SIMONDS made the following comment on these remarks:

> "It is sufficient to say that the general proposition that it is the duty of the court to find out the intention of Parliament—and not only of Parliament but of ministers also—cannot by any means be supported. The duty of the court is to interpret the words that the legislature has used; those words may be ambiguous, but, even if they are, the power and duty of

[10] P. 27 supra.

the court to travel outside them on a voyage of discovery are strictly limited..."

Lord Morton said:

> "Insofar as the intention of Parliament or of ministers is revealed in Acts of Parliament or Orders, either by the language used or by necessary implication, the courts should, of course, carry these intentions out; but it is not the function of any judge to fill in what he conceives to be the gaps in the Act of Parliament. If he does so he usurps the function of the legislature."

In the Court of Appeal DENNING, L.J., had spoken of his remarks about his impatience with an ultra-legalistic interpretation as "heroics". In the House of Lords Lord SIMONDS spoke of filling in gaps in a statute as a "naked usurpation of the legislative function under the thin disguise of interpretation". Of course he did not suggest that this was hyperbole but he might have done so. There is an element of gap-filling in a great deal of interpretation. The simple truth is that some judges are prepared to go further than others. Lord RADCLIFFE's dissenting speech in the House of Lords in *Magor and St. Mellons Rural District Council* v. *Newport Corporation* shows that the result achieved by DENNING, L.J., could also have been achieved by more orthodox methods. His view was that, immediately the Newport Extension Act came into force, the Rural District Councils of Magor and St. Mellons each acquired a right to adjustment which could be quantified according to methods of calculation which could have been stated there and then. Those were the rights passed on to the new Rural District Council and the claim to be arbitrated simply concerned calculation. Lord RADCLIFFE in effect invoked the golden rule on the footing that there was a choice of meanings, and the meaning which produced the more just result was to be preferred. For PARKER, J., the majority of the Court of Appeal and the majority of the House of Lords there was no choice of meanings because they had no doubt about the applicability of the literal meaning. The point at which judges feel doubts of this sort is naturally variable. This is why there is not, and probably never can be, anything meriting the description of a coherent body of case-law on statutory interpretation as a whole as distinct from the interpretation of a particular statute.

In *Black-Clawson International, Ltd.* v. *Papierwerke Waldhof-Aschaffenburg A.G.*[11] Lord REID said: "We often say that we are looking for the intention of Parliament, but that is not quite accurate. We are seeking the meaning of the words which Parliament used. We are seeking not what Parliament meant but the true meaning of what they said." This is not one of Lord REID's most helpful remarks because if the

[11] [1975] 1 All E.R. 810, at p. 814.

true meaning of what someone says is not what he intended to say, it is difficult to know what it is. If for "true meaning" we substitute "plain meaning", that does not get us very far because, when in doubt, we must do our best to consult the author of the document, whoever he may be. However that may be, in view of the uniformity of judicial insistence that the intention of parliament, if there is such a thing, with regard to the particular situation before the court must be gathered from the words of the relevant statutory provision, there is no need to treat that intention as a dominant ingredient in any formulation of the basic rules of statutory interpretation.

G. THE MEANING OF INTERPRETATION

If the intention of parliament is not to be a dominant ingredient in the formulation of our basic rules of interpretation, some revision of Gray's definition of interpretation is called for. That definition was "the process by which a judge (or indeed any person, lawyer or layman, who has occasion to search for the meaning of a statute) constructs from the words of a statute-book a meaning which he either believes to be that of the legislature, or which he proposes to attribute to it."[12] It would be better to say that interpretation is the process by which the courts determine the meaning of a statutory provision for the purpose of applying it to the situation before them. The meaning the court ultimately attaches to the statutory words will frequently be that which it believes members of the legislature attached to them, or the meaning which they would have attached to the words had the situation before the court been present to their minds. The object of the statute, or a particular section of it, may be treated as part of its context, and, to the very limited extent discussed in Chapter VI, English courts may travel outside the four corners of the Act with which they are concerned in order to ascertain its object, but they may not go outside the statute in order to ascertain the meaning which members of the legislature attached, or would have attached, to a particular provision in its application to a particular situation. The following words of a South African judge surely hold good for English law:[13]

> "Evidence that every member who voted for a measure put a certain construction upon it cannot affect the meaning which the court must place upon the statute, for it is the product, not of a number of individuals, but of an impersonal Parliament."

To revert to the definition of interpretation, it is hardly necessary to add that the meaning which persons other than a judge trying a case would attach to a statutory provision for the purpose of applying

[12] P. 25 supra.

[13] Van Den Hever, J. A., in *Swart and Nicol* v. *De Kock* 1951 3 S.A. 589, at p. 611.

it to a given situation is dependent on their views of what the courts have done in similar situations, or would do in the situation were it to come before them. Throughout the rest of this book it is assumed that the word "interpretation" is only apt in its application to statutes when there is a dispute about the meaning of words. This excludes the discussion of two procedures which certainly have claims to be described as "interpretation", the process of declaring how words of undisputed meaning apply to an undisputed situation of fact and the process of applying words of undisputed meaning after a conclusion has been reached with regard to disputed facts.

The first of these processes takes place out of court. It is the process followed by legal advisers and any number of other kinds of adviser. Someone consults a solicitor about his rights under the intestacy of a parent or brother. The solicitor gives his advice with confidence on the assumption that the facts are as stated by his client. There is a sense in which the solicitor is interpreting the relevant statutory provisions for his client who may even have read the provisions without understanding them. If it be thought that, in the case of intestacy, these provisions are simple enough for anyone to understand, let the case be one in which a solicitor or accountant is consulted on a simple question of tax liability when the relevant statutory provisions are almost certain to be double dutch to the layman even though they are clear beyond the possibility of dispute to the expert adviser. Whether it be right or wrong to call this process "interpretation" it is the process to which statutes are most commonly subjected and one which renders it essential that the first rule of statutory interpretation should be that the courts must give effect to the ordinary, or, where appropriate, the technical meaning of statutory words. The fact that most statutes are "interpreted" in the sense mentioned in this paragraph out of court is one of the justifications of the restrictions on admissible evidence of the object of a statute mentioned in Chapter VI.

Courts spend more of their time applying words of undisputed meaning to facts which have been disputed than in interpreting statutory words of disputed meaning. To appreciate the truth of this assertion it is only necessary to think of the imposition of prison sentences within the maxima allowed by the various statutes, or the apportionment of damages in the ordinary case of contributory negligence. The point does not call for comment. It simply shows that, if the word is construed sufficiently broadly, "interpretation" is a many-sided process.

III

The Basic Rules Stated

This chapter begins with a statement of the basic rules of English law concerning statutory interpretation. The statement is made with all the diffidence, hesitancy and reservation that the subject demands. No guidance is to be derived from a statute for the Interpretation Act 1889 contains no general principles; there are no binding judicial decisions on the subject of statutory interpretation generally as opposed to the interpretation of particular statutes; all that there is is a welter of judicial dicta which vary considerably in weight, age and uniformity. Naturally it is the last of these variables which confronts anyone attempting a coherent account of the subject with most difficulty. To quote from the first paragraph of the preface to the 12th edition of Maxwell *On the Interpretation of Statutes:*

> "Maxwell might well be sub-titled 'The Practitioners' Armoury': it is, I trust, not taking too cynical a view of statutory interpretation in general, and this work in particular, to express the hope that Counsel putting forward diverse interpretations of some statutory provision will each be able to find in Maxwell dicta and illustrations in support of his case."

The practitioner's boon is the academic's bugbear. It shows no disrespect to the author and editor of that admirable work to say that Maxwell is useless for anyone hoping for a general view of the subject which has the remotest claim to coherence. Invaluable as those dicta and illustrations must be to a protagonist in search of authority, they cannot all be right for the simple reason that a large proportion of them are mutually contradictory. The academic must chance his arm at least to the extent of preferring some dicta to their opposites; but he owes it to his readers to make it clear when this has been done. He must also be on his guard against reading too much into the comparatively few dicta and illustrations which he selects. Warnings to which readers of this book are entitled are that the author may have attached too much importance to *A.-G.* v. *Prince Ernest Augustus of*

Hanover,[1] a decision of the House of Lords which will be mentioned shortly, and he may have minimised the significance of the dicta denying any power in the courts to decline to follow the clear meaning of statutory words on account of the absurdity of the results.[2]

Subject to these reservations it is submitted that the following is a reasonably brief and accurate statement of the rules of English statutory interpretation:

1. The judge must give effect to the ordinary or, where appropriate, the technical meaning of words in the general context of the statute; he must also determine the extent of general words with reference to that context.
2. If the judge considers that the application of the words in their ordinary sense would produce an absurd result which cannot reasonably be supposed to have been the intention of the legislature, he may apply them in any secondary meaning which they are capable of bearing.
3. The judge may read in words which he considers to be necessarily implied by words which are already in the statute and he has a limited power to add to, alter or ignore statutory words in order to prevent a provision from being unintelligible or absurd or totally unreasonable, unworkable or totally irreconcilable with the rest of the statute.[3]
4. In applying the above rules the judge may resort to the aids to construction and presumptions mentioned in Chapters V–VII of this book.

A very full statement of rules 1 and 2 is that of Lord SIMON OF GLAISDALE in *Maunsell* v. *Olins*:[4]

> "... in statutes dealing with ordinary people in their everyday lives, the language is presumed to be used in its primary ordinary sense, unless this stultifies the purpose of the statute, or otherwise produces some injustice, absurdity, anomaly or contradiction, in which case some secondary ordinary sense may be preferred, so as to obviate the injustice, absurdity, anomaly or contradiction or fulfil the purpose of the statute: while, in statutes dealing with technical matters, words which are capable of both bearing an ordinary meaning and being terms of art in the technical matter of the legislation will presumptively bear their primary meaning as such terms of art (or, if they must necessarily be modified, some secondary meaning as terms of art)."

---

[1] [1957] A.C. 436.

[2] See for example the dictum of Lord ESHER in *R.* v. *City of London Court Judge*, p. 30 *supra*.

[3] *Per* Lord REID in *Federal Steam Navigation Co., Ltd.* v. *Department of Trade and Industry*, [1974] 2 All E.R. 97, at p. 100.

[4] [1975] A.C. 373 at p. 391. The fact that it occurs in a dissenting speech in no way detracts from the authoritative nature of this statement which was made with the concurrence of Lord DIPLOCK, the other dissentient in the case.

The first three rules are fully illustrated in the next chapter. In this chapter something will be said about the context of a statute, the admissibility of evidence concerning the meaning of statutory words and different kinds of meaning between which the courts must choose in interpreting those words.

A. CONTEXT

For some time the law relating to statutory interpretation was bedevilled by the notion that it was wrong for a court to look beyond the words with which it was immediately concerned if their meaning was clear when they were considered in isolation. Blackstone had said that recourse should only be had to the context if the words "happen still to be dubious"[5] and the notion derived support from TINDAL, C.J.'s advice to the House of Lords in the *Sussex Peerage* case: "if the words of the statute are in themselves precise and unambiguous, then no more can be necessary than to expound those words in that natural and ordinary sense . . . but if any doubt arises from the terms employed by the legislature, it has always been held a safe means of collecting that intention to call in aid the ground and cause of the making of the statute. . . ."[6] It is difficult to believe that the notion of construction in complete isolation was ever taken wholly seriously, and we saw that TINDAL, C.J., was not above relying on the second section of the Royal Marriage Act 1772 as support for his construction of the first. Nonetheless, even in the 20th century, it has proved necessary for appellate courts to administer mild rebukes to judges for their isolationist approach to statutory construction.

For example, in *Re Bidie*,[7] a case concerned with a widow's application under the Inheritance (Family Provision) Act 1938, the deceased had died on 16th January 1945 and, no will having been found, a grant of administration was made to his widow and one of his children on 13th April 1945. A will was subsequently discovered and the grant of administration was revoked, a grant of probate to the executor named in the will being made on 7th September 1946. As the will contained no provision for her, the widow issued a summons under the 1938 Act on 8th January 1947. Section 2 (1) of the Act provided that "an Order under this Act shall not be made save on an application made within six months from the date on which *representation* in regard to the testator's estate for general purposes is first taken out". If the grant of administration was "representation" within the meaning of the subsection the summons was out of time and this was the

---

[5] P. 18 *supra*. [6] P. 13 *supra*.

[7] [1948] 2 All E.R. 995. See now Inheritance (Provision for Family and Dependants) Act, 1975, ss. 4 and 23.

conclusion reached by the trial judge. But his decision was reversed by the Court of Appeal on the ground that, in the context, "representation" meant representation in respect of a testamentary disposition for it was only by virtue of such a disposition that the court had jurisdiction under the Act. Lord GREENE said:[8]

> "In the present case, if I might respectfully make a criticism of the learned judge's method of approach, I think he attributed too much force to what I may call the abstract or unconditioned meaning of the word 'representation'... The real question which we have to decide is what does the word mean in the context in which we find it here, both in the immediate context of the subsection in which the word occurs and in the general context of the Act, having regard to the declared intention of the Act and the obvious evil that it is designed to remedy."

It has never been doubted that the date of a statute may be very relevant to its construction simply because the meaning of a word may change with the passage of time and the material time is generally said to be that at which the word was used. One of the stock examples is *The Longford*,[9] a case concerned with a private act of William IV's reign which provided that "no *action* in any of His Majesty's courts of law" should be brought against certain shipowners without a month's notice. The question was whether the word "action" was apt to cover an Admiralty action *in rem* and Lord ESHER gave the answer of the Court of Appeal in the following telling words:[10]

> "The first point to be borne in mind is that the act must be construed as if one were interpreting it the day after it was passed ... the word 'action' mentioned in the section was not applicable when the Act was passed to the procedure of the Admiralty Court. Admiralty actions were then called 'suits' or 'causes'; moreover, the Admiralty Court was not called and was not one of His Majesty's courts of law."

The rule that an Act must be construed as if one were interpreting it the day after it was passed is not inconsistent with the somewhat quaint statement that a statute is "always speaking". This appears to have originated in Lord THRING's exhortations to draftsmen concerning the use of the word "shall": "An Act of Parliament should be deemed to be always speaking and therefore the present or past tense should be adopted, and 'shall' should be used as an imperative only, not as a future".[11]

But Lord ESHER's words must undoubtedly be qualified in certain respects. The Telegraph Act 1869 was passed before telephones were invented, but, in *A.-G.* v. *Edison Telephone Co.*,[12] it was held that the

[8] [1948] 2 All E.R. 995, at p. 998. [9] (1889), 14 P.D. 34.

[10] *Ibid.*, at p. 36.

[11] *Practical Legislation* p. 32. See also *Re Pratt, Ex Parte Pratt* (1884), 12 Q.B.D. 334, at p. 340.

[12] (1880), 6 Q.B.D. 244.

privileges that the Act conferred on the Postmaster-General extended to messages sent by phone. STEPHEN, J., said:[13]

> "Of course no one suspects that the legislature intended to refer specifically to telephones many years before they were invented, but it is highly probable that they would, and it seems to us that they actually did, use language embracing future discoveries as to the use of electricity for the purpose of conveying intelligence."

No one would suggest that a written constitution should be construed for all time as if the court were sitting the day after it was enacted, and, when considering the question whether the British North America Act 1869 empowered the Canadian legislature to abolish the right of appeal from Canadian courts to the Privy Council, Lord JOWETT said:[14]

> "It is, as their Lordships think, irrelevant that the question is one which might have seemed unreal at the date of the British North America Act. To such an organic statute the flexible interpretation must be given that changing circumstances require."

Again, the use of general words such as "cruelty", as in the successive Matrimonial Causes Acts from 1937 to 1965, necessarily implies that much is to be left to the courts.

The above examples merely illustrate the point that Parliament may, and often does, evince an intention that the meaning to be attributed to its words should not be ossified on the day on which they were enacted, but *Dyson Holdings, Ltd.* v. *Fox*[15] goes much further. Section 12 (1) (*g*) of the Rent and Mortgage Interest Restriction Act 1920 (re-enacted by the Rent Act 1968) provided that:

> "The expression 'tenant' includes the widow of a tenant . . . who was residing with him at the time of his death, . . . or where a tenant leaves no widow, or is a woman, such member *of the tenant's family* so residing as aforesaid as may be decided in default of agreement by the County Court."

In 1950 the Court of Appeal decided, in *Gammans* v. *Ekins*,[16] that the tenant's "common law husband" who had had no children by her was not a member of her family within the meaning of the subsection in spite of a prolonged residence with her. In the *Dyson Holdings* case, the same Court held 25 years later that a tenant's childless "common law wife" who had been residing with him for a long time when he died in 1961 was a member of his family. BRIDGE, L.J., said:

> "If the language can change its meaning to accord with changing social attitudes, then a decision on the meaning of a word in a statute before

[13] (1880), 6 Q.B.D. 244, at p. 254.
[14] *A.-G. for Ontario* v. *A.-G. for Canada*, [1947] A.C. 127, at p. 154.
[15] [1975] 3 All E.R. 1030.
[16] [1950] 2 K.B. 328, [1950] 2 All E.R. 140.

such a change should not continue to bind thereafter, at all events in a case where the courts have constantly affirmed that the word is to be understood in its ordinary accepted meaning."[17]

Remarks of this nature could herald the erosion of the rule, or at least its restriction to cases in which the original statutory words were not used in a popular sense; but it would be rash to jump to conclusions because no reference was made to the requirement that a statute must be construed as though the court was sitting the day after it was passed.

Even if it is not as unqualified as Lord ESHER might have thought, this requirement must still be regarded as a very important one. It does not only affect the meaning to be given to statutory words for it may also have an important bearing on the question whether the court should depart from their ordinary meaning on the ground that adherence to it would lead to absurd results. The question of absurdity must also be considered as at the time when the statute was passed. This was made very clear by the decision of the House of Lords (affirming the decision of the Court of Appeal) in *A.-G.* v. *Prince Ernest Augustus of Hanover*.[18] In 1955 the Prince sought a declaration that he was a British subject by virtue of his lineal descent from the Electoress Sophia of Hanover. The validity of his claim depended on the construction of a statute of Queen Anne's reign which provided that the Electoress and the issue of her body "and all persons lineally descended from her *born or hereafter to be born* be, and shall be deemed to be, natural born subjects of this kingdom". The preamble stated that: "to the end that the said princess and the heirs of her body and all persons lineally descended from her may be encouraged to become acquainted with the laws and constitutions of this realm it is just and highly reasonable that they *in your Majesty's lifetime* should be naturalised". The preamble could be invoked in support of an argument that the words "in your Majesty's lifetime" should be read into the enacting part of the statute after the words "hereafter to be born." This argument was accepted by the trial judge, VAISEY, J., who refused to make the declaration sought by the Prince. VAISEY, J., took the view that it is not permissible to take account of the preamble when the enacting words are clear but, in this instance, he thought them unclear because they led to absurd results:[19]

"To suppose that Parliament thought that every descendant, however remote in time or distant in kinship of the Electoress, ought to study English law is really rather absurd, however salutary the topic would have been to the immediate successors of Queen Anne."

---

[17] [1975] 3 All E.R. 1030, at p. 1036.
[18] [1957] A.C. 436, [1957] 1 All E.R. 49.
[19] [1955] Ch. 440, at p. 449.

The Court of Appeal also commented on the absurd effects of the statute in the 20th century:[20]

"If the construction of the Act for which the plaintiff contends is the right one, it would follow that the German Kaiser Wilhelm II 'was a British subject and that there are some four hundred persons scattered about Europe who are entitled to British nationality by virtue of this statute'."

But the Court of Appeal held that Prince Ernest was a British subject because the question whether the enacting words led to an absurdity was to be determined by the conditions prevailing when the statute was passed. The House of Lords affirmed the decision of the Court of Appeal in favour of the Prince:[1]

"The question is one of interpretation, and it is not in doubt that the Act must be construed as it would have been construed immediately after it became law."

The Hanover case is of special importance on account of the views expressed in the House of Lords concerning the use that may be made of a preamble when there is one, and further reference is made to this aspect of the decision in Chapter V. The case is also important because of the broad views taken in the House of Lords, notably by Viscount SIMONDS and Lord SOMERVELL concerning the context of a statute. They suggest that account may be taken of the general context, including the object of a statute, in determining the meaning of the statutory provision before the court in the first instance, and not merely at a later stage, should it become necessary to do so on account of the ambiguity of the provision. The remarks are to some extent revolutionary and no apology is made for quoting them at length. Viscount SIMONDS said:[2]

"... words and particularly general words, cannot be read in isolation, their colour and content are derived from their context. So it is that I conceive it to be my right and duty to examine every word of a statute in its context, and I use 'context' in its widest sense, which I have already indicated as including not only other enacting provisions of the same statute but its preamble, the existing state of the law, other statutes *in pari materia*, and the mischief which I can, by those and other legitimate means, discern the statute was intended to remedy."

Lord SOMERVELL said:[3]

"It is unreal to proceed as if the court looked first at the provision in dispute

---

[20] [1956] Ch. 188, at p. 216, *per* ROMER, L.J. It seems to follow that the Kaiser could have been prosecuted for treason after the 1914 war.

[1] [1957] A.C. 436, at p. 465, *per* Lord NORMAND.

[2] *Ibid.*, at p. 461.

[3] *Ibid.*, at p. 473. The citation from Sir John NICHOLL is from *Brett* v. *Brett* (1826), 3 Add. 210, at p. 216.

without knowing whether it was contained in a Finance Act or a Public Health Act. The title and general scope of the Act constitute the background of the context. When a court comes to the Act itself, bearing in mind any relevant extraneous matters, there is, in my opinion, one compelling rule. The whole or any part of the Act may be referred to and relied on. It is, I hope, not disrespectful to regret that the subject was not left where Sir John Nicholl left it in 1826.

> 'The key to the opening of every law is the reason and spirit of the law—it is the "*animus imponentis*" the intention of the lawmaker, expressed in the law itself, taken as a whole. Hence to arrive at the true meaning of any particular phrase in a statute, that particular phrase is not to be viewed, detached from its context in the statute: it is to be viewed in connection with its whole context—meaning by this as well the title and preamble as the purview or enacting part of the statute.' "

Lord SIMONDS's words were cited by Lord UPJOHN in his speech in favour of the majority decision of the House of Lords in *Director of Public Prosecutions* v. *Schildcamp*,[4] a case which shows that the place in a statute occupied by a particular provision may be decisive with regard to its construction. Section 332 of the Companies' Act 1948 appears among a group of sections under the cross-heading "Offences Antecedent to and in course of Winding-Up". Section 332 (1) provides that "if *in the course of the winding-up* of a company it appears that any business has been carried on with intent to defraud creditors or for a fraudulent purpose" the court may declare that some of its officers are personally responsible for its debts. Section 332 (3) reads: "where any business of a company is carried on with such intent or for such purpose as is mentioned in sub-section (1) of this section every person who is knowingly a party to the carrying on of the business in manner aforesaid shall be liable on conviction on indictment to imprisonment..." Is it an essential prerequisite of a conviction under the sub-section that a winding-up order should have been made? The answer of the majority was in the affirmative.

The unanimous decision of the Court of Appeal in *Engineering Industry Training Board* v. *Samuel Talbot (Engineers), Ltd*[5] must have been almost, if not entirely, as disconcering as the *Schildcamp* case to those who believed that the context of a statutory provision is only relevant when it is ambiguous. Section 326 (2) of the Companies' Act 1948 provides that: "where under an execution ... the goods of a company are sold ... the sheriff shall ... retain the balance for fourteen days, and if within that time notice is served on him ... of a meeting having been called *at which there is to be proposed a resolution for the compulsory winding-up of the company* and ... a resolution is passed ... for the winding-up of the company the sheriff shall pay the balance to the liquidator, who shall be entitled to retain it as against the execution creditor".

---

[4] [1971] A.C. 1, at p. 23.
[5] [1969] 2 Q.B. 270.

The plaintiff, a judgment creditor, levied execution on the defendant company, and the sheriff sold sufficient goods to pay the debt. He had been sent a copy of the notice convening a creditors' meeting which, in accordance with the ordinary procedure in a creditors' voluntary winding-up, was summoned to appoint a liquidator on the same day as the members' meeting at which the resolution for the winding-up of the company was passed. It was held that the money in the sheriff's hands should be paid over to the liquidator because all that s. 326 (2) required was that the sheriff should be given notice that a creditors' voluntary winding-up was imminent. By no stretch of imagination could he be said to have been served with notice of a meeting having been called at which there was to be proposed a resolution for the voluntary winding-up of the company. What the sheriff got was a notice from which it could be inferred by anyone cognisant of company law that such a meeting had been summoned. This was sufficient because, to quote Lord DENNING, "... we no longer construe acts of Parliament according to their literal meaning. We construe them according to their object and intent".[6]

The above discussion justifies us in regarding the context of a statutory provision as including the whole of the statute in which it is contained, title and preamble, if any, as well as the enacting parts; the place occupied by the provision within the statute; other statutes *in pari materia*; the circumstances in which the statute was passed, and its object. A few words may be added about the latter.

The significance of the object of the statute in the sense of the mischief to be remedied and the remedy provided has of course been appreciated since the days of *Stradling* v. *Morgan and Heydon's* case.[7] It will have been observed, however, that Lord SIMONDS spoke of ascertaining the mischief which the statute was intended to remedy from the whole enactment (including the preamble), and existing state of the law, other statutes and "other legitimate means". This was a reference to the restrictions to be discussed in Chapter VI on the use which the courts may make of such extrinsic materials as reports of committees and Parliamentary debates. These restrictions, coupled with the almost total absence of preambles in modern statutes, mean that the courts' opportunities of appreciating to the full the object of complicated legislation is limited. At the other extreme, there is a danger that references to the object of a statute will become trivial simply because they are so obvious. There is not much point in exhorting a judge to keep in mind the object of the generality of the provisions in such statutes as the Offences Against the Person Act 1861, the Theft Act 1968 and the Criminal Damage Act 1971. They

[6] [1969] 2 Q.B. 270, at p. 274.
[7] Pp. 8–9 *supra*.

are all aimed at the suppression of various types of crime. A further difficulty arises from the dimensions of many statutes. One Act often deals with a multitude of subjects and, even when it is confined to a single subject, it may deal with many aspects of that subject. For example it is inept to speak of "the object" of Companies' Acts, Local Government Acts and Finance Acts. It is only possible to seek out the object of particular provisions and, even when this has been done, it may be necessary to recognise that a single provision has more than one object.

Subject to reservations such as those which have just been expressed, it would be difficult to exaggerate the importance of the bearing which the object of statutes or statutory provisions has upon their interpretation. The significance of the speeches in the *Hanover* case lies in their recognition of the fact that the object is something to be taken into account in arriving at the ordinary meaning of a provision and not, as the words of TINDAL, C.J., in the *Sussex Peerage* case suggest, merely something to be considered "if any doubt arises from the terms employed by the legislature".[8] The notion that the ordinary meaning of statutory words is something to be arrived at by a purely semantic process or, at most, with the aid of the other enacting parts of the statute in which they occur, has been finally exorcised. This does not mean that the object of the statute has no bearing on the resolution of doubt in cases in which the courts are confronted with a choice of ordinary meanings, or a choice between the primary and secondary meaning of a word. The object is material at two stages of the judge's deliberations, that at which he enquires whether the words are "in themselves precise and unambiguous", and that at which, having answered this question in the negative, he is seeking to resolve doubts arising from the terms employed by the legislature. To put the same point in a different way, the mischief rule is both a primary and a secondary canon of interpretation.[9]

This distinction is subtle but not, it is believed, over-subtle. It is also difficult to illustrate from the *ipsissima verba* of judges for, on the whole, judges are not accustomed to give details of every stage of their reasoning when deciding a point of interpretation, and the attempt to subdivide their reasoning into stages would often be unreal. It is frequently perfectly right and proper for a judge to begin by saying that he has had doubts concerning which of two meanings is the correct one for the purpose in hand, and then to express a preference for one of them on a variety of grounds including, in some cases, the object of the particular provision. On other occasions it will be equally right and proper simply to say that such and such a meaning is the

---

[8] P. 13 *supra*.

[9] See *per* Lord SIMON OF GLAISDALE in *Maunsell* v. *Olins*. [1975] A.C. 373, at p. 385.

natural one in the context and to refer to the object as one of the reasons for this conclusion.

Lord PARKER's judgment in *Bowers* v. *Gloucester Corporation*[10] can be regarded as a case of the latter type. Bowers was a licensed hackney-carriage proprietor and the licensing authority had power to revoke his licence under the Town Police Clauses Act 1847 if he were convicted for the second time "of *any offence*" under the Act and various bye-laws. He had been convicted of several offences relating to hackney-carriages under the Act and bye-laws, but never twice for the same offence. The authority revoked his licence, but the Recorder had held that it was not entitled to do so because the words of the Act were ambiguous as they could be read as applying only to a conviction for the second time of the same offence and the ambiguity ought to be resolved in favour of Bowers. The Divisional Court was, however, of opinion that there was no ambiguity and so did not have to consider how it should be resolved. Lord PARKER said: "When I first read these words it seemed to me that 'any offence' means what it says, 'any offence' ... that is so on general principles of construction". After saying that there was no ambiguity or doubt, he justified his conclusion by reference to the ordinary meaning of the words and the object of the provision "which is clearly that this strict control should be kept on taxicab drivers ... together with the complete absurdity which arises, bearing in mind the mischief aimed at, if a man can show himself to be utterly unfitted to be a taxicab driver ... by committing 30, 40 or 50 offences and yet not have his licence revoked because he has always committed a different offence".[11]

When the object of the statute is called in aid to resolve an ambiguity, it has the force of a mere presumption that a construction which tends to suppress the mischief and advance the remedy is to be preferred to one that does not have these effects. This is a presumption which is liable to be defeated by other presumptions, and, in criminal cases, it frequently is defeated by the presumption in favour of a strict construction of penal statutes. That is what tilted the scales in favour of the narrower meaning of "engine" as a mechanical contrivance in *R.* v. *Munks*.[12] By contrast the presumption in favour of the advancement of the statutory purpose triumphed in *Adler* v. *George*.[13]

B. EVIDENCE

The ordinary meaning of words, a matter of obvious concern to the law of interpretation, is a question of fact. Thus, in *Brutus* v. *Cozens*,[14]

---

[10] [1963] 1 Q.B. 881. [11] *Ibid.*, at p. 887.
[12] P. 10 *supra*. [13] P. 32 *supra*.
[14] [1973] A.C. 854 [1972] 2 All E.R. 1297.

the defendant was charged with an offence under s. 5 of the Public Order Act 1936 on the ground that he had used "insulting behaviour" whereby a breach of the peace was likely to be occasioned in a public place. To the annoyance of the spectators, he had interrupted play in a match at the Wimbledon Tennis Championships by going on to the court. His action was a protest against the participation of a South African player in the tournament, but the prosecution's case was that it was the spectators who had been insulted. The magistrates dismissed the case on the ground that the defendant's behaviour had not been "insulting". The Divisional Court reversed their decision because what the defendant had done evinced disrespect or contempt for the rights of others which reasonable people would foresee was likely to cause a protest. The House of Lords restored the decision of the magistrates on the ground that it is incorrect to say that conduct evincing a disrespect or contempt for the rights of others is always insulting and, the question being one of fact, the magistrates were entitled to decide the case as they did.

But, although the meaning of ordinary words is a question of fact, it is very far from being an ordinary fact for legal purposes. In the first place one is apt to think of questions of fact as something upon which evidence can be called on each side. This is certainly not the law of statutory interpretation so far as the ordinary meaning of words is concerned. In *Marquess of Camden* v. *Inland Revenue Commissioners*[15] the evidence of a valuer with regard to the meaning of "a nominal rent" was held to have been inadmissible, PHILLIMORE, L.J., disposing of the matter with the remark that "it is enough to say that in construing a modern statute, not dealing with the particular customs of a particular locality, or with the practice of a particular trade, but of general application, evidence such as is sought to be adduced in this case is inadmissible".[16] Lord ESHER stated the theoretical position with regard to the admissibility of evidence concerning the meaning of words on questions of interpretation when he said:[17]

> "If the Act is directed to dealing with matters affecting everybody generally, the words used have the meaning attached to them in the common and ordinary use of language; if the Act is one passed with reference to a particular trade, business, or transaction, the words are used as everybody conversant with that trade, business or transaction knows and understands to have a particular meaning in it, then the words are to be construed as having that particular meaning, though it may differ from the common or ordinary meaning of the words."

These remarks come from a case in which the question was whether

---

15 [1914] 1 K.B. 641.

16 *Ibid.*, at p. 650.

17 *Unwin* v. *Hanson*, [1891] 2 Q.B. 115, at p. 119.

the power conferred upon justices by s. 65 of the Highway Act 1835 to direct trees near the highway to be "pruned or lopped" was confined to directions to cut off lateral branches or whether it extended to "topping". It was held that the justices' powers did not extend that far. Evidence had been called on the difference between lopping and topping, but it was said to be unnecessary because every countryman is familiar with the distinction. It may therefore be assumed that evidence of the ordinary meaning of statutory words is theoretically inadmissible,[18] although it may be received in practice comparitively frequently. When it is agreed or contended that statutory words have a technical meaning, evidence with regard to that meaning is unquestionably admissible, and it should generally be preferred to information gleaned from other sources such as dictionaries.[19]

The second reason why the meaning of ordinary words is no ordinary question of fact is that it is the subject of judicial notice. This has at least two highly significant consequences. The first is that, although the direct evidence of witnesses concerning the ordinary meaning of statutory words is inadmissible, recourse may be had to all the other sources of information which a judge may tap when considering whether a fact is one of which judicial notice should be taken. These include dictionaries. To take one among many examples, in *R.* v. *Peters*,[20] the question before the Court for Crown Cases Reserved was whether "credit" had been obtained by an undischarged bankrupt. He had simply bought a horse from an Irish dealer who delivered it on to a steamer, the horse being duly received by the accused. There was no formal stipulation for the giving of credit for the price which had not in fact been paid. Nonetheless the majority of the court decided the credit had been obtained. Lord COLERIDGE said that he was well aware that dictionaries were not to be taken as authoritative expositions of the meanings of words used in acts of Parliament, "but it is a well-known rule of courts of law that words should be taken to be used in their ordinary sense, and we are therefore sent for instruction to these books".[1] He then reached his conclusion after citing Johnson's definition of credit as "correlative to debt" and Webster's reference to it as "trust, the transfer of goods in confidence of future payment". Textbooks and the practice of the business com-

[18] For cases in which evidence of the ordinary meaning of words has been held inadmissible, see *R.* v. *Calder and Boyars, Ltd.*, [1969] 1 Q.B. 151; [1968] 3 All E.R. 644; *R. v. Anderson*, [1972] 1 Q.B. 304; [1971] 3 All E.R. 1152. *R.* v. *Stamford*, [1972] 2 Q.B. 391; [1972] 2 All E.R. 430. The difficulty is that the distinction between an ordinary and a technical meaning is not at all easy to draw.

[19] *Prophet* v. *Platt Brothers & Co., Ltd.*, [1961] 2 All E.R. 644; *Central Press Photos Ltd.* v. *Department of Employment and Productivity*, [1970] 3 All E.R. 775.

[20] (1886), 16 Q.B.D. 636.

[1] *Ibid.*, at p. 641.

munity or conveyancers may be called in aid on similar principles. Where they are relevant assistance may also be gained from historical works and purely literary sources. In *London and North Eastern Rail Co.* v. *Berriman*,[2] for instance, a will of 1587 and Milton's *Paradise Lost* were cited to the House of Lords to help them decide the question whether a railway worker was engaged in "repairing" within the meaning of rules made under the Railway Employment Prevention of Accidents Act 1900 when engaged on the routine oiling and maintenance of the apparatus in a signal box.

The other highly significant consequence of the ordinary meanings of statutory words being the subject of judicial notice is that decisions with regard to them, unlike other decisions on questions of fact, become binding precedents so far as the construction of the statute in question is concerned. Let it be granted that it is a question of fact whether behaviour is "insulting" within the meaning of s. 5 of the Public Order Act 1936, it is now a rule of English law that behaviour is not necessarily insulting because it shows a contempt for other people's rights. Similarly, after the decision of the majority of the House of Lords in *Berriman's* case that routine oiling and maintenance of signalling apparatus was not "repairing" within the rules with which the House was concerned, all courts had to hold that such work fell outside the protection afforded to those who were "repairing" within the meaning of the rules. In *Carter* v. *Bradbeer*[3] three law lords out of a House consisting of five held that every bar counter from which intoxicating liquor may be bought is necessarily a "bar" for the purposes of s. 76 (5) of the Licensing Act 1964. Lord DIPLOCK was not prepared to express so categorical a view, but, no question of principle being involved, he saw no point in delivering a dissenting judgment since the words of a statute mean whatever a majority of the appellate committee dealing with the case say they mean.

There is a further reason, not directly connected with the meaning of words, why the practice of taking judicial notice is of great importance in relation to statutory interpretation. The courts' powers of investigating the object of a statute are restricted by the fact that there are certain types of evidence, such as parliamentary debates, which may not be considered.

> "In this country we do not refer to the legislative history of an enactment as they do in the United States of America. We do not look at the explanatory memoranda which preface the Bills before Parliament. We do not have recourse to the pages of Hansard. All that the courts can do is to

---

[2] [1946] A.C. 278; [1946] 1 All E.R. 255.
[3] [1975] 3 All E.R. 158.

take judicial notice of the previous state of the law and of other matters generally known to well-informed people."[4]

C. THE DIFFERENT KINDS OF MEANING

At the end of the last chapter interpretation was spoken of as the process by which the courts determine the meaning of a statutory provision for the purpose of applying it to the situation before them.[5] Something must now be said about the different kinds of meaning with which this process is concerned.[6]

It is assumed that when judges speak, as they frequently do, about the "ordinary" or "natural" meaning of words and phrases they have in mind the meaning which would be attached to those words and phrases by the normal speaker of English at the time when the statute was passed. This is taken to have been the meaning intended by the draftsman or, after due allowance has been made for the metaphor, by Parliament. It is not uncommon for a judge to ask himself the direct question what the ordinary man would have understood by the words; but there are limits to the utility of this process in the case of disputed interpretation because everything depends on the context and there is often a choice of ordinary meanings. For example, s. 3 (1) of the Extradition Act 1870 provides that "a fugitive criminal shall not be surrendered if the offence in respect of which his surrender is demanded is one of a *political character*". If the ordinary man were asked the meaning of the words "an offence of a political character", he might, after a good deal of prompting, finish up by saying "an offence committed as part of a plan to overthrow a government": but what if the offence were attempted murder of an official of the regime to be overthrown while on a visit to the country requesting extradition? Having been told that attempted murder is an offence for which extradition can be sought and, if the offence is of a political character, refused, would the ordinary man say "for the purposes of the Extradition Act the offence must have been part of a plan to overthrow the government of the requesting state in order that it should be an offence of a political character?" In *Cheng* v. *Governor of Pentonville Prison*,[7] Lord SIMON OF GLAISDALE answered this question in the negative. He was confident that the most harassed commuter from Clapham would say "of course the offence was of a political charac-

---

[4] *Escoigne Properties, Ltd.* v. *Inland Revenue Commissioners*, [1958] A.C. 549, at p. 565, *per* Lord DENNING.

[5] P. 40 *supra*.

[6] The best introduction to this subject for lawyers is provided by the articles on "Language and the Law" by Professor Glanville Williams in 61 Law Quarterly Review 71; 179; 293; 384; and 62 Law Quarterly Review 387.

[7] [1973] A.C. 931, at p. 951.

ter". But Lord SIMON's was a dissenting speech and the effect of the majority decision is that, for the purposes of s. 3 (1) of the 1870 Act "offence of a political character" means an offence designed to overthrow the government of the requesting state.

The ordinary meaning of a term may be a question of fact, albeit a somewhat special one, but the construction of a statute is a question of law and an issue with regard to the choice of ordinary meanings in a particular context is concerned with statutory construction. The judge takes judicial notice of ordinary meanings and chooses the one which he considers to be the most appropriate in the context. The normal speaker of English is not often of much assistance with regard to the choice, although he may have rendered yeoman service in indicating what were possible and impossible ordinary meanings just as he renders yeoman service as the yardstick of statutory interpretation, if that be the right word, where there is no problem simply because there is no possibility of a choice of meanings.[8]

Nothing need be said at this stage about the distinction between an ordinary and technical meaning, but something must be said about "fringe meaning" and the cognate problem of the restrictions to be placed on the interpretation of general words. Problems of fringe meaning are sometimes spoken of as "problems of the penumbra", the point being that, in the case of a great many words, there is no doubt about the hard core of their meanings, but different views may well be taken on the question whether the word is applicable to things or situations outside that hard core. No-one doubts that a chair is furniture, but what about linoleum? A fully equipped motor-car is certainly a vehicle, but what if the engine and wheels are removed? Is a bicycle a carriage? Different minds may take different views concerning the answer to these and countless similar questions. In a great many cases the answer will of course vary according to the context in which the problem arises and the courts will be guided by the object of the legislation they are considering, but very frequently the judge can do little more than say that a line has to be drawn somewhere and that he has decided to draw it beyond or short of the facts of the case before him.

Fringe meaning raises the question how far words extend in ordinary language as well as in law. There is the converse question, usually, though by no means always, an exclusively legal one, of whether any limit should be placed upon the generality of statutory words.

---

[8] In "The Theory of Legal Interpretation", 12 Harvard Law Review 417, Holmes says: "But the normal speaker of English is merely a special variety, a literary form, so to speak, of our old friend the prudent man". In the case of statutory interpretation, the existence of a legal context which can sometimes be very complicated makes the analogy somewhat questionable.

We have already had an example of this kind of question in *Re Bidie*[9] where the nature of the jurisdiction conferred by the Inheritance (Family Provision) Act 1938 led the Court of Appeal to limit the words "representation" to grants of representation in respect of testamentary dispositions. The problem is, however, frequently solved by recourse to very strong presumptions, such as the presumption that statutes do not, in the absence of express provision, deprive an accused of the general defences to a criminal charge, or to less strong presumptions such as the presumption that *mens rea* is required by the definition of every crime. No statutory crime is defined in such a way as to admit in ordinary language of such defences as insanity, duress and necessity, but it has never been contended that these defences are not available. Quite a lot of statutory crimes are defined in absolute terms, but it is by no means uncommon for the courts to imply a requirement of guilty knowledge. The problem of the limitations, if any, to be placed upon general words is not exclusively a legal one for we shall see in Chapter V that there is an important rule of language, the *ejusdem generis* rule, which restricts the apparently general effect of words and phrases such as "whatsoever", "any other" or "all other".

The distinction between primary and secondary meaning turns on that between usual and less usual meanings. Many words and phrases have more than one usual meaning since allowance has to be made for a lot of different contexts. But a time comes when it is permissible to say that, though a word is capable of bearing such and such meaning, that meaning is unusual, i.e. secondary. For example, the statement "it happened by accident" has a number of usual meanings. In criminal law it may mean either that the accused did not intend the harm or else that he neither intended nor was guilty of negligence with regard to it. In industrial law an employee's injury may be said to have been an "accident arising out of and in the course of his employment" even though it was deliberately inflicted, as when thugs murder a cashier while robbing him,[10] or pupils murder their schoolmaster.[11] But, if someone says "X inherited a fortune by accident", meaning "so many contingencies in the way of sudden deaths of relations had to occur that the settlor cannot be said to have intended X to inherit anything", the reply might well be, "I see what you mean but your use of the word 'accident' is rather odd." "He acquired a fortune by the accident of his birth" is a statement involving the use of the word accident in what must now be regarded as its secondary meaning of "chance", although etymologically the word means

[9] P. 44 *supra*.
[10] *Nisbet* v. *Rayne and Burn*, [1910] 2 K.B. 689.
[11] *Trim Joint District School Board of Management* v. *Kelly*, [1914] A.C. 637.

"anything that happens"; but, if someone were to say "X's winning the race was more of an accident than Y's coming second", the reply would have to be "you are giving the word accident a meaning it will not bear. You should say 'the odds against X's coming first were higher than those against Y coming second.''

The distinctions between the different usual meanings of words and phrases is important for interpreters of statutes because they have to decide which sense is most appropriate in the particular context. The distinction between usual or ordinary meaning on the one hand, and a secondary meaning on the other hand, is important for interpreters of statutes because, from time to time, they have to opt for a secondary meaning on account of the inconvenience, injustice or absurdity of applying any of the primary meanings to the situation before them. The question whether a particular "interpretation" gives the words a meaning they will not bear is crucial because to do that is not interpretation; but there is a no-man's land between interpretation and making statutory provisions not made by the legislature where words are "read in" to a section of a statute.

A kind of meaning which has yet to be mentioned is the "literal" meaning. It is frequently used as a synonym for the natural or ordinary meaning, as in the phrase "literal rule" which figured in Chapter I. But, when applied to the construction of statutes, it is often used pejoratively. Then it is the meaning which results from giving to each word an ordinary meaning without much reference to the context and applying the provision to a particular situation without any regard to its object. Reference has already been made to s. 8 of the Road Traffic Act 1972. It reads in part as follows:

> "A constable in uniform may require any person *driving or attempting to drive* a motor vehicle on a road or other public place to provide a specimen of breath for a breath test there or nearby if the constable has reasonable cause (*a*) to suspect him of having alcohol in his body...."

The literal meaning of this provision is that, if cases of attempted driving are excluded, a constable can only make the request for a breath test while the driver is driving. It would therefore be open to a motorist stopped by a constable who had every reason to suspect him of having alcohol in his body to retort with the subsequent blessing of the court, "Too late, I am stinking drunk but I am not, by any stretch of the imagination, 'driving'."

Section 38 (1) of the Children and Young Persons Act 1933 enables a child of tender years to give unsworn evidence in criminal cases. The following is the proviso·

> "Provided that where evidence admissible by virtue of this section is given on behalf of the prosecution the accused shall not be liable to be convicted

of the offence unless that evidence is corroborated by some other material evidence in support thereof implicating him."

Unquestionably the effect of this proviso, "literally construed", is that a conviction for burglary would have to be quashed notwithstanding the fact that three adult witnesses gave overwhelming evidence against the accused, if the prosecution had called a child to give uncorroborated unsworn evidence on some minor point.[12] Few people, whether or not they happen to be lawyers, would dissent from Lord DIPLOCK's statement that "so preposterous an intention cannot reasonably be ascribed to Parliament'".[13] Some such words as "in consequence of such evidence" must be read in after the word "offence". The House of Lords has held that the object of the proviso is to prevent a conviction based on nothing but the unsworn evidence of children, accordingly the words "other evidence" must be given the slightly restricted meaning of "evidence admissible otherwise than by virtue of this section."[14]

So far as appears from reported cases no-one has tried to argue that a conviction is unlawful if it resulted from a trial at which any uncorroborated evidence had been given by an unsworn child of tender years however peripheral that evidence may have been, but, when a wholly different provision was under consideration, the Appellate Division of the Supreme Court of Alberta was once confronted with an argument in favour of a construction no less literal. The case concerned the construction of a bye-law directing that "all drug shops shall be closed at 10 p.m. on each and every day of the week". It was contended for the defendants that there was no infringement if a drug shop were closed at 10 p.m. and opened a few minutes later on the same day. This contention was dismissed with the contempt it deserved and with the observation that no-one but a lawyer would ever have thought of imputing such a meaning to the bye-law.[15] Presumably this is the kind of thing which STEPHEN, J., had in mind when he said that it is not enough for the drafting of Acts of Parliament to attain to a degree of precision which a person reading them in good faith can understand, "but it is necessary to attain, if possible, to a degree of precision which a person reading in bad faith cannot misunderstand".[16] The words "if possible" were well chosen. Relatively little of what has to be said in a statute can be said in such a way that it may not be reduced to utter nonsense by a strictly literal and wholly unimaginative construction.

---

[12] *Cross on Evidence*, 4th Edn, p. 172.
[13] *Director of Public Prosecutions* v. *Hester*, [1973] A.C. 296, at p. 323.
[14] *Director of Public Prosecutions* v. *Hester*, *supra*.
[15] *R.* v. *Liggetts-Finlay Drug Stores, Ltd.*, [1919] 3 W.W.R. 1025.
[16] In *Re Castioni*, [1891] 1 Q.B. 149, at p. 166.

IV

The Basic Rules Illustrated

It is now proposed to illustrate the basic rules set out on page 43 by treating some of the more important or more instructive cases on statutory interpretation as involving choices of the different kinds of meaning mentioned in the last section of the previous chapter. The first three sections of this chapter illustrate the first of our basic rules: "The judge must give effect to the ordinary or, where appropriate, the technical meaning of words in the general context of the statute; he must also determine the extent of general words with reference to that context". The remaining two sections of the chapter illustrate the second and third of the basic rules.

A. CHOICE BETWEEN ORDINARY MEANINGS IN THE CONTEXT

In a number of cases the choice between ordinary meanings in the context is not a very difficult one. These are often criminal appeals in which the point of statutory construction causing the case to be reported was the last resort or forlorn hope of the appellant. In *Abrahams* v. *Cavey*,[1] for example, the Ecclesiastical Court's Jurisdiction Act 1860 was under consideration in a case in which the defendant had caused a disturbance at a Sunday morning church service at which some leading politicians were present by shouting out criticisms of their policy. The relevant provision penalises "any person who shall be guilty of riotous, violent or *indecent* behaviour at divine service." No doubt "indecent" often means "obscene", but it can also be used by ordinary people in the sense of "unbecoming" and it is difficult to believe that it took the Divisional Court much time to reach the conclusion that, in the particular context, the word bore the latter

[1] [1968] 1 Q.B. 479; [1967] 3 All E.R. 179.

meaning. The court treated the word as a species of the genus creating a disturbance in a sacred place. In *Mills* v. *Cooper*[2] the defendant was charged with a contravention of s. 127 of the Highways Act 1959 under which it is an offence "if without lawful authority or excuse a *gypsy* encamps on a highway." Some four months earlier the defendant had been acquitted on a similar charge. If "gypsy" in this context means a member of the Romany race a plea of issue estoppel might well have succeeded, but not if it means a person leading a nomadic life of no fixed employment or abode, because the defendant might have taken to that mode of life between the two charges. The court adopted the second meaning on account of the other provisions of the section which were solely concerned with interferences with the amenities of the highway. There was a choice between the dictionary and colloquial meanings of the word "gypsy" and "it is difficult to think that Parliament intended to subject a man to a penalty in the context of causing litter and obstruction on the highway merely by reason of his race".[3]

There were differences of judicial opinion in the cases mentioned in Chapter III which partly turned on the meaning of the word "accident" in relation to workmen's compensation. Was it confined to injury suffered without fault on anybody's part, or did it apply to injuries deliberately inflicted on an employee? The latter conclusion was largely dictated by the context which was one of insurance against risks incidental to employment, and the differences of judicial opinion were more concerned with the question whether the accident arose "out of and in the course of" the claimant's employment than with the meaning of "accident".[4] Another case which gave rise to differences of judicial opinion about the choice between the ordinary meanings of statutory words is *Ealing London Borough* v. *Race Relations Board*.[5] The Ealing Borough Council gave priority to British subjects when allocating the housing accommodation at their disposal. They sought a declaration that this discrimination was not an infringement of the Race Relations Act 1968. Under s. 1 (1) of that Act

> "A person discriminates against another for the purposes of this Act if, on the ground of colour, race, or ethnic or *national origins* he treats that other in any situation to which section 2, 3, 4 or 5 below applies less favourably than he treats or would treat other persons."

Section 5 prohibits discrimination with regard to housing. The test

---

[2] [1967] 2 Q.B. 459, [1967] 2 All E.R. 100.

[3] *Per* Lord PARKER, C.J., [1967] 2 Q.B. 459, at p. 467.

[4] *Nisbet* v. *Rayne and Burn*, [1910] 2 K.B. 689; *Trim Joint District School Board of Management* v. *Kelly*, [1914] A.C. 637; p. 58 *supra*.

[5] [1972] A.C. 342.

case was that of a Polish national resident in Ealing whose name was not placed on the council's housing list. Stated concisely the issue was whether "national origins" means citizenship at birth or something akin to race. SWANWICK, J., held that the phrase referred to citizenship and accordingly made no declaration, but the House of Lords held by a majority of 4 to 1 that the phrase meant something akin to race and accordingly made the declaration sought by the council. "The ground of the discrimination was that he [the Polish national] was not a British subject. It was his nationality at the time when he applied, not his national origins which led to the refusal to put him on to the waiting list."[6] Discrimination against a naturalised British subject on the ground of his nationality at birth would no doubt have constituted an infringement of the Act, and the same might well have been true of discrimination against a British subject one of whose parents was a foreigner. The context of the Act suggested a concentration on racial rather than national discrimination, but there is plainly force in the argument which commended itself to SWANWICK, J., that present nationality and national origins are usually the same with the result that the practical effect of the council's rule was that the vast majority of people of other national origins were treated less favourably than people of British or Commonwealth origins.

London North Eastern Rail Co. v. *Berriman*[7] is another case which produced a marked difference of judicial opinion about the ordinary meaning of words. The issue was whether a railway worker was engaged in "relaying or repairing" the permanent way within the meaning of rules made under the Railway Employment Prevention of Accidents Act 1900 when he was engaged in oiling and cleaning an apparatus which worked the points. He was standing on the line when he was knocked down and killed by a train. If he was "repairing", his widow was entitled to damages under the Fatal Accidents Act not otherwise. The case turned on the question whether "repairing" in this context meant putting right something that was wrong and no more, or whether it could include maintaining something in good order. By a majority of 3 to 2 the House of Lords were in favour of the first answer. There is plainly much to be said for the second in the context of legislation aimed at protecting railway workers, but the statute and rules made the Railway Company's failure to provide an adequate system of warning persons in the position of the deceased a crime, and the conflict of the mischief rule with the presumption in favour of a strict construction of penal statutes lies at the root of some of the most controversial cases on statutory interpretation.

---

[6] *Per* Lord DILHORNE, *ibid.*, at p. 349.
[7] [1946] A.C. 278; [1946] 1 All E.R. 255.

Some cases can be treated equally well as deciding that words are incapable of bearing the meaning for which one of the parties was contending or as decisions that one of two possible meanings is to be preferred. *Bourne* v. *Norwich Crematorium, Ltd*[8] is an example. The issue was whether a crematorium was an "industrial building" within the meaning of s. 271 (1) (*c*) of the Income Tax Act 1952. If it was, the company by which it was managed was entitled to a tax allowance. The subsection defined "an industrial building" as a building in use "for the purpose of a trade which consists in the manufacture of goods or materials or *the subjection of goods or materials to any process.*" STAMP, J., emphatically rejected the claim to tax relief in the following words:[9]

> "What has to be decided here is whether what is done by the taxpayer viz. the consumption or destruction by fire of the dead body of a human being is within the phrase "the subjection of goods or materials to any process". I can only say that, giving the matter the best attention that I can, I conclude that the consumption by fire of the mortal remains of homo sapiens is not the subjection of goods or materials to a process within the definition of industrial buildings in s. 271 (1) (*c*) of the Income Tax Act 1952."

Perhaps it is unrealistic to talk about the ordinary meaning of "the subjection of goods or materials to any process", but it does seem that there was more to be said in favour of the claim to relief than STAMP, J., allowed. It is arguable that there were two linguistic issues; (i) is a dead body "goods or materials"? and (ii) is destruction by fire a "process"? If the answer given to (i) were that a dead body may properly be described as "materials" and to (ii) that destruction by fire can properly be described as a process, it is difficult to see how language would have been distorted in the context of taxation. STAMP, J., protested against "subjecting the English language, and more particularly a simple English phrase to this kind of process of philology and semasiology". He did not appear to consider the context and this may be an instance in which the letter was unnecessarily allowed to prevail over the spirit in the court's answer to a question of statutory interpretation.

B. CHOICE BETWEEN AN ORDINARY AND A TECHNICAL MEANING

Many cases bear out the distinction taken by Lord ESHER in the following passage which has already been quoted:

> "If the Act is directed to dealing with matters affecting everybody generally, the words used have the meaning attached to them in the common

[8] [1967] 2 All E.R. 576.
[9] *Ibid.*, at p. 578.

and ordinary use of language. If the Act is one passed with reference to a particular trade, business, or transaction, and words are used which everybody conversant with that trade, business or transaction knows and understands to have a particular meaning in it then the words are to be construed as having that particular meaning, though it may differ from the common or ordinary meaning of the words."[10]

To take the second half of the passage first in *Jenner* v. *Allen West & Co., Ltd.*[11] the court of appeal held that "crawling boards" within the meaning of the Building (Safety, Health and Welfare) Regulations 1948 meant boards with battens on them to prevent workmen who used such boards when placed over portions of a building from which the roof had been removed from slipping. The trial judge heard evidence on the point and the ordinary meaning of plain boards on which workmen could crawl was rejected. Similarly in *Prophet* v. *Platt Brothers & Co. Ltd.*[12] HARMAN, L.J., made the point that the meaning of the word "fettling" as used in the schedule to the Protection of Eyes Regulations 1938 was not to be gathered from looking at a dictionary (from which it might have appeared that the word referred to the lining of a furnace). The "fettling of metal castings" appeared from the evidence to be "a kind of trimming up of the castings as they come from the foundry".[13] A more controversial case to which reference has already been made is *Fisher* v. *Bell*[14] where the expression "offers for sale" in s. 1 (1) of the Restriction of Offensive Weapons Act 1959 was held not to apply to the placing of a flick-knife in a shop window. The court had a choice between the technical meaning of that term as used in the law of contract and a popular meaning according to which goods placed in shop windows are offered for sale. It could perhaps be said without undue exaggeration that the Act being to a large extent addressed to shopkeepers it was passed with reference to a particular trade within the meaning of Lord ESHER's dictum, but the decision is best regarded as one more example of the resolution of the conflict between the mischief rule and the presumption that penal statutes should be strictly construed in favour of the presumption.

It will be recollected that Blackstone tells us that, although words are generally to be understood in their "usual and most known signification", terms of art must be "taken according to the acceptation of the learned in each art, trade and science".[15] He illustrates this latter point by reference to the Act of Settlement limiting the Crown

---

[10] *Unwin* v. *Hanson*, [1891] 2 Q.B. 115, at p. 119.
[11] [1959] 2 All E.R. 115.
[12] [1961] 2 All E.R. 644.
[13] *Ibid.*, at p. 648.
[14] [1961] 1 Q.B. 394; [1960] 3 All E.R. 731, p. 11 *supra*.
[15] P. 18 *supra*.

of England to the Princess Sofia and the heirs of her body, being Protestants. "It becomes necessary to call in the assistance of lawyers to ascertain the precise idea of the words 'heirs of her body' which in a legal sense comprise only certain of her lineal descendants".[16] In the case of quite a large number of statutes it is clear that words are used in their technical legal sense; but occasionally there are cases in which the point in issue is a choice between a legal and a popular meaning. Thus the strict legal meaning of "hospital" is an eleemosynary institution in which persons benefited form a corporate body. Nonetheless it was held in *Lord Colchester* v. *Kewney*[17] that the exemption of hospitals from land tax by statutes of 1797 and 1798 extended to all establishments popularly known as hospitals including an asylum for orphans. Similarly, in *London County Council* v. *Cutts*.[18] it was held that the provision in s. 69 (1) of the London County Council (General Powers) Act 1933 that consent to the establishment of petrol filling stations adjacent to any street shall not be refused "in the case of any proposed petroleum-filling station unless in the opinion of the local authority the petroleum-filling station if established would cause *obstruction* to traffic" referred to any interference with traffic and not to obstruction on the highway in the strict common law sense.

Section 18 (5) of the Rent Act 1968 accords a measure of protection against eviction to a sublessee whose protected tenancy has been terminated by the death of his lessor. The subsection protects him against eviction by the head lessor "where a dwelling house (*a*) forms part of *premises* which have been let as a whole on a superior letting but do not constitute a dwelling house let on a protected tenancy and (*b*) is itself let on a protected tenancy or statutory tenancy". Does the word "premises" bear its usual legal meaning in the common law context of landlord and tenant of that which constitutes the subject matter of a lease? The House of Lords answered this question in the negative in *Maunsell* v. *Olins*[19] but only by a majority of 3 to 2. The plaintiff owned a farm comprising a hundred acres of land on which there was the farmhouse and two tied cottages. He let the farm to B who was allowed to sublet the cottages. B sublet one of the cottages to the first defendant, and it was not disputed that, as between B and the first defendant the latter's tenancy was protected by the Rent Act. B died and his tenancy of the farm terminated. The plaintiff claimed possession of the cottage from the first defendant. Obviously he failed

---

[16] *Commentaries*, 1813 edition, vol. 1, p. 79.
[17] (1867), L.R. 1 Ex Ch. 368.
[18] [1961] 1 All E.R. 600.
[19] [1975] A.C. 373.

if the word "premises" was to be given its common law meaning in such a context and Lord SIMON OF GLAISDALE supported this conclusion in a vigorous dissenting speech in which Lord Diplock concurred. From the sociological point of view the speech derived its strength from the fact that, when problems arise, persons affected by s. 18 (5) are likely to seek legal advice. The majority reached the conclusion that the subsection only applied to premises which, for the purposes of the 1968 Act, are to be treated as dwelling houses, for more than one reason. The lease to B was governed by the Agricultural Holdings Act and it would be odd if the Rent Act had much to do with agricultural lettings; there is a presumption against any greater alteration of the common law than is required by the ordinary meaning of the words of the statute; and, if asked what he understood by the word "premises", a farmer would probably not include farm land as distinct from farm buildings.

C. FRINGE MEANING AND THE EXTENT OF GENERAL WORDS

Stock examples of the problem of fringe meaning are provided by *Newberry* v. *Simmonds*[20] and *Smart* v. *Allan*.[1] Each case turned on the construction of s. 15 (1) of the Vehicles (Excise) Act 1949; "if any person uses or keeps on a public road any *mechanically propelled vehicle* for which a licence under this Act is not in force he shall be liable . . ." In *Newberry* v. *Simmonds* a car which was kept standing on a road, and the engine of which had been stolen, was held to be a mechanically propelled vehicle requiring a licence. In *Smart* v. *Allan* the defendant bought a car for £2 as scrap and left it on a road. The engine was rusted and did not work; three tyres were flat and one was missing; there was no gear box or electrical accessories and the car could not move under its own power. It was held not to be a mechanically propelled vehicle, Lord PARKER, C.J., saying:[2]

> "It seems to me as a matter of common sense that some limit must be put, and some stage must be reached, when one can say: 'This is so immobile that it has ceased to be a mechanically propelled vehicle'. Where, as in the present case, and unlike *Newberry* v. *Simmonds*, there is no reasonable prospect of the vehicle ever being made mobile again, it seems to me that, at any rate at that stage, a vehicle has ceased to be a mechanically propelled vehicle."

No useful purpose would be served by providing a multiplicity of illustrations of fringe meaning, but it must be emphasised that the solution of problems of this nature is one of the most common tasks

---

[20] [1961] 2 Q.B. 345; [1961] 2 All E.R. 318.
[1] [1963] 1 Q.B. 291; [1962] 3 All E.R. 893.
[2] [1963] 1 Q.B. 291, at p. 298.

of the courts in relation to statutory interpretation. Is a bicycle a "carriage"?[3] Is a goldfish an "article"?[4] Is orange juice pressed from fresh oranges a "manufactured beverage"?[5] Is a toffee apple "confectionery"?[6] Conundrums of this sort are part of the daily bread of judges and practitioners. In solving them the courts usually pay due regard to the context, but, in many instances, the answer must, in Lord PARKER's words, be treated as a matter of common sense. The fact that a substantial proportion of the problems of statutory interpretation which confront them cannot be answered on principle is something to be borne in mind when the manner in which the courts perform their interpretative function is under discussion. The dictates of common sense are notoriously liable to produce different answers by different people to the same question, but this is not the kind of difficulty which can be overcome by law reform.

In the context of statutory interpretation the expression "general words" is a broad one. It applies to any word, phrase or provision which refers to actions, persons or things as a class rather than individually. Plowden's report of *Stradling* v. *Morgan* tells us that the sages of the law have construed statutes "which comprehend all things in the letter . . . to extend but to some things, . . . and those which include every person in the letter they have adjudged to reach some persons only".[7] A good modern example of this process is the construction of s. 1 of the Sex Disqualification (Removal) Act 1919 adopted by the majority of the House of Lords' Committee of Privileges at the hearing of *Viscountess Rhondda's claim* to be entitled to be summoned to sit in the House as a peeress in her own right.[8] On the previous occasions when women have claimed that they were entitled to exercise such public functions as voting at Parliamentary elections they had been defeated by the express words of the statutes upon which they relied. General words like "any person" were used, but persons subject to any legal incapacity were excepted, and women were held to be legally incapacitated from exercising public functions at common law.[9] The words of the 1919 Act are, however, perfectly general in their terms; "a person shall not be disqualified by sex or marriage from the exercise of any public function." The basis of the decision against the claim was that the creation of a new right must be distin-

[3] *Corkery* v. *Carpenter*, [1951] 1 K.B. 102; [1950] 2 All E.R. 745.
[4] *Daly* v. *Cannon*, [1954] 1 All E.R. 315.
[5] *Customs and Excise Commissioners* v. *Savoy Hotel, Ltd.*, [1966] 2 All E.R. 299.
[6] *Candy Maid Confections, Ltd.* v. *Customs and Excise Commissioners* [1969] 1 Ch. 611; [1968] 3 All E.R. 773.
[7] Pp. 8–9, *supra*.
[8] [1922] 2 A.C. 339.
[9] *Chorlton* v. *Lings* (1869), L.R. 4 C.P. 373; *Nairn* v. *St. Andrews University*, [1909] A.C. 147.

guished from the removal of a disqualification and specific words, such as those used in earlier statutes conferring the right to exercise public functions on women, were necessary for the former purpose.

Another striking illustration of the manner in which the effect of broad general words may be limited by the courts is the treatment accorded by a 4 to 1 majority of the House of Lords to s. 154 (4) of the Companies' Act 1929 in *Nokes* v. *Doncaster Amalgamated Collieries, Ltd.*[10] According to the subsection "property" includes "proprietary rights and powers of every description". An order made under s. 153 of the Act had transferred all the property of the Hickleton Collieries, Ltd to the Doncaster Company, but the House of Lords held that this did not transfer rights under a contract of personal service. The principle that a servant cannot be obliged to work for another master against his will has not been abrogated by s. 154 (4).

The maxim "*generalia specialibus non derogant*" expressing the rule, mentioned in the introduction, that general words in a later statute do not repeal an earlier statute dealing with a special subject, is a further illustration of the cautious approach adopted by the courts to the interpretation of broad provisions. The leading case is *The Vera Cruz* in which Lord SELBORNE said:

> "Now if anything be certain it is this, that where there are general words in a later Act capable of reasonable and sensible application without extending them to subjects specially dealt with by earlier legislation, you are not to hold that earlier and special legislation indirectly repealed, altered, or derogated from merely by force of such general words, without any indication of a particular intention to do so."[11]

Of course general provisions are often given their full general effect for in this, as in most other cases, the courts pay due regard to the context. Section 26 (1) of the Factories Act 1961 requires compliance with certain safety provisions "as respect every chain, rope or lifting tackle used for the purpose of *raising* or lowering persons, goods, or materials." In *Ball* v. *Richard Thomas and Baldwins, Ltd.*[12] it was held that the loosening and lifting of the molten metal which spilt on to the floor of a steel works amounted to "raising materials". If that were not so, "... this operation of carrying the scab by the use of a crane, which is admittedly a regular and recognized method of procedure ... fraught with some degree of danger, would be completely outside the scope of the Factories Act 1961 and any regulations made thereunder".[13]

In at least one instance the context and historical background has

---

[10] [1940] A.C. 1014; [1940] 3 All E.R. 549.
[11] (1884), 10 App. Cas. 59, at p. 68.
[12] [1968] 1 All E.R. 389.
[13] *Per* WILMER, L.J., *ibid.*, at p. 397.

led to a vast extension of the meaning of general words. Section 1 of the Affiliation Proceedings Act 1957 provides that: "a *single woman* who is with child or has been delivered of an illegitimate child, may apply by complaint to a Justice of the Peace for a summons to be served on the man alleged by her to be the father of her child." The effect of a series of cases going back for 150 years is that a married woman living apart from her husband,[14] even if they occupy the same house,[15] may apply for a summons and obtain an order against another man. The section derives from statutes of Elizabeth I, and the justification for the extended meaning of the phrase single woman is "public policy". "The law, differently interpreted, would fail to reach a very large proportion of illegitimate children".[16] The basic idea is that the child in respect of whom the order is sought should have been born outside matrimony and this was made clearer in the earlier statutes. It has even been held that a woman living apart from her husband under a separation order can obtain an affiliation order against him in respect of a child born a few hours before her previous marriage had been finally dissolved by decree absolute and therefore not legitimated by her subsequent marriage.[17] DEVLIN J. said: [18]

> "The artificiality of the construction which the courts have given to the expression 'single woman' is brought into high relief when a wife asserts against her own husband that she is a single woman. Nevertheless once the point is reached when the fact of singleness is determined by looking at the actual state to which the woman has been reduced and not at her status in the eyes of the law, it seems to me that a woman whose husband has deserted her or cast her off can say to him, with as much force as she can say it to anyone else, that he has reduced her to living as a single woman."

By the use of some kind of general words Parliament inevitably confers considerable legislative power upon the courts. When such words as "desertion" or "cruelty" were used in statutes providing for matrimonial relief it was apparent that the courts were being given a free hand and the resultant case law was enough to fill a book. The same proved to be true of the expression "accident arising out of and in the course of the employment" used in the Workmen's Compensation Acts. The judicial exegesis of such phrases as "just and equitable", "imputations on the character of the prosecutor or the witnesses for the prosecution" and "just cause or excuse" may not fill a book, but the least prescient reader would realise that there is little hope of

---

[14] *R.* v. *Luffe* (1807), 8 East 193.
[15] *Whitton* v. *Garner*, [1965] 1 All E.R. 70.
[16] *Per* DENMAN, J., in *R.* v. *Collingwood and Tomkins* (1848), 12 Q.B. 681, at p. 687.
[17] *Kruhlak* v. *Kruhlak*, [1958] 2 Q.B. 32. The law was altered by the Legitimacy Act 1959.
[18] *Ibid.*, at p. 37.

understanding the statutes in which they occur without a comprehensive reference to the law reports.

Occasionally the courts propose a test for determining the side of a line on which a particular situation falls, but then there is always the danger that the test will become a substitute for the statutory words which it is the judges' duty to apply to the cases that come before them. Illustrations are provided by the way in which the courts have grappled with what is now s. 8 of the Road Traffic Act 1972. It reads:

> "A constable in uniform may require any person *driving* or attempting to drive a motor vehicle on a road or other public place to provide a specimen of breath for a breath test there or nearby if the constable has reasonable cause (*a*) to suspect him of having alcohol in his body, or (*b*) to suspect him of having committed a traffic offence while the vehicle was in motion."

We have already seen that it would be absurd to construe the word "driving" in such a way as to render it necessary for the vehicle to be in motion when the test is required.[19] At one time the solution favoured by the Court of Appeal was to ask whether the person required to undergo the test could be said to have been the driver of the vehicle at the material time. We undoubtedly speak of someone being the driver of a car although it is not moving and even after he has got out of the driving seat, but the word to be construed is "driving" and the Court of Appeal's solution was rejected by the House of Lords in *Pinner* v. *Everett*.[20] In that case a police officer stopped the defendant at night because the rear numberplate of his car was not illuminated. The defendant got out of his car and had a conversation with the officer. After some lapse of time the officer suspected that he had been drinking and required a breath test which proved positive. Clearly if, at the time when the test was required, someone had asked who was the driver of the car, the reply would have been "the defendant". This was the basis of the Divisional Court's judgment against him; but the House of Lords quashed his conviction by a majority of 4 to 1. The majority treated the problem raised by the case as one of fringe meaning. Lords REID and GUEST gave examples of cases falling on different sides of the line determining whether the defendant was driving when the officer's suspicions were aroused. It was said that someone who, while held up in a traffic jam, got out of his car in order to buy a paper would still be driving, whereas someone who drew his car into the kerb and went into a shop would not be driving. These examples were treated with reserve in a subsequent case heard by the House of Lords.[1] The decision of that case turned on what is now s. 8 (1) (*b*) of the 1972 Act under which

[19] P. 27 *supra*. [20] [1969] 3 All E.R. 257.

[1] *Sakhuja* v. *Allen*, [1973] A.C. 152; [1972] 2 All E.R. 311.

the driver must be suspected of having committed a traffic offence. A constable in uniform observed the defendant driving at an estimated speed of 90 mph and gave chase. The defendant ultimately stopped outside his house, got out of his car and approached the constable who required a breath test at once. The test proved positive and the House of Lords unanimously affirmed the decision of the Divisional Court upholding the defendant's conviction by the magistrates. The *ratio decidendi* of the House of Lords was that the defendant's driving, the constable's observation of what appeared to be a traffic offence during that driving and the request for a breath test formed part of one transaction. *Pinner* v. *Everett* was said to have decided no more than that the driving in that case had ceased before the constable's suspicions were aroused. This book is not concerned with the labyrinthine details of the case law on the Road Safety Act 1967 now re-enacted in the Road Traffic Act 1972 and, at the time of writing, a strong candidate for reform. It is of course tempting to blame the courts and the draftsman but due allowance must be made for the conflict between the desire to promote road safety and the wish to protect motorists from undue harrassment which underlies the legislation. At the time it was passed there was a strongly expressed public dislike of random tests and what is now s. 8 was something of a compromise. Considerations of the kind which have just been mentioned may well have affected the statutory drafting and even the decisions of the courts.

The danger that tests proposed by the courts for determining the meaning of general statutory words would be treated as a substitute for those words is further illustrated by cases turning on the construction of s. 2 (1) of the Race Relations Act 1968:

> "It shall be unlawful for any person concerned with the provision to the public or a *section of the public* (whether on payment or otherwise) of any goods, facilities or services to discriminate against any person seeking to obtain or use those goods, facilities or services by refusing or deliberately omitting to provide him with any of them or to provide him with goods, services or facilities of the like quality in the like manner and on the like terms on which the former normally makes them available to other members of the public."

In *Charter* v. *Race Relations Board*[2] the East Ham Conservative Club rejected the application for membership of an Indian on the casting vote of the chairman of the Club's Committee who indicated that he regarded the applicant's colour as a relevant consideration. Any man of 18 was eligible for membership if he was a conservative and duly proposed and seconded. The County Court judge held that

[2] [1973] A.C. 868; [1973] 1 All E.R. 512.

s. 2 (1) of the 1968 Act did not apply because members of the Club were not a section of the public to whom the Club provided facilities or services. This decision was reversed by the Court of Appeal, but it was reinstated by the House of Lords. In the Court of Appeal Lord Denning said:[3]

> "... over the years the courts have evolved a test for determining what is 'a section of the public' as distinct from a private group ... it is this: look at the group of persons concerned. Make sure that there are quite a number of them (they must not be numerically negligible). See what is the quality which they have in common—the quality which distinguishes them as a group from the public at large. Then ask whether the quality is essentially impersonal or essentially personal. If it is impersonal, the group will rank as a 'section of the public'. If it is personal, it will rank as a private group, and not a section of the public."

But the House of Lords by a majority of 4 to 1 treated the words "public or a section of the public" as words which limit what would otherwise be the completely general terms of s. 2 (1). The provision of facilities and services to some people must be outside the subsection and, a club being a private association of individuals, is outside the subsection if its election rules provide a genuine process of selection which is followed in practice.

The dangers of the test propounded by Lord DENNING are illustrated by *Applin* v. *Race Relations Board*[4] which came before the County Court judge while the appeal to the House of Lords in *Charter's* case was pending. The judge held that registered foster parents would not be infringing s. 2 (1) by discriminating against black children in care because children in care were not a "section of the public" within Lord DENNING's test. The Court of Appeal reversed this decision after the House of Lords had allowed the appeal in *Charter* v. *Race Relations Board*, and the decision of the Court of Appeal in *Applin's* case was affirmed by a majority of 4 to 1 in the House of Lords.

A unanimous House of Lords was, unlike the Court of Appeal, unable to distinguish *Charter* v. *Race Relations Board* in *Dockers' Labour Club and Institute, Ltd* v. *Race Relations Board*.[5] In that case a dockers' club which operated a colour bar was linked with 4,000 other working men's clubs in an association affording admission to a member of any associated club as an associate member of any other. A coloured member of one of the associated clubs was asked to leave the dockers' club. The Race Relations Board obtained a declaration from the County Court judge that s. 2 (1) of the 1968 Act had been infringed and the judge's decision was upheld by the Court of Appeal where

[3] [1972] 1 Q.B. at p. 555.
[4] [1975] A.C. 259; [1974] 2 All E.R. 73.
[5] [1974] 3 All E.R. 592.

Charter's case was distinguished on the ground that, although club members elected by a *bona fide* process constituted a private group, something like a million members of other clubs had associate members' rights in the dockers' club without being personally approved by it. The House of Lords took the view that the policy of the Act was to separate the public from the private sphere, and numbers as such were therefore irrelevant. A notice on the door of the dockers' club reading "Members of the public not admitted" would have been as appropriate as such a notice would be in the case of a much smaller club. The result of the construction adopted by the House of Lords was in many ways disastrous, but the results of a test distinguishing between small clubs and big clubs and clubs which did or did not supply personal services would have been even more disastrous. A new Race Relations Act may well become law before this book is published, but this will not mean that the cases mentioned above will be any less instructive so far as statutory interpretation is concerned.

D. CHOICE BETWEEN PRIMARY AND SECONDARY MEANING

The second of our basic rules set out on page 43 must now be illustrated: "If the judge considers that the application of the words in their ordinary meaning would produce an absurd result which cannot reasonably be supposed to have been the intention of the legislature he may apply them in any secondary meaning which they are capable of bearing". To repeat a quotation from one of Lord Reid's speeches:[6]

> "In determining the meaning of any word or phrase in a statute the first question to ask always is what is the natural or ordinary meaning of that word or phrase in its context in the statute. It is only when that meaning leads to some result which cannot reasonably be supposed to have been the intention of the legislature that it is proper to look for some other permissible meaning of the word or phrase."

This is of course substantially similar to Lord Wensleydale's golden rule as stated in *Grey* v. *Pearson*;[7] "... the grammatical and ordinary sense of the words is to be adhered to, unless that would lead to some absurdity, or some repugnance or inconsistency with the rest of the instrument, in which case the grammatical and ordinary sense of the words may be modified, so as to avoid the absurdity and inconsistency, but no further." More recently Lord Simon of Glaisdale in *Maunsell* v. *Olins* said:[8]

> "... the language is presumed to be used in its primary ordinary sense,

[6] *Pinner* v. *Everett*, [1969] 3 All E.R. 257, at p. 258.
[7] (1857), 6 H.L. Cas. 61, at p. 106; p. 15 *supra*.
[8] [1975] 1 All E.R. 16, at p. 25.

unless this stultifies the purpose of the statute, or otherwise produces some injustice, absurdity, anomaly or contradiction, in which case some secondary ordinary sense may be preferred ..."

The question whether words like "repugnance", "inconsistency", "absurdity", "anomaly" and "contradiction" are, for the purposes of brief exposition properly subsumed under the word "absurdity" in rule 2 set out at the beginning of this section is best considered after the propositions embodied in the above quotations have been illustrated.

It must be emphasised at the outset that it is only when a secondary meaning is available that there can be any question of the courts' abandoning a primary meaning because it produces an absurdity. No judge can decline to apply a statutory provision because it seems to him to lead to absurd results nor can he, for this or any other reason, give words a meaning they will not bear. These points are vividly illustrated by the unanimous decision of the House of Lords in *Inland Revenue Commissioners* v. *Hinchy*.[9] Section 25 (3) of the Income Tax Act 1952 provided that "a person who neglects or refuses to deliver ... or wilfully makes delay in delivering a true and correct list, declaration or return which he is required under the preceding parts of this chapter to deliver shall (*a*) if proceeded against by action in any court forfeit the sum of £20 and treble *the tax which he ought to be charged under this Act*". In his tax return for 1952 Hinchy included savings bank interest of £18 6s. instead of the amount actually received by him, £51 5s 9d. The tax payable on the amount omitted was £14 5s. The tax payable on Hinchy's entire income for the year (including the £51 5s 9d) was £139 11s 6d. The Inland Revenue Commissioners claimed £438 14s 6d, being three times £139 11s 6d plus £20. DIPLOCK J. awarded them only £20 because the deficiency had been made good before the action was begun; the Court of Appeal awarded £62 15s (three times the tax due on the interest not included in the return plus £20); and the House of Lords awarded the Commissioners the £438 14s 6d which they claimed. All three tribunals recognised the absurdity of the results of the construction contended for by the Commissioners and adopted by the House of Lords. To quote Lord REID:[10]

"A man might be properly chargeable to £5,000 tax on his actual return, and properly chargeable to £5,100 on the correct return. If the appellants are right the penalty will be £15,300. If the other view is the right one [i.e. that of the Court of Appeal], it would only be £320."

---

[9] [1960] A.C. 748.
[10] *Ibid.*, at p. 767.

Owing to other provisions in the Act, a man might incur a penalty of three times the tax with which he was chargeable plus £20 by merely failing to send in a correct list of his employees. These absurdities caused DIPLOCK, J., to seek a secondary meaning of the words "treble the tax which he ought to have been charged under this Act", and, in effect, he added the words "at the commencement of the proceedings". The weakness of this approach lies in the fact that the offence in respect of which the penalty was provided was completed when the return was made. The absurdities caused the Court of Appeal, in effect, to add some such words as "on the difference between the income returned and that which should have been returned"; but tax is only chargeable after an assessment has been made and the Court of Appeal's construction presupposes an incorrect assessment followed by a correct one after the error has been discovered. In *Hinchy's* case the error was discovered before any assessment was made. There is the further unanswerable point that the Court of Appeal's construction could not be applied to a case of wilful delay in making any kind of return. In the House of Lords, Lord REID said:[11]

> "What we must look for is the intention of Parliament, and I also find it difficult to believe that Parliament ever really intended the consequences which flow from the appellants' contention. But we can only take the intention of Parliament from the words which they have used in the Act, and therefore the question is whether these words are capable of a more limited construction. If not, then we must apply them as they stand, however unreasonable and unjust the consequences, and however strongly we may suspect that this was not the real intention of Parliament. . . . One is entitled and indeed bound to assume that Parliament intends to act reasonably and therefore to prefer a reasonable interpretation of a statutory provision if there is any choice. But I regret to say that I am unable to agree that this case leaves me with any choice."

In the context of statutory interpretation the word most frequently used to indicate the doubt which a judge must entertain before he can search for and, if possible, apply a secondary meaning is "ambiguity". In ordinary language this term is often confined to situations in which the same word is capable of meaning two different things, but, in relation to statutory interpretation, judicial usage sanctions the application of the word "ambiguity" to describe any kind of doubtful meaning of words, phrases or longer statutory provisions. *Hinchy's* case prompted the suggestion that, if, in a particular context, words convey to different judges a different range of meanings "derived from, not fanciful speculations or mistakes about linguistic usage, but from true knowledge about the use of words, they are ambi-

[11] [1960] A.C. 748, at pp. 767–8. An entirely new scheme of penalties is now in force.

guous".[12] The author of the suggestion was not satisfied with the following answer which had already been provided by Lord SIMONDS:[13]

> "Each one of us has the task of deciding what the relevant words mean. In coming to that decision he will necessarily give great weight to the opinion of others, but if at the end of the day he forms his own clear judgment and does not think that the words are 'fairly and equally open to divers meanings' he is not entitled to say that there is an ambiguity. For him at least there is no ambiguity and on that basis he must decide the case."

It has since been said to be difficult to justify Lord SIMONDS' answer on logical grounds,[14] but it is hard to see what logic has to do with the matter. There is a rule of law according to which the judge must apply the ordinary and natural meaning of statutory words in their context unless that would produce a result which cannot reasonably be supposed to have been intended by the legislature. There is of course general agreement about the ordinary and natural meaning of statutory words, but the agreement is not universal, a point which is borne out by the fact that a question of statutory interpretation is being litigated. In borderline cases judges are apt to disagree about the ordinary meaning of words and they are equally apt to form different opinions on the question whether there is sufficient doubt to warrant the application of a secondary meaning. This point was put very clearly by Lord REID when dealing, in a later case,[15] with an argument that he should act on the presumption that penal statutes are to be construed strictly:

> "But it only applies where after full inquiry and consideration one is left in real doubt. It is not enough that the provision is ambiguous in the sense that it is capable of having two meanings. The imprecision of the English language, and so far as I am aware of any other language, is such that it is extremely difficult to draft any provision which is not ambiguous in that sense. This section [s. 37 of the Criminal Justice Act 1967] is clearly ambiguous in that sense, the Court of Appeal (Criminal Division) attach one meaning to it, and your lordships are attaching a different meaning to it. But if, after full consideration, your lordships are satisfied, as I am, that the latter is a meaning which Parliament must have intended the words to convey, then this principle does not prevent us from giving effect to our conclusion."

Barnard v. *Gorman*[16] was a case in which the wording of the statute cried out for the application of a secondary meaning and the most surprising feature of the entire litigation is the fact that a majority of the Court of Appeal stuck to the primary meaning. Section 186 of the Customs

---

[12] Professor A. L. Montrose, 76 Law Quarterly Review 350.
[13] *Kirkness* v. *John Hudson & Co., Ltd.*, [1955] A.C. 696, at p. 712.
[14] Odgers, *Construction of Deeds and Statutes*, 5th Ed., p. 449.
[15] *Director of Public Prosecutions* v. *Ottewell*, [1970] A.C. 642, at p. 649.
[16] [1941] A.C. 378.

Consolidation Act 1876 provided that: "every person who shall ... knowingly harbour any ... uncustomed goods with intent to defraud Her Majesty of any duties thereon shall for each offence forfeit either treble the value of the goods, including the duty payable thereon, or £100 at the election of the Commissioners of Customs; and the *offender* may either be detained or proceeded against by summons". Gorman was a steward on a British ship who was arrested on suspicion of knowingly harbouring uncustomed goods with intent. He was subsequently charged and acquitted whereupon he claimed damages for wrongful arrest. The House of Lords held that the action failed because, in the context, "offender" included a person suspected on reasonable grounds to have committed an offence. To quote Lord ROMER:[17]

> "That the ordinary meaning of the word 'offender' is a person who has in fact offended must be conceded, but the context in which a word is found may be, and very often is, strong enough to show that it is intended to bear other than its ordinary meaning and such a context is in my opinion to be found in the present case for the section provides that the offender may be proceeded against by summons, and to give the word 'offender' in this connection its ordinary meaning would be to render the provision nonsensical. It would mean that before issuing the summons the magistrate would have to decide that the offence had in fact been committed."

The action might well have failed even if there had been no provision with regard to summoning the offender for s. 186 would have been largely unworkable if "offender" was not read as "apparent offender", and this was the construction subsequently placed by the Court of Appeal upon a similar provision in *Wiltshire* v. *Barrett*.[18] That case was concerned with s. 6 (4) of the Road Traffic Act 1960 under which a police constable might arrest without warrant "a person committing an offence under this section". The section dealt with driving when unfit through drink, and the defendant had reasonable grounds for believing that the plaintiff was guilty of this offence when he arrested him; but the officer at the police station would not accept the charge with the result that there was no prosecution. The plaintiff then claimed damages for assault and the validity of his claim depended upon the answer to the question whether he had been lawfully arrested. The Court of Appeal held that the arrest was lawful because "a person committing an offence under this section" must be read as "a person apparently committing an offence under this

---

[17] [1941] A.C. 396.
[18] [1966] 1 Q.B. 312. The relevant provision with the same wording is now s. 5 (3) of the Road Traffic Act 1972.

section". The following observation of Lord DENNING is ample justification of such a construction.[19]

> "The police have to act at once on the facts as they appear on the spot, and they should be justified by the facts as they appear to them at the time and not on any *ex post facto* analysis of the situation. ... If every motorist who is acquitted is to have an unanswerable claim for damages against the police, I should think the police would soon give up trying to arrest anyone; and that would be very bad for us all."

It has been said that in this case the line between judicial construction and judicial legislation was very fine,[20] but, unless courts are to make nonsense of statutes by a rigid application of the literal meaning of the words, any other construction would have been preposterous. It would be the equivalent of construing a bye-law according to which "all drug shops shall be closed at 10 p.m. on each and every day of the week" as permitting the opening of such shops immediately after a momentary closure at 10 p.m.[1]

Barnard v. *Gorman* and *Wiltshire* v. *Barrett* are examples of the application of an extended meaning in order to avoid an absurdity. A further example of the same kind, though concerned with very different facts, is *Luke* v. *Inland Revenue Commissioners*.[2] Sections 160 and 161 of the Income Tax Act 1952 were aimed at preventing company directors from enjoying tax immunities in respect of expense allowances and payments in kind. The effect of s. 161 (1) was to render a director liable to tax in respect of expense incurred by the company "in or in connection with the provision of living or other accommodation or of other benefits or facilities of whatsoever nature". These words were wide enough to cover a case where a house was let by a company to one of its directors under a lease at a fair rent and, dry rot having been discovered, the company spent £5,000 on remedying it. This expenditure might be of no permanent benefit to the director whose tenancy might terminate shortly after the removal of the dry rot, yet he would be liable to tax on £5,000 in the absence of any saving clause to be found in some other provision of the statute. The facts of *Luke's* case were not as vivid as those which have just been mentioned, but the House of Lords was none the less confronted with the question whether a director who leased a house from a company was liable for tax on expenses incurred by the company in carrying out repairs which are normally executed by a landlord. A majority of 3 to 2 found a saving clause in s. 162 (1) of the 1952 Act under which "any expense incurred by a body corporate

---

[19] [1966] 1 Q.B. 312, at p. 321.
[20] Odgers, *op. cit.*, p. 447.
[1] P. 60 *supra*.
[2] [1963] A.C. 557.

in the acquisition or production of an asset which remains its own property shall be left out of account for the purposes of the last preceding section". It is almost an abuse of language to describe repairs as the production of an asset, but it is hard to believe that s. 161 was intended to render a director liable to tax in respect of expenditure which was of no benefit to him personally. Considerations of this nature led Lord REID to say:[3]

> "To apply the words literally is to defeat the obvious intention of the legislation and to produce a wholly unreasonable result. To achieve the obvious intention and produce a reasonable result we must do some violence to the words. This is not a new problem, though our standard of drafting is such that it rarely emerges. The general principle is well settled. It is only where the words are absolutely incapable of a construction which will accord with the apparent intention of the provision and will avoid a wholly unreasonable result that the words of the enactment must prevail."

Two examples of restrictive interpretation to avoid absurdity are provided by *Thompson* v. *Thompson*[4] and *Richard Thomas and Baldwins, Ltd.* v. *Cummings*.[5]

In the first of these cases the petitioner sought a decree of presumption of death and dissolution of marriage under s. 16 of the Matrimonial Causes Act 1950.[6] The petition was presented on 24th February 1955 and the respondent was last seen alive on 17th February 1948. In these circumstances the petitioner relied on s. 16 (2) which read as follows:

> "The fact that for a period of seven years or upwards the other party to the marriage has been continually absent from the petitioner, and the petitioner has no reason to believe that the other party has been living *within that time*, shall be evidence that he or she is dead until the contrary is proved."

Did this mean that it was necessary for the petitioner to have had no reason to believe, within the period of seven years and upwards that the other party was alive? This is the natural interpretation but, if it were right, the subsection would have been valueless on the facts of the case, for the petitioner had every reason to believe that his wife, who was only 49 and strong enough to come to court to collect maintenance on 17th February 1948, was alive for at least a few weeks after that day. SACHS, J., in effect read in the words "derived from matters occurring during the period of seven years" after the word "reason". He did this because the natural construction "would produce inconvenience and hardship to a petitioner contrary to the

---

[3] [1963] A.C. 577.
[4] [1956] P. 414; [1956] 1 All E.R. 603.
[5] [1955] A.C. 321.
[6] Now s. 19 of the Matrimonial Causes Act 1973.

apparent intentions of the legislature and would indeed reduce subsection 2 to an absurdity."[7]

Richard Thomas and Baldwins, Ltd. v. *Cummings*[8] was concerned with the construction of s. 16 of the Factories Act 1937 which required the fencing of dangerous parts of machines "to be constantly maintained and kept in position while the parts required to be fenced or safeguarded are *in motion* or use". There was an exception permitting exposure of the dangerous parts for examination and lubrication or adjustment shown by examination to be immediately necessary, but this clearly did not apply to repairs and Cummings had lost a finger in consequence of an injury sustained while repairing an unfenced machine which had been out of use for three weeks. He had turned the machine by hand in order to get it into position for repairing and repairs could not have been effected if the machine were fenced in accordance with the requirements of the Act. Clearly there was a sense in which the machine could be said to have been "in motion", but the House of Lords interpreted these words restrictively so as to exclude a mere transitory manual turning. Referring to the impossibility of effecting repairs if "in motion" were held to include any movement of the parts, however small, however brief and however caused, Lord Reid said:[9]

> "The fact that the interpretation for which the respondent contends would lead to so unreasonable a result is, in my opinion, sufficient to require the more limited meaning of 'in motion' to be adopted unless there is very strong objection to it, and none was suggested. It is true that the Factories Act is a remedial statute and one should therefore lean towards giving a wide interpretation to it, but that does not justify interpreting an ambiguous provision in a way which leads to quite unreasonable results."

We are now in a position to answer two questions which have been left open. (i) Does the word "absurdity" as used in various statements of the golden rule mean something wider than repugnance or inconsistency with the rest of the instrument? (ii) Can such words as "repugnancy", "inconsistency", "anomaly" and "contradiction" be properly subsumed under the word "absurdity" for the purposes of a brief exposition of the rules of statutory interpretation? If the answer to the first question is in the affirmative, the answer to the second must also be in the affirmative for our rules of interpretation have fortunately not reached such a degree of sophistication as to require distinctions of so great subtlety to be drawn. The construction of s. 186 of the Customs Consolidation Act 1876 adopted by the House of Lords

---

[7] [1956] P. 414, at p. 423.
[8] [1955] A.C. 321.
[9] *Ibid.*, at pp. 334–5.

in *Barnard* v. *Gorman*[10] avoided a repugnancy between the requirement that the offender should actually have committed the offence and the provision that he might be proceeded against by summons; the construction of s. 161 (1) of the Income Tax Act 1952 adopted in *Luke* v. *Inland Revenue Commissioners*[11] avoided an anomaly and the construction of s. 16 (2) of the Matrimonial Causes Act 1950 adopted in *Thompson* v. *Thompson*[12] removed an internal inconsistency; but, in each instance, it is true to say that an absurdity was also avoided.

It is submitted that the answer to the first question is in the affirmative, "absurdity" in this context does mean something wider than repugnance or inconsistency with the rest of the instrument, although cases of repugnancy and inconsistency may be subsumed under the conception of absurdity. *Richard Thomas and Baldwins, Ltd.* v. *Cummings*[13] seems to afford conclusive support for the submission as a holding, contrary to that of the House of Lords, to the effect that the machine was in motion would, so far from being inconsistent with, or repugnant to, the rest of the statute, have furthered its object, the protection of workmen. The submission is none the less made with diffidence because the contrary has been argued with much force by Mr E A Driedger. His contention is that Lord WENSLEYDALE's statement of the golden rule must, if it is to represent the present law, be amended to read: "The grammatical and ordinary sense of the words is to be adhered to, unless that would lead to some absurdity *in relation to*, or some repugnance to or inconsistency with the rest of the instrument".[14] There is certainly no lack of dicta in support of Mr Driedger's view,[15] but he recognises that it cannot be reconciled with the notoriously hesitant, though frequently cited, speech of Lord BLACKBURN in *River Wear Commissioners* v. *Adamson*.[16] That case was concerned with the construction of s. 74 of the Harbours, Docks, and Piers Clauses Act 1847, the relevant part of which reads:

> "The owner of every vessel, or float of timber, shall be answerable to the undertakers for any damage done by such vessel or float of timber, or by any person employed about the same, to the harbour, dock, or pier, or the quays or works connected therewith; and the master, or person having the charge of such vessel or float of timber, through whose wilful act or negligence any such damage is done, shall also be liable to make good the same. . . ."

Without fault on anybody's part the defendant's ship was driven ashore while endeavouring to make the port of Sunderland in a storm.

---

[10] P. 77 *supra*.

[11] P. 79 *supra*. [12] P. 80 *supra*. [13] P. 81 *supra*.

[14] *The Construction of Statutes*, p. 29.

[15] For example, Lord ESHER in *R.* v. *City of London Court Judge*, p. 30 *supra*; Sir George JESSEL in *Nuth* v. *Tamplin* (1881), 8 Q.B.D. 247, at p. 253; Lord MACMILLAN in *Altrincham Electric Supply, Ltd.* v. *Sale Urban District Council* (1936), 154 L.T. 379, at p. 388.

[16] (1877), 2 App. Cas. 743, at pp. 764–5.

After the officers and crew had been taken off with difficulty, the ship drifted as a wreck, striking a pier owned by the plaintiffs. The Court of Appeal and a majority of 4 to 1 in the House of Lords held that the defendant was not liable. The case is probably now best regarded as authority for nothing more than the narrow proposition that a ship-owner is not liable under the section if his vessel was not under human control and it caused damage to the harbour, dock or pier;[17] but the preponderant view in the House of Lords was that clearer words were necessary for the statutory imposition of civil liability without fault. The following remark of Lord BLACKBURN enlarging upon the terms in which Lord WENSLEYDALE formulated the golden rule may be taken to have been made in furtherance of that conclusion:[18]

> "... I believe that it is not disputed that what Lord Wensleydale used to call the golden rule is right, viz., that we are to take the whole statute together, and construe it altogether, giving the words their ordinary signification, unless when so applied they produce an inconsistency, or an absurdity or inconvenience so great as to convince the court that the intention could not have been to use them in their ordinary signification, and to justify the court in putting on them some other signification, which, though less proper, is one which the court thinks the words will bear."

There is much force in Mr Driedger's suggestion that Lord BLACKBURN refused to believe that Parliament meant what it said,[19] and, over the years, the courts have undoubtedly become less squeamish over the question of statutory impositions of civil liability without fault,[20] but these considerations do not alter the fact that there appear to be more dicta according to which an absurdity sufficient to justify a departure from the ordinary meaning of statutory words need not be "in relation to the rest of the statute" than there are dicta to the contrary effect. Lord BLACKBURN went on to stress the point that the value of the golden rule is reduced by the fact that different minds are liable to take different views about what constitutes an absurdity, but this is a type of infirmity to which a great many legal rules are subject. Mr Driedger suggests that judges should stop saying that an absurdity justifies a departure from the grammatical and ordinary sense unless they go on to explain clearly what they mean by an absurdity,[1] but it is questionable whether it is possible to improve upon the word "unreasonable" which is repeatedly used by judges in this context.

---

[17] *Great Western Rail. Co.* v. *S.S. Mostyn (Owners)*, [1928] A.C. 57; *Workington Harbour and Dock Board* v. *S.S. Towerfield (Owners)*, [1951] A.C. 112.

[18] (1877), 2 App. Cas. 743, at pp. 764–5, *per* Lord BLACKBURN.

[19] *Op. cit.*, p. 36.

[20] See for example *Kensington Borough Council* v. *Walters*, [1960] 1 Q.B. 361; [1959] 3 All E.R. 652.

[1] *Op. cit.*, p. 44, n. 37.

The actual decision in the *Wear Commissioners* case did not turn on the choice between a primary and secondary meaning so much as on the question whether words implying fault should be read into the section. For example, Lord CAIRNS favoured a view according to which "damage" should be read as "actionable damage" because the section was purely procedural. The undertakers were to be given the opportunity of suing the owner whenever anyone would have been liable at common law, leaving the owner with a remedy over against the person who was at fault. On this basis the case is an illustration of the reading of words into a statute, a matter which must now be discussed.

E. READING WORDS IN AND OUT OF A STATUTE

This brings us to the illustration of the third of the basic rules set out on page 43; the judge may read in words which he considers to be necessarily implied by words which are already in the statute and he has a limited power to add to, alter or ignore statutory words in order to prevent a provision from being unintelligible, absurd or totally unreasonable, unworkable, or totally irreconcilable with the rest of the statute.

Words may be said to be necessarily implied by other words when their express statement merely clarifies a secondary meaning of those other words. Several instances of necessary implication have already been given. In *Adler* v. *George*[2] the court took the view that, in the context of the obstruction of airfields, the words "in the vicinity of" were apt to cover someone on a field; the words "in or" were implied with the result that an offence could be committed by someone "in or in the vicinity". In *Wiltshire* v. *Barrett*,[3] in the context of arrest on suspicion, the words "a person committing an offence under this section" were held to extend to people believed by the person making the arrest to be committing an offence; the word "apparently" could, as a matter of necessary implication, be assumed to precede the words "committing an offence". Were this not so, the grant of a power to arrest without warrant under what is now s. 5 (5) of the Road Traffic Act 1972 would be pointless. The companion case of *Barnard* v. *Gorman*[4] shows that the clarification of the secondary meaning of even a single statutory word may necessarily imply further words. In order to make sense of s. 186 of the Customs Consolidation Act 1876 "offender" had in effect to be read as "apparent offender". Similarly in *Re Bidie*,[5] the single word "representation" was held, in the context

[2] P. 32 *supra*.
[3] P. 78 *supra*.
[4] P. 77 *supra*.
[5] P. 44 *supra*.

of the Inheritance (Family Provision) Act 1938 to imply the words "in respect of a testamentary disposition". In many cases it is possible to apply the secondary meaning of a single word without there being any question of implying further words. In the context of mediaeval papal usurpations there was no question of implication when "provisions" were construed to mean nominations to benefices rather than victuals,[6] just as, in *R.* v. *Webb*,[7] in the context of the Sexual Offences Act 1956, the offence of procuring a woman to become a "common prostitute" was held, without the necessity of supplying further words, to have been committed by someone employing a masseuse who performed lewd acts with men although there was no suggestion of sexual intercourse. "Lewd hireling" is a recognised secondary meaning of the word "prostitute". The reading in of statutory words is, however, a very frequent concomitant of giving a secondary meaning to a statutory provision of any length.

The reason why the process is mentioned in rule 3 is that there are inevitably cases in which it is debatable whether the court was giving effect to a secondary meaning or adding words in order to prevent unreasonable results. The construction of the proviso to s. 38 of the Children and Young Persons Act 1933 mentioned on page 59 may be taken as an example. The proviso reads:

> "Provided that where evidence admissible by virtue of this section is given on behalf of the prosecution the accused shall not be liable to be convicted of the offence unless that evidence is corroborated by some other material evidence in support thereof implicating him."

When, in *Director of Public Prosecutions* v. *Hester*,[8] the House of Lords treated the words "some other material evidence in support thereof" as the equivalent of "some other material evidence admissible otherwise than by virtue of this section" they were certainly doing no more than stating expressly what was already implied in the statutory words; but what about the reading in of some such words as "in consequence of such evidence" after the word "offence" in order to prevent the preposterous result that an accused would, on a literal construction of the proviso, not be liable to be convicted in a case in which there was an abundance of evidence against him admissible otherwise than by virtue of s. 38 and some peripherally relevant evidence of an uncorroborated unsworn child? The phrase "that evidence" means, in its verbal context, "any evidence admissible by virtue of s. 38". If a court holds that, in its legal context, "that evidence" means "evidence in consequence of which the accused is liable to be convicted", is it giving effect to a secondary meaning, or is it

---

[6] P. 18 *supra*.
[7] [1964] 1 Q.B. 357; [1963] 3 All E.R. 177.
[8] [1973] A.C. 296; [1972] 3 All E.R. 1056.

exercising a power to add words in order to prevent a wholly unreasonable result? This is a silly question in the context of the present discussion because it makes no difference what the answer is. The words "in consequence of such evidence" must be read into the proviso in either event.

An example of the exercise of the power to add to the words of a statute in order to prevent a provision from being wholly unreasonable or totally irreconcilable with the plain intention of the rest of the statute is the course canvassed by Lord DENNING in *Eddis* v. *Chichester Constable*[9] of assuming that the words "or its value" were inserted in the proviso to s. 26 of the Limitation Act 1939 after the word "property"; but this was no more than a judicial suggestion, and we must not forget Lord SIMONDS's ominous words in *Magor and St Mellon's Rural District Council* v. *Newport Corporation*, warning against a naked usurpation of the legislative power.[10] In fact these words, reinforced by Lord MORTON's speech in the same case, could be treated as authority for the proposition that the courts have no power to read words into a statute which are not already there by necessary implication; but some allowance must at least be made for obvious drafting errors. For example, s. 33 of the Fines and Recoveries Act 1833 provided that, if the protector of a settlement should be convicted of felony, or an infant, the Court of Chancery should be the protector in lieu of the infant. The convicted felon was obviously omitted in error, and, in *Re Wainwright*,[11] Lord LYNDHURST held that the omission should be made good by supplying the words "in lieu of the person who shall be convicted" before the reference to the infant."

Even in this class of case judges will sometimes go to remarkable lengths in order to avoid saying that they are adding words to a statute. In *A.-G.* v. *Beauchamp*[12] the defendant was charged under a statute which provided that:

> "Every person who shall print ... any paper which shall be meant to be published or dispersed and who shall not print upon such paper his or her name and place of abode or business, and every person who shall publish or disperse ... any printed paper ... on which the name and place of abode of the person printing the same shall not be printed as aforesaid, shall for every copy so printed by him or her, forfeit a sum of not more than £5."

The defendant was the publisher, but not the printer, of a paper which did not bear the name and place of abode or business of the printer. He was held liable to a penalty under the statute by the Divisional Court notwithstanding the omission of the words "or published or

---

[9] P. 32 *supra*.
[10] P. 37 *supra*.
[11] (1843), 1 Ph. 258.
[12] [1920] 1 K.B. 650.

dispersed" before the words "by him or her" at the end of the section. ROWLATT, J., thought the omission was an obvious error which could be made good; but the other two members of the court preferred to treat the words "so printed by him or her" as referring to the "person printing the same" in order to avoid adding words. ROWLATT, J.'s retort, not accepted by the other members of the court, was that their construction would mean that anyone who only published one copy of an offending paper would be liable to a penalty in respect of every copy printed by the printer.

A much bolder approach was adopted in a far less clear case by JAMES, L.J., in *Ex parte Walton.*[13] Section 23 of the Bankruptcy Act 1869 provided that:

> "When any property of the bankrupt acquired by the trustee under this Act consists of lands of any tenure burdened with onerous covenants, ... the trustee may, ... by writing under his hand, disclaim such property, and, upon the execution of such disclaimer, the property disclaimed shall, if the same is ... a lease, be deemed to have been surrendered on the [date of the order of adjudication]."

No problem arose under the section in cases in which a lease had been granted to the bankrupt and he had not sublet the property comprised in it. A notional surrender took place on the date of adjudication and the lessor could prove in the bankruptcy for any arrears of rent. But difficulties did arise where the lessee had sublet the property before going bankrupt. According to the ordinary law of landlord and tenant, the head lessor may enter the land which has been sublet and distrain for rent due under the head lease. He would forfeit this right if he accepted a surrender of the head lease, and he would ordinarily only do so on being satisfied with regard to the payment of rent already due to him. Did s. 23 mean that a landlord lost his right to distrain for rent due under the head lease at the date of adjudication if the trustee in the head lessee's bankruptcy exercised his right of disclaimer? The answer of the Court of Appeal in *Ex parte Walton* was in the negative. JAMES, L.J., used strong words about the apparent effect of s. 23 and was equally forthright about the manner in which the problem should be solved. He said:[14]

> "Now, when a statute enacts that something shall be deemed to have been done, which in fact and truth is not done, the court is entitled and bound to ascertain for what purposes and between what persons the statutory fiction is to be resorted to. Now the bankruptcy law is a special law having for its object the distribution of an insolvent's assets equitably amongst his creditors and persons to whom he is under liability, and, upon this *cessio bonorum*, to release him under certain conditions from future liability in

[13] (1881), 17 Ch.D. 746.
[14] *Ibid.*, at p. 756.

respect of his debts and obligations. That being the sole object of the statute, it appears to me to be legitimate to say that, when the statute says that a lease which was never surrendered in fact (a true surrender requiring the consent of both parties, the one giving up and the other taking), is deemed to have been surrendered, it must be understood as saying so with the following qualification, which is absolutely necessary to prevent the most grievous injustice, and the most revolting absurdity 'shall as between the lessor on the one hand, and the bankrupt, his trustee and estate on the other hand, be deemed to have been surrendered'."

JAMES, L.J.'s words were quoted with approval in the House of Lords in *Hill* v. *East and West India Dock Co.*[15] but the majority appears to have taken the view that the words he would have added to the statute were already there by necessary implication. After characterising the choice before the House as one between interpreting the provision to mean that the disclaimer should, to all intents and purposes, have the same effect as a real surrender, and interpreting it to mean that the disclaimer should operate as a surrender "so far as is necessary to effectuate the purposes of the Act", Lord BLACKBURN spoke of the meaning canvassed by JAMES, L.J., as the more natural, more reasonable and more correct.[16] On this one can agree with the passage in the dissenting speech of Lord BRAMWELL in which he said that what the majority was proposing was not a modification of the words, but a "positive addition to the language"[17] without disapproving of the decision of the majority that the original lessee remained liable on his covenant to pay the rent after the lease had been disclaimed by the trustee in bankruptcy of an assignee.

Although the cases happen to be concerned with the substitution rather than the addition of words, modern judges are generally prepared to describe what they are doing in more realistic terms than their predecessors. One of the frankest statements concerning the power to go further than merely giving a statutory provision a secondary meaning and stating expressly what was already implied is that of MACKINNON, L.J., in *Sutherland Publishing Co., Ltd.* v. *Caxton Publishing Co., Ltd.*:[18]

"When the purpose of an enactment is clear, it is often legitimate, because it is necessary, to put a strained interpretation upon some words which have been inadvertently used and of which the plain meaning would defeat the obvious intention of the legislature. It may even be necessary, and therefore legitimate, to substitute for an inept word or words that which such intention requires. The most striking example of this I think is one passage in the Carriage of Goods by Sea Act 1924, where to prevent a result so nonsensical that the legislature cannot have intended it, it has been held

[15] (1884), 9 App. Cas. 448.
[16] *Ibid.*, at p. 459.
[17] *Ibid.*, at p. 468.
[18] [1938] Ch. 174, at p. 201.

necessary and legitimate to substitute the word 'and' for the word 'or'. The violence of this operation has, I think, been minimised by saying that in this place the word 'or' must be taken to mean 'and'. That is a cowardly evasion. In truth one word is substituted for another. For 'or' can never mean 'and'."

MACKINNON, L.J., was presumably referring to *R. F. Brown & Co., Ltd.* v. *T. and J. Harrison*[19] where, as MACKINNON, J., he had held that, in a provision of the Carriage of Goods by Sea Act 1924, "or" could not be read as conjunctive, although he was prepared to treat "and" as substituted for "or". He omitted to say that, although the Court of Appeal affirmed his decision, they did so on the ground that "or" could sometimes be construed conjunctively in order to avoid an absurdity, ATKIN, L.J., feeling constrained to characterise the argument that "or" could never mean "and" as the worst point that had ever been taken in the Court of Appeal in his time. MACKINNON, L.J., was partially vindicated by the decision of the House of Lords in *Federal Steam Navigation Co., Ltd.* v. *Department of Trade and Industry*,[20] where Lord REID agreed that "or" can never mean "and", adding that decisions suggesting that, as a matter of construction, it could do so were wrong; but he reaffirmed the existence of a power to substitute "and" for "or" although he was one of the two dissentients who thought that it ought not to have been exercised on the particular facts. Both defendants were charged with contravening s. 1 of the Oil in Navigable Waters Act 1955 which read in part as follows: "If any oil ... is discharged from a British ship ... into a part of the sea which is a prohibited sea area ... *the owner or master* of the ship shall be guilty of an offence." The defendants were respectively the owner and master of a British ship from which oil had been discharged into a prohibited sea area. Both of them were convicted and they appealed unsuccessfully to the Court of Appeal. In the House of Lords a majority of 3 to 2 was in favour of dismissing their appeals. All the law lords agreed that the House had power to treat the section as though the relevant words were "the owner and the master or each of them" or, to put it more shortly, "the owner and or the master". What divided the House was the question whether the concept of a criminal offence with regard to which the prosecution had an unfettered discretion to select which of two persons should be proceeded against was such a legal monstrosity that it had to be avoided by the application to the section of what Lord WILBERFORCE, a member of the majority, regarded as "surgery rather than therapeutic".[1] MACKINNON, L.J.'s vindication has been described as partial because Lord

[19] (1927), 43 T.L.R. 394, affirmed by the Court of Appeal at p. 633.
[20] [1974] 2 All E.R. 97.
[1] *Ibid.*, at p. 111.

SALMON expressly, and Lords MORRIS and SIMON by implication, did not commit themselves on the linguistic question whether "or" could ever mean "and". Granted that a court has power to substitute "and" for "or" in the reading of a statute the linguistic question is legally irrelevant.

R. v. *Oakes*[2] is the converse of *Federal Steam Navigation Co., Ltd.* v. *Department of Trade and Industry*, for "or" was substituted for "and". Oakes was charged with doing an act preparatory to the commission of an offence under the Official Secrets Act 1911. Section 7 of the Official Secrets Act 1920 reads:

> "Any person who attempts to commit any offence under the Official Secrets Act 1911, or this Act, or solicits or incites or endeavours to persuade another, or aids or abets *and* does any act preparatory to the commission of an offence under the Official Secrets Act 1911 or this Act shall be guilty...."

It was unsuccessfully argued at first instance and on appeal that the indictment disclosed no offence because Oakes was not charged with attempting, inciting, aiding or abetting the commission of an offence in addition to doing a preparatory act. Lord PARKER's answer was:[3]

> "It seems to this Court that where the literal reading of a statute, and a penal statute, produces an intelligible result, clearly there is no ground for reading in words or changing words according to what may be the supposed intention of Parliament. But here we venture to think that the result is unintelligible."

The courts seem to have had fewer inhibitions about ignoring statutory words than about adding to and altering them. It is only necessary to mention two very strong cases, *Salmon* v. *Duncombe*[4] and *Re Lockwood*.[5] The first is a strong case because some words were ignored and others treated as necessarily implied by the words that were left, and the second is a strong case because an entire subsection of a modern statute was totally disregarded.

Salmon v. *Duncombe* was concerned with the construction of a Natal Ordinance of 1856. The title and preamble made it clear that the object of the Ordinance was to enable natural born British subjects resident in Natal to make wills free from the restrictions on testation imposed by Roman Dutch law. Mrs Duncombe, a natural born British subject, had made a will in favour of her second husband while she was resident in Natal. Her estate consisted of real property situated in Natal, and the question was whether the second husband was entitled to the entire estate or whether the children of Mrs Duncombe's first marriage were entitled to portions of it in accordance

---

[2] [1959] 2 Q.B. 350. [3] *Ibid.*, at p. 354.
[4] (1886), 11 App. Cas. 627.
[5] [1958] Ch. 231; [1957] 3 All E.R. 520.

with Roman Dutch law which had been adopted in Natal. Section 1 (1) of the Ordinance read:

> "Any natural born subject of Great Britain and Ireland resident within this district may exercise all and singular the rights which such natural born subject could or might exercise according to the laws and customs of England in regard to the disposal by last will and testament of property, both real and personal, *to all intents and purposes as if such natural born subject resided in England.*"

The draftsman had failed to make allowance for the provisions of English private international law according to which gifts by will of immovable property are governed by the law of the country where the property is situated. If Mrs Duncombe had been resident in England when she made her will it would have been subject to the restrictions of Roman Dutch law in favour of the children of her first marriage so far as her real property in Natal was concerned. There was no finding with regard to Mrs Duncombe's domicile at the time of her death. But it may be added that, by English law, the validity of dispositions of movable property is governed by the law of the testator's last domicile; accordingly the will of a natural born British subject resident and domiciled in Natal would be subject to the restrictions imposed by Roman Dutch law on account of the last nine words of the Ordinance. The judicial committee of the Privy Council got over the difficulties occasioned by the draftsman's apparent ignorance of English private international law by disregarding the last nine words of the Ordinance and implying the words "over property subject to such laws and customs" after the word "England". In justification of this course Lord HOBHOUSE said: "It is very unsatisfactory to be compelled to construe a statute in this way, but it is much more unsatisfactory to deprive it altogether of meaning".[6]

In *Re Lockwood*[7] Lockwood died intestate and his only next of kin were issue of uncles and aunts of the whole blood. Under s. 46 and the early part of s. 47 of the Administration of Estates Act 1925, the issue of deceased uncles and aunts of the intestate are entitled to share in his estate, but s. 47 (5) (inserted by the Intestate Estates Act 1952) raises doubts with regard to cases in which there are no surviving uncles and aunts. The subsection reads:

> "It is hereby declared that where the trusts in favour of any class of the relatives of the intestate other than issue of the intestate, fail by reason of no member of that class acquiring an absolutely vested interest, the residuary estate of the intestate ... shall ... go devolve and be held under the provisions of this part of this Act as if the intestate had died without leaving any member of that class *or issue of any member of that class* living at the death of the intestate."

---

[6] (1886), 11 App. Cas. 627, at p. 635.
[7] [1958] Ch. 231.

On the strength of this subsection the Crown claimed the deceased's estate as *bona vacantia*. *Prima facie* its case was unanswerable. The trusts in favour of Lockwood's uncles and aunts had failed because none of them had acquired a vested interest, accordingly the estate was to go and devolve as if no issue of uncles and aunts had been living at the date of Lockwood's death. There were no next of kin of the half blood, hence the Crown must succeed on the strength of the plain language of s. 47 (5). This conclusion is sufficiently odd to give pause for thought, but consequences thought by some to be even more capricious would follow from giving effect to the subsection. If one uncle of the whole blood had survived, the issue of dead uncles and aunts would have been entitled to the shares their parents would have received had they survived; if Lockwood had been survived by an uncle of the half blood in addition to the issue of uncles and aunts of the whole blood, that uncle would have been entitled to the whole estate. HARMAN, J., decided to disregard the section, saying: "I take this course because I am convinced that Parliament in laying down rules for ascertaining next of kin cannot have intended to promote those more remote over those nearer in blood".[8] The chosen course was rendered all the more bold by the fact that HARMAN, J., was unable to think of any situation to which the subsection might properly be applied.

The power to add to, alter or ignore statutory words is an extremely limited one. Generally speaking it can only be exercised where there has been a demonstrable mistake on the part of the draftsman or where the consequence of applying the words in their ordinary, or discernible secondary, meaning would be utterly unreasonable. Even then the mistake may be thought to be beyond correction by the court, or the tenor of the statute may be such as to preclude the addition of words to avoid an unreasonable result. *Inland Revenue Commissioners* v. *Ayrshire Employers' Mutual Insurance Association, Ltd.*[9] is a case in which the draftsman's mistake was treated as being past correction by the addition of words. It was not disputed that s. 31 of the Finance Act 1933 was intended to provide that mutual insurance companies were liable to income tax on the annual surplus arising from transactions with their members; but the draftsman had mistakenly assumed that these companies were already liable to tax on profits derived from insurance transactions with non-members and this assumption formed the basis of subsection (1):

> "In the application to any society or company of any provision or rule relating to profits or gains chargeable under case I of Schedule D which relates to trades, any reference to profits or gains shall be deemed to include

[8] [1958] Ch. 238.

[9] [1946] 1 All E.R. 637.

a reference to a profit or surplus arising from transactions of the company or society with its members and shall be included in profits or gains for the purpose of that provision or rule as if those transactions were transactions with non-members. ..."

A unanimous House of Lords held that the Association's profits from transactions with its members were not liable to tax because, according to the case law, profits of mutual insurance companies were immune from tax on the ground that they belonged to the contributors whether they were members of the Association or not. Lord MACMILLAN said that the legislature had "plainly missed fire".[10] To this Lord DIPLOCK has since retorted extrajudicially that if, as in this case, the courts can identify the target of Parliamentary legislation, "their proper function is to see that it is hit; not merely to record that it has been missed".[11] There is obvious force in this remark but there is also much to be said for the following observations of Lord SIMONDS in the *Ayrshire Insurance* case itself:[12]

"The section ... is clearly a remedial section, if that is a proper description of a section intended to bring further subject matter within the ambit of taxation. It is at least clear what is the gap that is intended to be filled and hardly less clear how it is intended to fill that gap. Yet I can come to no other conclusion than that the language of the section fails to achieve its apparent purpose and I must decline to insert words or phrases which might succeed where the draftsman failed."

Lord DIPLOCK's comment implies that it is the courts' sole function to ascertain the intention of Parliament and give effect to it. No doubt this is true so far as most statutes are concerned, but, in the case of some statutes, notably those creating crimes but possibly also those imposing taxes, surely the courts have the further function of ensuring that citizens are only deprived of their liberty or their money by reasonably clearly worded provisions or, at least by provisions which, though poorly phrased, are susceptible of comparatively easy rectification. With the best will in the world rectification of s. 31 of the Finance Act 1933 would have been far from easy.

Cartledge v. *E. Jopling & Sons, Ltd.*[13] is a case in which the clear express provisions of a statute precluded any addition to its words in order to avoid an unreasonable result. Under s. 2 (1) (*a*) of the Limitation Act 1939, actions in tort were barred "after the expiration of six years from the date on which the cause of action *accrued*". Section 26 provides that, where the action is based on fraud or mistake, time does not begin to run until the plaintiff discovers the fraud or mistake or could have done so with reasonable diligence. In October 1957

[10] *Ibid.*, at p. 641.
[11] *Courts and Legislators*, p. 10.
[12] [1946] 1 All E.R. 637, at p. 641.
[13] [1963] A.C. 758; [1963] 1 All E.R. 341.

Cartledge and other workmen, suffering from pneumoconiosis contracted in the course of their employment, issued writs claiming damages from their employers for negligence or breach of statutory duty by failing to take adequate precautions against the inhalation of dust by their workmen. No negligence or breach of duty took place after the 1st October 1950 by which time the plaintiffs had suffered substantial harm from inhalation of dust but were unaware of this fact, pneumoconiosis not having developed until a later date. The Court of Appeal and House of Lords were unanimous in dismissing the action although they thought that there should be legislation to allow for such cases.[14] Section 26 was conclusive against the addition of any words in the 1939 Act. To quote Lord REID: "The necessary implication from that section is that, where fraud or mistake is not involved, time begins to run whether or not the damage could be discovered".[15] A further objection to action by the Courts in such a situation is the difficulty of specifying the precise words which should be added. On facts such as those of *Cartledge* v. *E. Jopling & Sons, Ltd.*, should time begin to run from the date at which the workmen became aware of the existence of their causes of action or from the date at which they became aware of relevant facts?

Were it not for a passage in Lord REID's speech in *Federal Steam Navigation Co., Ltd.* v. *Department of Trade and Industry*[16] no attempt would have been made in the formulation of rule 3 of the basic rules set out on page 43 to classify the cases to which it applies. It confers a wholly exceptional power of what is in effect rectification of a statute, and the wiser course might have been to refrain from further formulation. Lord REID said:[17]

> "Cases where it has properly been held that a word can be struck out of a deed or statute and another substituted can as far as I am aware be grouped under three heads: where without such substitution the provision is unintelligible or absurd or totally unreasonable; where it is unworkable; and where it is totally irreconcilable with the plain intention shown by the rest of the deed or statute."

Perhaps it is permissible to extend these remarks to cases of addition and alteration. Examples have been given of all three of the categories mentioned by Lord REID. Section 7 of the Official Secrets Act 1920 is unintelligible without the substitution of "or" for "and" adopted in *R.* v. *Oakes*;[18] the addition of the reference to a convicted felon

---

[14] As there was in the Limitation Act 1963; see now the Limitation Act 1975.
[15] [1963] A.C. 758, at p. 772.
[16] [1974] 2 All E.R. 97.
[17] *Ibid.*, at p. 100.
[18] P. 90 *supra*.

in *Re Wainwright*[19] prevented an absurdity, and the effect of s. 23 of the Bankruptcy Act 1869 would have been totally unreasonable without the emendation canvassed by JAMES, L.J., in *Ex parte Walton.*[20] The Natal Ordinance with which *Salmon* v. *Duncombe*[1] was concerned would have been unworkable without the drastic action taken by the Privy Council. Section 47 (5) of the Administration of Estates Act 1925 is plainly at variance with the scheme of the Act under which relations of the whole blood are preferred to relations of the half blood and this was the justification of the action of HARMAN, J., in *Re Lockwood.*[2]

Lord REID also made the point that it would not always be proper to strike words out even when the case fell within one of the above categories. There can be little doubt that different judges have taken different views with regard to the exercise of the exceptional power of rectification. It is far from clear that all courts would give their blessing to the emendation of the proviso to s. 26 of the Limitation Act 1939 proposed by Lord DENNING in *Eddis* v. *Chichester-Constable.*[3] On the other hand there are reported decisions in which the power was not exercised although other judges might have acted differently. In support of this statement it is only necessary to refer to *Altrincham Electric Supply, Ltd.* v. *Sale Urban District Council,*[4] a case which excited a remarkable difference of judicial opinion. The company supplied electricity to the urban district of Sale and to parts of the rural district of Bucklow. The Sale Urban District Council served notice exercising its statutory option to purchase so much of the company's undertaking as operated in the area of Sale. The case turned on the assessment of the purchase price which depended on the true construction of the following extract from s. 58 of the Ashton-on-Mersey Electric Lighting Ordinance 1896:

> "The price payable by the Local Authority shall be ascertained as follows: If the accumulated profits of the undertaking shall at the expiration of notice amount to or exceed a return of 7½% per annum on the total expenditure of the undertakers upon the undertaking, including the cost of additions and alterations, the purchase money shall be a sum equal to such total expenditure."

If, as the company contended, "the total expenditure of the undertakers upon the undertaking" meant the expenditure of the whole of its undertaking, including those parts of it which operated in Bucklow, the sum due was nearly twice as much as would have been due

[19] P. 86 *supra.*
[20] P. 87 *supra.*
[1] P. 90 *supra.*
[2] P. 91 *supra.*
[3] P. 32 *supra.*
[4] (1936), 154 L.T. 379.

if the words were so construed (or altered) as to mean "the total expenditure of the undertakers upon the undertaking or such parts thereof as are included in the notice". It was of course the contention of the Sale Urban District Council that the Order should be so construed. The arbitrator and FARWELL, J., decided in favour of the company on the ground that the words were clear and unambiguous. A majority of the Court of Appeal decided in favour of the Urban District Council and the House of Lords allowed the company's appeal by a majority of 3 to 2. It is true that the minority in the House of Lords appears to have treated the case as one in which the limitation on the meaning of undertaking was necessarily implied, but it is difficult to escape the conclusion that some modern judges would have regarded the case as one in which the power of rectification might be exercised on the ground that adhering to the ordinary meaning of the words would have been something that was totally unreasonable. However the contrary view was expressed with great force by Lord Russell who said:[5]

> "In the present case, notwithstanding the alleged impossible results which are said to flow from the plain meaning of the words used (e.g. the duplication which would necessarily accompany the hypothetical case of simultaneous notices and purchases by Sale and Bucklow), I find myself without any materials, evidential or otherwise, which enable me to assert that the words in s. 58 cannot possibly have been intended by their authors to bear the only meaning which they naturally convey."

Lord MACMILLAN pinned his faith to the following passage from Lord HALSBURY's speech in *Income Tax Special Purposes Commissioner* v. *Pemsel*:[6]

> "Whatever the real fact may be I think a court of law is bound to proceed on the assumption that the legislature is an ideal person that does not make mistakes. It must be assumed that it has intended what it has said, and I think any other view of the mode in which we must approach the interpretation of a statute would give authority for the interpretation of the language of Parliament which would be attended with the most serious consequences."

What, it may be asked, would Lord HALSBURY have done in *Salmon* v. *Duncombe*?[7] Would he have acquitted the accused in *R.* v. *Vasey and Lapley*[8] on the ground that the statutory provision under which they were charged was gibberish which did not define a crime in relation to salmon rivers? Section 13 of the Salmon Fisheries Act 1873 read:

> "The provisions of s. 32 of the Malicious Injuries to Property Act 1861

[5] (1936), 154 L. T. 388.
[6] [1891] A.C. 531, at p. 549.
[7] P. 90 *supra*.
[8] [1905] 2 K.B. 748.

so far as they relate to poisoning any water with intent to kill or destroy fish shall be extended and applied to salmon rivers, as if the words 'or in any salmon river' were inserted in the said section in lieu of the words 'private right of fishery' after the words 'noxious material in any such pond or water'."

Unfortunately the words "any private right of fishery" did not follow the words "noxious material in any pond or water" but occurred at a point in the verbiage of s. 32 before the putting of noxious material into water with intent to kill or destroy fish had been reached. The Court for Crown Cases Reserved did not care whether the words in s. 13 of the 1873 Act from "as if" on were ignored or whether the proposed amendment was inserted at a point at which it made sense. But the Court did carry out the obvious intention of the legislature and held that in consequence of s. 13 of the 1873 Act, it was a misdemeanour under s. 32 of the 1861 Act unlawfully and maliciously to put noxious materials into any salmon river with intent to destroy fish.

Would Lord HALSBURY have concluded that, on the true construction of the Criminal Appeal Act 1907, an accused who pleaded guilty could appeal against sentence although the Court of Criminal Appeal had no power to substitute another sentence if the original one were quashed? This certainly appeared to be the effect of the words of the Act. Under s. 3 a person convicted on indictment might appeal against a sentence passed on his conviction. Section 4 (3) provided that "on an appeal against sentence the Court of Criminal Appeal shall, if they think a different sentence should have been passed, quash the sentence passed at the trial, and pass such other sentence warranted in law by the *verdict* (whether more or less severe) in substitution therefore as they think ought to have been passed". Plainly no other sentence is warranted in law "by the verdict" in the case of someone who pleaded guilty, but the Court of Criminal Appeal avoided this difficulty in *R.* v. *Ettridge*[9] by "striking out" those words.

Of course there must be an exceptionally strong case for the exercise of the wholly exceptional power of rectification, and of course it is essential that the Courts should so far as possible stick to the ordinary meaning of statutory words, but this does not mean that they should throw their hands up in despair, not always unmingled with satisfaction, when the ordinary meaning produces a preposterous result. It is difficult to see any difference between the literal meaning approved by the majority in the *Altrincham case* and the interpretation of the bye-law requiring all drug shops to be closed at 10 p.m. on each and every day of the week as permitting a momentary closure at 10 p.m. to be followed by a reopening on the same day.[10] It was said that

[9] [1909] 2 K.B. 24.
[10] P. 60 *supra*.

no-one but a lawyer would ever have thought of imputing such an intention to the bye-law. Who but a lawyer would have thought of imputing to Parliament the intention attributed to it by the majority in the *Altrincham case?* As often as not it is a matter of taste whether such results are avoided by the technique of necessary implication or by rectification, but avoided they should be like the plague.

V

Internal Aids to Construction

The internal aids to construction will be briefly discussed under the heads of the enacting parts of the same statute, other parts of the same statute (preamble, headings, title etc.) and rules of language such as the *ejusdem generis* rule.

A. ENACTING PARTS OF THE SAME STATUTE

It is scarcely necessary to cite authority for the proposition that Acts must be construed as a whole. Guidance with regard to the meaning of a particular word or phrase may be found in other words and phrases in the same section or in other sections although the utility of an extensive consideration of other parts of the same statute will actually vary from case to case. Speaking of the Income Tax Act 1952, Lord REID said:[1]

> "It is no doubt true that every act should be read as a whole, but that is, I think, because one assumes that in drafting one clause of a bill the draftsman had in mind the language and substance of other clauses, and attributes to Parliament a comprehension of the whole act. But where, as here, quite incongruous provisions are lumped together and it is impossible to suppose that anyone, draftsman or Parliament, ever considered one of these sections in the light of another, I think it would be just as misleading to base conclusions on the different language of different sections as it is to base conclusions on the different language of sections in different Acts."

Changes of language do, however, frequently have a decisive effect on the construction of the statutory provision. For example, s. 102 of the Mental Health Act 1959 empowers the judge to do or secure the doing of all such things with respect to the property and affairs of a patient as appear necessary or expedient: "(*b*) for the mainten-

[1] *Inland Revenue Commissioners* v. *Hinchy*, [1960] A.C. at p. 766.

ance or other benefit of members of the patient's family; or (*c*) for making provision for other persons or purposes for whom or which the patient might be expected to provide if he were not mentally disordered". In *Re D. M. L.*[2] CROSS, J., said: "The contrasting language of sub-clauses (*b*) and (*c*) suggests to my mind that the legislature considered that the word 'family' consisted of persons for all of whom the patient might *prima facie* be expected to make some provision. This, I think, indicates that the word does not include collateral relatives". The result was that a scheme to avoid death duties under which benefits were conferred on the patient's nephews and nieces could not be sanctioned under s. 102 (*b*) although it was sanctioned under s. 102 (*c*).

There is a presumption that the same word or phrase bears the same meaning throughout the same statute. In *Coward* v. *Motor Insurers' Bureau*,[3] for example, the words "for hire or reward" in s. 36 (1) (*b*) (ii) of the Road Traffic Act 1930 were held to require a legally enforceable agreement and so to exclude a case in which payments were made by a pillion passenger in the absence of such an agreement to a motor cyclist who gave him lifts to and from work. The phrase "for hire or reward" was used elsewhere in the Act in a context which clearly referred to a legally enforceable agreement and *prima facie* it should bear the same meaning throughout the statute. The presumption is, however, of the mildest kind for it is easy to point to cases in which the same word has been held to have different meanings in different sections, or even the same section, of a single statute. A stock example of the first type of case is provided by the different meanings of the word "premises" in the Landlord and Tenant Act 1954. Sometimes it is used in its popular sense of buildings while at other points in the statute it bears the technical meaning of that which may form the subject matter of the habendum of a lease with the result that land with or without buildings on it may be included.[4] The stock example of the use of the same verb in different senses in the same section is s. 57 of the Offences Against the Person Act 1861 which provides that: "whosoever, being married, shall *marry* any other person during the life of the former husband or wife" shall be guilty of bigamy. Although "being married" means being validly married, "shall marry" necessarily means no more than "go through a marriage ceremony".[5]

It would be pointless to multiply examples of the effect of a change of language, or the use of identical language, within the same section or statute. Everything depends on the context and it is impossible

[2] [1965] Ch. 1113, at p. 1137. [3] [1963] 1 Q.B. 259; [1962] 1 All E.R. 531.
[4] *Bracey* v. *Read*, [1963] Ch. 88; [1962] 3 All E.R. 472.
[5] *R.* v. *Allen* (1872), L.R. 1 C.C.R. 367.

to make useful generalisations; but something must be said about the effect that one section of a statute may have on the construction of another section of the same statute as a matter of substance rather than language.

To begin with, two sections may be repugnant to each other. If the repugnancy is total and wholly inescapable, a rule of thumb has to be applied under which the later section prevails, "*leges posteriores priores contrarias abrogant*"; but this is very much a last resort and there are various techniques of construction which may be employed in order to avoid a repugnancy. One of these, the technique of finding a secondary meaning for one or more of the words or phrases in question has already been discussed. Two others mentioned in Maxwell are the technique of treating apparently conflicting provisions as dealing with distinct matters, and the technique of holding that one section apparently in conflict with another merely provides for an exception to the general rule contained in that other.[6] The first is illustrated by *R.* v. *Forest Justices, ex parte Dallaire*,[7] the second by *Gelberg* v. *Miller*.[8] In *R.* v. *Forest Justices* the problem was how to reconcile s. 158 (2) and s. 166 (2) of the Housing Act 1957. Section 158 (2) empowered a local authority to obtain possession of buildings owned by it under the Small Tenements Recovery Act 1838 by means of a notice of intention to apply for a warrant of possession which could be signed by the landlord's "agent", a term considerably broader than the clerk to a Local Authority or his lawful deputy, the officer by whom, according to s. 166 (2), "a notice, demand or other written document proceeding from a Local Authority under this Act" had to be signed. The Divisional Court solved the problem by holding that s. 166 (2) did not apply to a notice given pursuant to s. 158 (2).

In *Gelberg* v. *Miller* a minor problem was how to reconcile s. 54 (6) with s. 63 of the Metropolitan Police Act 1839. Section 54 (6) created the offence of obstructing the thoroughfare, and made it "lawful for any constable ... to take into custody, without warrant, any person who shall commit any such offence within the view of any such constable". Section 63 applies to all offences under the Act, but its requirements are more exacting. It reads: "It shall be lawful for any constable ... to take into custody, without a warrant, any person who within view of any such constable shall offend in any manner against this Act, and whose name and residence shall be unknown to such constable, and cannot be ascertained by such constable". Lord Parker solved the problem by concluding that "it is reasonably plain

[6] Maxwell, *On the Interpretation of Statutes*, 12th Edn., pp. 187 *et seq.*
[7] [1962] 2 Q.B. 629; [1961] 3 All E.R. 1138.
[8] [1961] 1 All E.R. 291.

that s. 63 is in effect dealing with other offences than those which are covered by s. 54".

One section may affect the construction of another as a matter of substance when account is taken of the fact that a particular construction of the section before the court which is not absurd would lead to a construction of other sections which would be absurd. Whether considerations of this nature are proper in a criminal case is perhaps questionable, but the outstanding instance is undoubtedly *R.* v. *Prince.*[9] Prince was charged with abduction contrary to s. 55 of the Offences Against the Person Act 1861 according to which it was an offence to "unlawfully take ... any unmarried girl, being under the age of 16 years, out of the possession and against the will of her father or mother. ..." He was found by the jury to have believed on reasonable grounds that the girl he abducted was over 16, but by a majority of 14 to 1, the Court for Crown Cases Reserved held that this was no defence. Under s. 50 of the 1861 Act it was a felony to "carnally know and abuse any girl under the age of 10 years", and s. 51 made it a misdemeanour to "carnally know and abuse any girl being above the age of 10 years and under the age of 12 years". The principal argument used in the leading majority judgment delivered by BLACKBURN, J., is contained in the following passage:[10]

> "It seems impossible to suppose that the intention of the legislature in those two sections [s. 50 and s. 51] could have been to make the crime depend upon the knowledge of the prisoner of the girl's actual age. It would produce the monstrous result that a man who had carnal connection with a girl, in reality not quite 10 years old, but whom he on reasonable grounds believed to be a little more than 10, was to escape altogether. He could not, in that view of the Statute, be convicted of the felony, for he did not know her to be under 10. He could not be convicted of the misdemeanour because she was in fact not above the age of 10. It seems to us that the intention of the legislature was to punish those who had connection with young girls, though with their consent, unless the girl was in fact old enough to give a valid consent. ... The 55th section, on which the present case arises, uses precisely the same words as those in ss. 50 and 51, and must be construed in the same way."

In a sense Prince was the victim of bad drafting, for, quite apart from any issue concerning the niceties of *mens rea*, there is something seriously wrong with two such provisions as ss. 50 and 51 of the Offences Against the Person Act 1861 if a man charged with unlawful intercourse with a girl above 10 and under 12 should have the cast iron defence that she was in fact under 10. Section 51 should simply have prohibited intercourse with girls under 12. Allowing for the substitu-

---

[9] (1875), L.R. 2 C.C.R. 154.
[10] *Ibid.*, at pp. 171–2.

tion of the ages of 13 and 16 for 10 and 12, this is the result achieved by ss. 5 and 6 of the Sexual Offences Act 1956, as amended by the Criminal Law Act 1967. Section 5 punishes intercourse with girls under 13 with a maximum of imprisonment for life, and s. 6 punishes intercourse with girls under 16 with a maximum of two years' imprisonment. The failure of the draftsman of the 1861 Act to appreciate the merits in certain situations of a statutory overlap may have been a significant cause of the proliferation of offences of strict liability.

Two types of clause to be found in the enacting parts of many statutes require special consideration as aids to interpretation. They are the interpretation (or definition) clause and the proviso.

Interpretation clauses

Modern statutes frequently contain, generally, in the case of English statutes, at the end, provisions to which the marginal note is "Interpretation". These clauses usually take one of two forms, either they state that a particular word or phrase "shall mean ..." (or "bears the meaning" assigned to it by the clause), or else they state that a particular word or phrase "includes ..."; both forms are implied in s. 50 (1) of the Courts' Act 1971. "The 'appointed day' means the commencement of this Act"; "'sentence', in relation to an offence, includes any order made by a court when dealing with an offender". There is usually some such saving clause as "unless the context otherwise requires", nevertheless the distinction is important because, when an interpretation clause states that a word or phrase "means ...", any other meaning is excluded, whereas the word "includes" indicates an extension of the ordinary meaning which continues to apply in appropriate cases.

> "The word 'include' is very generally used in interpretation clauses in order to enlarge the meaning of words or phrases occurring in the body of the statute; and when it is so used these words or phrases must be construed as comprehending, not only such things as they signify according to their natural import, but also those things which the interpretation clause declares that they shall include. But the word 'include' is susceptible of another construction, which may become imperative, if the context of the Act is sufficient to show that it was not merely employed for the purpose of adding to the natural signification of the words or expressions defined. It may be equivalent to 'mean and include' and in that case it may afford an exhaustive explanation of the meaning which, for the purposes of the Act, must invariably be attached to these words or expressions."[11]

The justice's failure to appreciate the implications of the distinction between "means" or "means and includes" on the one hand, and "includes" on the other hand, was partly responsible for the appeal

---

[11] *Dilworth* v. *Stamps Commissioner*, [1899] A.C. 99, at pp. 105–6, *per* Lord WATSON.

in *Carter* v. *Bradbeer*.[12] According to s. 201 (*a*) of the Licensing Act 1964 " 'bar' includes any place exclusively or mainly used for the consumption of intoxicating liquor". Carter was the holder of a special hours' certificate under which he was permitted to serve drinks in a club outside the normal licensing hours, but s. 76 (5) of the Act provides that a special hours' certificate does not permit the service of drinks at a "bar". Two rooms in a club managed by Carter contained a counter across which drinks were served outside normal licensing hours. These rooms were also used for dancing and the consumption of meals. The justices concentrated on s. 201 (*a*) and convicted Carter on the ground that the rooms could be subdivided into different areas, those near the counters being places exclusively or mainly used for the consumption of intoxicating liquor. The conviction was affirmed by the House of Lords, but not on the basis of the distinction drawn by the justices. The counters were treated as bars within the ordinary meaning of the term.

Interpretation clauses may bring the most incongruous things within the operation of a statute. This point was made by CHANNELL, J., in the course of holding that the Savoy Hotel was a shop.[13] In spite of its seeming oddity, the effect of the decision was beyond criticism for it brought persons under 18 within the protection against excessive working hours accorded by the Shops Act 1892 under which "shop" included "licensed public houses and refreshment houses of any kind". None the less, it is presumably the apparently bizarre nature of conclusions of this sort which have led to criticisms of interpretation clauses. Lord BROUGHAM spoke of them as "the famous freak of modern law givers",[14] and BLACKBURN, J., said that they frequently do a great deal of harm because they give a non-natural sense to words which are afterwards used in a natural sense.[15] BLACKBURN, J., was speaking of the "expression ... shall include" type of clause, but his observation would apply to the "means and includes" type. Interpretation clauses are comparatively modern, but they have been a common form of legislation for the last 100 years and they must have been responsible for a great deal of economy of drafting.

Provisos

A proviso is frequently not an aid to construction, although the terms of the section to which it is a proviso are usually of considerable aid to its construction. To discuss the subject under the head of aids to construction is rather like putting the cart before the horse. But

---

[12] [1975] 3 All E.R. 158.
[13] *Savoy Hotel Co.* v. *London County Council*, [1900] 1 Q.B. 665, at p. 669.
[14] Parliamentary Debates, 3rd series, vol. 68, col. 888 (1848).
[15] *Lindsay* v. *Cundy* (1876), 1 Q.B.D. 348, at p. 358.

the adoption of this course has its conveniences. The reason why the main clause affects the construction of the proviso is that there is a presumption based on the ordinary use of language that the scope of the proviso is affected by the scope of the main clause. The leading case is *Thompson* v. *Dibdin*.[16] After enacting that no marriage between a man and his deceased wife's sister should be, or be deemed to have been, void or voidable as a civil contract by reason of such affinity, s. 1 of the Deceased Wife's Sister's Marriage Act 1907[17] continued:

> "Provided always that no clergyman in holy orders of the Church of England shall be liable to any suit, penalty or censure, whether civil or ecclesiastical, for anything done or omitted to be done by him in the performance of the duties of his office to which suit, penalty or censure he would not have been liable if this Act had not been passed."

Did this mean that a clergyman could refuse holy communion to a man and his deceased wife's sister who had intermarried, as he could have done before the Act? Read without reference to what preceded it, this would have been the effect of the proviso, but, having regard to the fact that s. 1 was solely concerned with the contract of marriage, the Court of Appeal and House of Lords held that a clergyman was not entitled to refuse holy communion in the circumstances:

> "... A proviso must *prima facie* be read and considered in relation to the principal matter to which it is a proviso, that is the marriage contract. It is not a separate or independent enactment. The words are dependent on the principal enacting words to which they are tacked as a proviso. They cannot be read as divorced from their context."[18]

It has been said that if Parliament had in plain terms stated in the proviso that a clergyman might do just what the clergyman in *Thompson* v. *Dibdin* had claimed to do, the courts would not have been entitled to refuse to give effect to that enactment on the ground that the draftsman had broken a rule which he should have observed.

> "The courts have not, and certainly do not claim, the right to say to Parliament or its draftsmen: 'Observe the rules which we lay down, or, though your meaning may be perfectly clear, we will teach you a lesson by interpreting your language in a sense which you obviously did not intend.'"[19]

This is of course perfectly true, but the courts are entitled to say to the draftsman: "If you don't observe common linguistic practice, you are liable to be misunderstood." The point is that the ordinary reader

---

[16] [1912] A.C. 533.

[17] See now Marriage (Enabling) Act 1960.

[18] [1912] A.C. 533, at p. 544, *per* Lord ASHBOURNE.

[19] *No-Nail Cases Propriety, Ltd.* v. *No-Nail Boxes, Ltd.*, [1944] 1 K.B. 629, at p. 637, *per* DU PARCQ, L.J.

would expect a proviso to qualify in some way the words which precede it.

The ordinary reader would not expect a proviso to control the construction of the main section and, although enactments containing provisos must be construed as a whole like all enactments, "each portion, if need be, throwing light on the rest",[20] warnings have from time to time been given against allowing a proviso to exercise an undue influence over the construction of the main section. To quote Lord WATSON:[1]

> "I am perfectly clear that if the language of the enacting part of the statute does not contain the provisions which are said to occur in it, you cannot derive those provisions by implication from a proviso, . . . I perfectly admit that there may be and are many cases in which the terms of an intelligible proviso may throw considerable light on the ambiguous import of the statutory words."

It is possible to point to at least one case of which the *ratio decidendi* was the avoidance of a construction which would have rendered a proviso otiose,[2] but if a proviso is clearly otiose, it cannot be right to allow it to influence the construction of the main section. Yet this is precisely what the Court of Criminal Appeal did in *R.* v. *Wheat* and *R.* v. *Stocks.*[3] Section 57 of the Offences Against the Person Act 1861 defines bigamy as the offence committed by someone who

> "being married, shall marry any other person during the life of the former husband or wife . . . provided that nothing in this section contained shall extend to any person marrying a second time whose husband or wife shall have been continually absent from such person for a space of seven years last past and shall not have been known by such person to have been living within that time; or shall extend to any person who at the time of such second marriage shall have been divorced from the bond of the first marriage."

In *R.* v. *Tolson*[4] the Court for Crown Cases Reserved construed the main section in such a way as to allow for the defence of a reasonable, though mistaken, belief in the death of the first spouse even though the second ceremony took place less than seven years after his disappearance. In *R.* v. *Wheat* and *R.* v. *Stocks*[5] the Court of Criminal Appeal held that a reasonable, though mistaken, belief that the first marriage had been terminated by divorce was no defence because the second proviso, unlike the first, contained no reference to the

---

[20] *Jennings* v. *Kelley*, [1940] A.C. 206, at p. 229, *per* Lord WRIGHT.
[1] *West Derby Union* v. *Metropolitan Life Assurance Society*, [1897] A.C. 647, at p. 652.
[2] *R.* v. *Governor of Leeds Prison, Ex parte Stafford*, [1964] 2 Q.B. 625; [1964] 1 All E.R. 610.
[3] [1921] 2 K.B. 119.
[4] (1889), 23 Q.B.D. 168.
[5] [1921] 2 K.B. 119.

accused's state of mind; but the second proviso was wholly unnecessary and ought not to have been allowed to have any bearing on the construction of the main section. *R.* v. *Wheat* and *R.* v. *Stocks* has been overruled[6] but not before generations of law students had been tortured by demands to perform the impossible task of reconciling the decision with *R.* v. *Tolson.*

B. OTHER PARTS OF THE SAME STATUTE

Matters calling for discussion under this head are the long title, preamble (if any) and short title, cross-headings, side-notes (or marginal notes) and punctuation. Nowadays it is probably true to say that each one of the above items has some value as an aid to construction in some circumstances, but they all have less value than the items mentioned in the previous section simply because they do not enact anything. There is a distinction between the first and second groups of items because the first three are clearly part of the Act and could be amended by Parliament when dealing with the Bill whereas this is not true of the remaining three. The theoretical upshot of this distinction is that, although the first three (or at any rate the first two) of the above items can be described as "aids to the ascertainment of the intention of Parliament", the last three merely indicate the intention of the draftsman.

There is a bewildering mass of conflicting dicta on the question whether some of the above items can be treated as aids to construction at all and, when it is conceded that they may be so treated, upon their weight. This is due to a failure to distinguish between two stages in the process of interpretation at which the aids may be relevant. The first stage is that at which the judge has to decide whether he has any real doubt about the meaning of the word, phrase or passage which he is called upon to interpret. At this point it is hard to believe that he can or should have any inhibitions concerning the parts of the statute which he will read. No doubt he will begin with the section containing the word, phrase or passage in dispute. He can hardly help taking account of the punctuation and sidenote. If he is to fulfil his duty of reading the whole Act, when it is necessary to do so in order to determine whether there is an ambiguity, he must look at the long title, preamble (if any), short title and cross-headings. If, after this performance, the judge is satisfied that the word, phrase or passage the meaning of which is in dispute really only has one meaning in the context, he must apply that meaning; but if he has doubts on the subject he will think again. It is at this point that the

---

[6] *R.* v. *Gould*, [1968] 2 Q.B. 65; [1968] 1 All E.R. 849.

distinction between the enacting parts of a statute and the other parts becomes crucial. If the sole cause of doubt is a disparity between the otherwise clear and unambiguous words and a title, preamble, heading or side-note, the judge must disregard his doubts and apply the otherwise clear and unambiguous words. This is because there is a rule of law according to which, although the parts of the statute which do not enact anything may be consulted as a guide to Parliamentary intent and hence to the meaning of the enacted words, effect must not be given to any doubts which they may raise about the meaning of those words. If, however, the judge has doubts about the meaning of the statutory provision he is considering for some such other reason as its lack of clarity or apparent pointlessness, he may take the title, preamble, heading or side note into consideration in determining how those doubts should be resolved. As we shall see, reservations have been expressed about the propriety of taking any of the above items into consideration, and it is necessary to be especially cautious when endeavouring to state the law with regard to the extent to which the short title and side-notes, not to mention punctuation, may be taken into consideration, but it is submitted that the following remarks of Lord UPJOHN in *Director of Public Prosecutions* v. *Schildkamp*[7] amply justify the above general account of the relevance of the items mentioned at the beginning of this section to the judicial process of interpretation. The remarks were made with special reference to cross-headings:

> "When the court construing the Act is reading it through to understand it, it must read the cross-headings as well as the body of the Act and that will always be a useful pointer to the intention of Parliament in enacting the immediately following sections. Whether the cross-heading is no more than a pointer or label, or is helpful in assisting to construe, or even in some cases to control, the meaning or ambit of those sections must necessarily depend on the circumstances of each case and I do not think it is possible to lay down any rules."

The matter must now be considered in slightly greater detail.

Long title and preamble

The long title is set out at the beginning of the statute and usually contains a general statement of the legislative purpose. For example the long title of the Theft Act 1968 reads: "An Act to revise the law of England and Wales as to theft and similar or associated offences, and in connection therewith to make provision as to criminal proceedings by one party to a marriage against the other and to make certain amendments extending beyond England and Wales in the Post Office Act 1953 and other enactments; and for other purposes connected

[7] [1971] A.C. 1, at p. 28.

therewith." In modern times all enactments have something like a long title, but preambles have for a long time been something of a rarity. An exception is the Parliament Act 1911, the preamble to which reads:

> "Whereas it is expedient that provision should be made for regulating the relations between the two Houses of Parliament: and whereas it is intended to substitute for the House of Lords as it at present exists a second Chamber constituted on a popular instead of hereditary basis, but such substitution cannot immediately be brought into operation: and whereas provision will require hereafter to be made by Parliament in a measure effecting such substitution for limiting and defining the powers of the new second Chamber, but it is expedient to make such provision as in this Act appears for restricting the existing powers of the House of Lords."

When there is a preamble, it sets out the facts and assumptions upon which the statute is based. The long title and preamble are discussed together because the law with regard to the use which may be made of each is the same, and what is strictly a long title is sometimes referred to as a preamble.[8]

The law concerning the use that may be made of the long title was succinctly stated by DONOVAN, J., in *R.* v. *Bates*:[9]

> "In many cases the long title may supply the key to the meaning. The principle as I understand it is that where something is doubtful or ambiguous the long title may be looked to to resolve the doubt or ambiguity, but, in the absence of doubt or ambiguity, the passage under construction must be taken to mean what it says so that, if its meaning be clear, that meaning is not to be narrowed or restricted by reference to the long title."

The law concerning the use that may be made of a preamble was stated by Lord NORMAND in the following terms in *A.-G.* v. *Prince Ernest Augustus of Hanover*:[10]

> "When there is a preamble it is generally in its recitals that the mischief to be remedied and the scope of the Act are described. It is therefore clearly permissible to have recourse to it as an aid to construing the enacting provisions. The preamble is not, however, of the same weight as an aid to construction of a section of the Act as are other relevant enacting words to be found elsewhere in the Act or even in related Acts. There may be no exact correspondence between preamble and enactment, and the enactment may go beyond or it may fall short of the indications that may be gathered from the preamble. Again, the preamble cannot be of much or any assistance in construing provisions which embody qualifications or exceptions from the operation of the general purpose of the Act. It is only when it conveys a clear and definite meaning in comparison with relatively obscure or indefinite enacting words that the preamble may legitimately prevail. The courts are concerned with the practical business of deciding a *lis*, and when the plaintiff puts forward one construction of an enactment

---

[8] E.g. in *Ward* v. *Holman, infra.*
[9] [1952] 2 All E.R. 842, at p. 844.
[10] [1957] A.C. 436, at p. 467; p. 47 *supra.*

and the defendant another, it is the court's business in any case of some difficulty, after informing itself of what I have called the legal and factual context including the preamble, to consider in the light of this knowledge whether the enacting words admit of both the rival constructions put forward. If they admit of only one construction, that construction will receive effect even if it is inconsistent with the preamble, but if the enacting words are capable of either of the constructions offered by the parties, the construction which fits the preamble may be preferred."

Lord NORMAND was speaking in a case in which the section of the statute of Anne which conferred British citizenship on the lineal descendants of the Electoress Sofia "born or hereafter to be born" was held to be unaffected by the reference to naturalisation in Queen Anne's lifetime in the preamble. The preamble itself was none too clear, but the Hanover case is clear authority for the proposition that the fact that the enacting words under consideration go beyond the scope of the purposes mentioned in the preamble is not a reason for declining to give effect to otherwise unambiguous statutory words.[11] It will be recollected that the case is also authority for the proposition that no-one is entitled to assert that statutory words are unambiguous until he has read them in their full context which includes the long title and preamble.

A further illustration of the rule that these parts of a statute cannot control otherwise unambiguous enacting words merely because those words fall outside their scope is provided by *Ward* v. *Holman*.[12] The long title of the Public Order Act 1936 is:

"An Act to prohibit the wearing of uniforms in connection with political objects and the maintainance by private persons of associations of military or similar character; and to make further provision for the preservation of public order on the occasion of public processions and meetings and in public places."

Under s. 5:

"Any person who in any public place or any public meeting uses threatening, abusive or insulting words or behaviour with intent to provoke a breach of the peace or whereby a breach of the peace is likely to be occasioned, shall be guilty of an offence."

Holman broke a window of a neighbour's house, stood in the street shouting abuse towards the house and, when members of the neighbour's family congregated in the street, challenged them to a fight. He was charged with an offence against s. 5 of the Act. Quarter Sessions, on the hearing of an appeal from the magistrates, held that he was not guilty because the Act was confined to public meetings, processions and the like; but the Divisional Court re-instated his con-

[11] See also *The Norwhale*, [1975] Q.B. 589; [1975] 2 All E.R. 501.
[12] [1964] 2 Q.B. 580; [1964] 2 All E.R. 729.

viction. Lord PARKER said: "It is impossible to look at the preamble [*sic*] of the Act as controlling the operative words of the Act itself unless those words are ambiguous".

This case may be contrasted with *Brett* v. *Brett*[13] which shows that the long title and preamble may be allowed to play their part in controlling apparently unambiguous enacted words when doubts about the meaning of those words arise from some other source. The Wills Act 1751 provided that beneficiaries who attested "any will or codicil" should be good witnesses but that gifts made to them in the will or codicil should be void. The words "any will or codicil" were of course apt to cover wills of personalty as well as realty, but the then state of the law naturally gave rise to doubts about their applying to wills of personalty because such wills did not require attestation at all. These doubts, coupled with the terms of a later section of the Act, and a reference to the long title and preamble both of which spoke only of wills and codicils of real estate were held by Sir John NICHOLL to warrant the reading in of the words "of real estate" after the word "codicil".

One of several examples of modern cases in which reference has been made to the long title as something which resolved a doubt about the meaning of an enacted word is *Fisher* v. *Raven*.[14] Did the word "credit" in the now repealed s. 13 (1) of the Debtors' Act 1869 which punished obtaining credit by fraud mean only credit in respect of the repayment of money, or did it extend to credit in respect of the future performance of services and delivery of goods? The long title of the Act is "An Act for the Abolition of Imprisonment for Debt, for the Punishment of Fraudulent Debtors, and for other purposes". This was held to support the conclusion of the House of Lords that "credit" in s. 13 meant and only meant credit in respect of the payment of money.

Short title

The short title is usually stated in a separate section towards the end of the statute. For example s. 36 (1) of the Theft Act says "This Act may be cited as the Theft Act 1968". As it is contained in the body of the Act and is, like the long title and preamble, subject to amendment by Parliament while the Bill is being passed, one would have thought that the short title should be treated in the same way as the long title and preamble; but the preponderance of authority suggests that it may never be relied on as something which may resolve a doubt. In support of this view it is urged that the short title is inserted as a mere identifying label, "a statutory nickname to obviate

[13] (1826), 3 Add. 210.
[14] [1964] A.C. 210; [1963] 2 All E.R. 389.

the necessity of always referring to the Act under its full and descriptive title".[15] But it is difficult not to feel considerable sympathy with the following remarks of SCRUTTON, L.J., made with reference to the issue whether the Vexatious Actions Act 1896 applied to criminal proceedings:[16]

> "I agree that the court should give less importance to the title than to the enacting part, and less to the short title than to the full title, for the short title being a label, accuracy may be sacrificed to brevity; but I do not understand on what principle of construction I am not to look at the words of the Act itself to help me to understand its scope in order to interpret the words Parliament has used in the circumstances in which they were legislating. It is by no means conclusive, but it is striking that if they were intending to deal with criminal proceedings they should call their Act the Vexatious Actions Act."

Headings

Headings are not voted on or passed by Parliament, but this does not appear to have prevented them from being treated in much the same way as the long title and preamble. Indeed in one of the cases in which great stress was placed on this lack of Parliamentary imprimatur, it was conceded that reference may be made to headings as aids in resolving an ambiguity. The case in question is *R.* v. *Hare*[17] in which a woman was charged with an offence against s. 62 of the Offences Against the Person Act 1861 under which "whosoever shall be guilty of any indecent assault upon a male person under the age of 16" is liable to be punished. Sections 61–3 of the Act were placed under the heading of "Unnatural offences", but the Court of Criminal Appeal none the less held that there was no ambiguity. In *Fisher* v. *Raven*,[18] the House of Lords took note of the fact that s. 13 of the Debtors' Act 1869 was included in Part II of the Act which was headed "Punishment of Fraudulent Debtors", and in *R.* v. *Bates*[19] DONOVAN, J., equated headings with the long title, at any rate for the purposes of the case before him. We have already seen that great importance was attached to the headings in the Companies Act 1948 by the majority of the House of Lords in *Director of Public Prosecutions* v. *Schildkamp*.[20] The fact that the heading of the group of sections which included s. 332 was "Offences Antecedent to and in the course of Winding-Up" supported the conclusion that the offence under s. 332 (3) could only be charged in a case in which a winding-up order had

[15] *Vacher & Sons Ltd.* v. *London Society of Compositors*, [1913] A.C. 107, at p. 128, *per* Lord MOULTON.
[16] *Re Boaler*, [1915] 1 K.B. 21, at pp. 40–1.
[17] [1934] 1 K.B. 354.
[18] [1964] A.C. 210; [1963] 2 All E.R. 389.
[19] [1952] 2 All E.R. 842.
[20] [1971] A.C. 1; [1969] 3 All E.R. 1640.

been made. The uncertainty concerned the scope rather than the meaning of the statutory words.

Side-notes

Chandler v. *Director of Public Prosecutions*[1] may be cited as conclusive authority for the proposition that side-notes (frequently spoken of as "marginal notes") cannot be used as aids to construction in any circumstances. The defendants, members of the Committee of One Hundred, the aim of which was to further nuclear disarmament, participated in a demonstration at an airfield with the object of grounding all aircraft. They were charged with and convicted of an offence against s. 1 (1) of the Official Secrets Act 1911 which punishes those who approach prohibited places for a purpose prejudicial to the safety of the State. The side-note reads "penalties for spying" and it was conceded that the defendants were not spying, but their appeal to the House of Lords was dismissed on the ground that they were acting for a purpose prejudicial to the safety of the State within the meaning of s. 1 (1). Lord REID said:[2]

> "In my view sidenotes cannot be used as an aid to construction. They are mere catch-words and I have never heard of it being supposed in recent times that an amendment to alter a sidenote could be proposed in either House of Parliament. Sidenotes in the original Bill are inserted by the draftsman. During the passage of the Bill through its various stages amendments to it or other reasons may make it desirable to alter a sidenote. In that event I have reason to believe that alteration is made by the appropriate officer of the House—no doubt in consultation with the draftsman. So sidenotes cannot be enacted in the same sense as the long title or any part of the body of the Act."

In spite of its great weight, three remarks may be made with regard to this passage. In the first place what Lord REID said would seem to be equally applicable to cross-headings, yet we have just seen that this has not prevented them from being treated in much the same way as the long title and preamble. Secondly, even if it is the case that side-notes cannot be called in aid in order to resolve doubts, it can hardly be the law that they are to be disregarded by the judge when he is perusing the Act with a view to ascertaining whether he has any doubts. No judge can be expected to treat something which is before his eyes as though it was not there. In the words of UPJOHN, L.J.: "While the marginal note to a section cannot control the language used in the section, it is at least permissible to approach a consideration of its general purpose and the mischief at which it is aimed with the note in mind".[3] Finally, Lord REID's remarks in *Chandler*

[1] [1964] A.C. 763.
[2] *Ibid.*, at p. 789.
[3] *Stephens* v. *Cuckfield Rural District Council*, [1960] 2 Q.B. 373, at p. 383.

v. *Director of Public Prosecutions* must be read in the light of his subsequent remarks in *Director of Public Prosecutions* v. *Schildkamp*:[4]

> "But it may be more realistic to accept the Act as printed as being the product of the whole legislative process, and to give due weight to everything found in the printed Act. I say more realistic because in very many cases the provision before the court was never even mentioned in debate in either House, and it may be that its wording was never closely scrutinised by any member of either House. In such a case it is not very meaningful to say that the words of the Act represent the intention of Parliament but the punctuation, crossheadings and sidenotes do not."

Punctuation

Lord Reid had previously expressed himself with great caution concerning punctuation:[5]

> "Before 1850 there was no punctuation in the manuscript copy of an Act which received the royal assent, and it does not appear that the printers had any statutory authority to insert punctuation thereafter. So even if punctuation in more modern Acts can be looked at (which is very doubtful), I do not think that one can have any regard to punctuation in older Acts."

The orthodox view with regard to punctuation, whatever be the date of the statute, is expressed in the following statement which is none the less telling for being completely untrue nowadays: "In an Act of Parliament there are no such things as brackets any more than there are such things as stops."[6] The more realistic view suggested by Lord Reid in *Director of Public Prosecutions* v. *Schildkamp* must surely be the right one, but, if it is to be adopted, it is to be hoped that the courts will continue to be prepared to ignore or insert punctuation where to do so is necessary to give effect to the purpose of the statute. The advantage of the present position under which the judge can pretend that the punctuation is not there is illustrated by two decisions mentioned in Maxwell.[7] In *Re Naranjansingh*,[8] the court was concerned with the construction of s. 10 of the Fugitive Offenders Act 1881 under which a court may refuse to return the alleged offender if:

> "By reason of the trivial nature of the case, or by reason of the application for the return of a fugitive not being made in good faith in the interests of justice or otherwise, it would, having regard to the distance, to the facilities of communication, and to all the circumstances of the case, be unjust. . . ."

[4] [1971] A.C. 1, at p. 10.

[5] *Inland Revenue Commissioners* v. *Hinchy*, [1960] A.C. 748, at p. 765.

[6] *Duke of Devonshire* v. *O'Connor* (1890), 24 Q.B.D. 468, at p. 478, *per* Lord Esher, M.R.

[7] *On The Interpretation of Statutes*, 12th Edn., p. 14.

[8] *R.* v. *Brixton Prison Governor, Ex parte Naranjansingh*, [1962] 1 Q.B. 211; [1961] 2 All E.R. 565.

As punctuated, the statutory words confine the power to refuse to return to trivial cases and cases in which the application is not made in good faith, but, aided by the references to distance and facilities which do not have much to do with good faith, the court was able to construe the words so as, in effect, to insert a comma after "justice". In *Luby* v. *Newcastle Upon Tyne Corporation*,[9] s. 133 (5) of the Housing Act 1957 was under consideration. It provided that "the Local Authority shall from time to time review rents and make such changes, either of rents generally or of particular rents, and rebates (if any) as circumstances may require." The comma after the word "rents" where it occurs for the third time suggests that the authority has power to make rebates rather than to make changes of rebates, but the subsection was read as though the comma was not there.

C. RULES OF LANGUAGE

Something must now be said about the rule of *ejusdem generis* ("of the same kind"), the maxim *noscitur a sociis* ("a thing is known by its companions"), the rule of rank and the maxim *expressio unius exclusio alterius* ("the mention of one thing is the exclusion of another"). *Noscitur a sociis* and the rule of rank can, roughly speaking, be respectively regarded as an extended and attenuated version of the *ejusdem generis* rule. These rules or maxims have attracted an unduly large quantity of case law because they are neither legal principles nor legal rules. It is hardly correct to speak of them as rules of language for they simply refer to the way in which people speak in certain contexts. They are no more than rough guides to the intention of the speaker or writer. To quote from an article by Mr. E A Driedger:[10] "Ordinarily a husband who authorised his wife to purchase a hat, coat, shoes and 'anything else you need' would not expect her to buy anything else but clothes." To exemplify the *expressio unius* maxim by the words of an even more generous hypothetical speaker, if someone were to say "I am going to give you my houses in London and York and the fixtures in my London house", the prospective donee could hardly hope for the fixtures in the York house.

Ejusdem generis[11]

The words of Mr. Driedger may again be quoted for a full formulation of the *ejusdem generis* rule:[12]

---

[9] [1965] 1 Q.B. 214; [1964] 3 All E.R. 169.

[10] 29 Canadian Bar Review at p. 841.

[11] See "The Origins and Logical Implications of the *Ejusdem Generis* Rule", by Glanville Williams, 7 Conv. (N.S.) 119.

[12] *On the Construction of Statutes*, p. 92.

> "Where general words are found, following an enumeration of persons or things all susceptible of being regarded as specimens of a single genus or category, but not exhaustive thereof, their construction should be restricted to things of that class or category, unless it is reasonably clear from the context or the general scope and purview of the Act that Parliament intended that they should be given a broader signification."

One of the shortest judicial statements of the rule is that of COCKBURN, C.J., in *R.* v. *Cleworth*: "According to well established rules in the construction of statutes, general terms following particular ones apply only to such persons or things as are *ejusdem generis* with those comprehended in the language of the legislature."[13]

Simple illustrations are provided by decisions on the Sunday Observance Act 1677 which read "no tradesman, artificer, workman, labourer, or other person whatsoever, shall do or exercise any worldly labour, business, or work of their ordinary callings upon the Lord's Day". This section was held not to apply to a coach proprietor,[14] farmer,[15] barber,[16] or estate agent,[17] the words "other person whatsoever" being confined to those following callings of the kind specified in the preceding words. One reason for the rule is that the draftsman must be taken to have inserted the general words in case something which ought to have been included among the specifically enumerated items had been omitted; a further reason is that, if the general words were intended to have their ordinary meaning, the specific enumeration would be pointless. For instance, in *Re Stockport Ragged Industrial and Reformatory Schools*[18] the question was whether Industrial Schools were included in the proviso to s. 62 of the Charitable Trusts Act 1853. If they were, the consent of the Charity Commissioners to their mortgages was required. The proviso referred to "any cathedral, collegiate, chapter, or *other* schools"; but it was held to be applicable only to the specified schools and those of a similar type. LINDLEY, M.R., said that he could not conceive why the legislature should have taken the trouble to specify particular schools except in order to show the type of school to which reference was being made.

For the rule to apply, it must be possible to construct a genus out of the specific words. *Allen* v. *Emmerson*[19] decided that the phrase "theatres and other places of public entertainment" used in s. 33 of the Barrow in Furness Corporation Act 1872 did not constitute a genus with the result that a fun fair required a licence under the sec-

---

[13] (1864), 4 B. & S. 927, at p. 932.
[14] *Sandiman* v. *Breach* (1827), 5 L.J. O.S. K.B. 298.
[15] *R.* v. *Cleworth* (1864), 4 B. & S. 927.
[16] *Palmer* v. *Snow*, [1900] 1 Q.B. 725.
[17] *Gregory* v. *Fearn*, [1953] 2 All E.R. 559.
[18] [1898] 2 Ch. 687.
[19] [1944] 1 K.B. 362.

tion although no charge was made for admission. The phrase "theatres and other places of public entertainment" was followed by words in parenthesis excepting from the requirement of a licence theatres to which admission was free, and it was argued that there was an excepted species or sub-genus of places of public entertainment admission to which was free; but ASQUITH, J., pointed out that words excepting a species from a genus are meaningless unless the species falls within the genus. "All hats other than top hats" makes sense. "All top hats other than bowler hats" does not. Nor does "all hats and other articles except gloves" if "other articles" is to be construed *ejusdem generis* with hats.[20]

Allen v. *Emmerson* lends no support to the suggestion that the *ejusdem generis* rule can never be applied to a "two word" phrase. It is sometimes said that the mention of a single species can never be treated as a reference to a genus. This was the view of SCOTT, L.J., in the Court of Appeal in *Alexander* v. *Tredegar Iron and Coal Co., Ltd.*[1] The case was concerned with the construction of s. 47 of the Coal Mines Act 1911 requiring every haulage road to be "kept clear as far as possible of pieces of coal and other obstructions". The question was whether a damaged truck being taken up the road for repair which collided with another truck and caused the death of a workman was an obstruction within the meaning of the section. SCOTT, L.J., said: "I cannot see that it [the *ejusdem generis* rule] has any application to s. 47. If one tries to apply it, one is at once met with the difficulty that, there being only one species, viz. pieces of coal, there is no basis for formulating a genus." The House of Lords also held that the *ejusdem generis* rule did not apply to s. 47, but not because of the difficulty of applying it to a two word phrase; the simple point was that s. 47 was not intended to deal with a traffic accident between two moving vehicles.[2]

Alexander v. *Tredegar Iron and Coal Co.* shows that the *ejusdem generis* rule which is at most a rule of language must yield to the basic duty of the Courts to have regard to the mischief aimed at by the statutory provisions they have to consider. *Skinner* v. *Shew*[3] shows that the mischief aimed at may require general words to be construed in their

---

[20] *Ibid.*, at p. 367.

[1] [1944] K.B. 390, at p. 396. The decision of the Court of Appeal was affirmed by the House of Lords, [1945] A.C. 286. See also a note by J. S. F. in 70 Law Quarterly Review 172 where other authorities are cited.

[2] The best known instance of the application of the *ejusdem generis* rule to a two word phrase is *Ashbury Railway Carriage and Iron Co.* v. *Riche* (1875), L.R. 7 H.L. 653 where, in a memorandum of association empowering the company to carry on business as "mechanical engineers and general contractors", the expression "general contractors" was construed *ejusdem generis* with "mechanical engineers".

[3] [1893] 1 Ch. 413.

most general sense in spite of the fact that they are preceded by specific items. Section 32 of the Patents, Designs, and Trademarks Act 1883 gave a right to an injunction against the continuance of threats "where any person claiming to be patentee of any invention, by *circulars, advertisements or otherwise* threatens any other person with any legal proceedings" unless the person making the threats brought his action with due diligence. It was held that the section applied to a threat by letter for its object was the protection of manufacturers and vendors of goods against unmeritorious threats to bring a patent action, conduct which could have the effect of paralysing their businesses. The reference to circulars and advertisements may have been made out of an abundance of caution so as to make it plain that threats contained in documents addressed to the public were included. In any event the mischief rule must prevail against the *ejusdem generis* rule. After referring to the latter, BOWEN, L. J., said:[4]

> "But there is an exception to that rule, if it be a rule and not a maxim of common sense, which is that although the words immediately around and before the general words are words which are *prima facie* confined, yet if you can see from a wider inspection of the scope of the legislation that the general words notwithstanding that they follow particular words, are nevertheless to be construed generally, you must give effect to the intention of the legislature as gathered from the entire section."

Noscitur a sociis

The *ejusdem generis* rule is an example of a broader linguistic rule or practice to which reference is made by the Latin tag *noscitur a sociis*. Words, even if they are not general words like "whatsoever" or "otherwise" preceded by specific words, are liable to be affected by other words with which they are associated. To quote STAMP, J.:[5]

> "English words derive colour from those which surround them. Sentences are not mere collections of words to be taken out of the sentence, defined separately by reference to the dictionary or decided cases, and then put back into the sentence with the meaning which you have assigned to them as separate words. . . ."

In other words due regard must be paid to the verbal context.

Two examples cited in Maxwell[6] are *Muir* v. *Keay*[7] and *Pengelly* v. *Bell Punch Co., Ltd.*[8] In the first of these cases it was held that on the true construction of s. 6 of the Refreshment Houses Act 1860 which dealt with houses "for public refreshment, resort and entertainment," "entertainment" meant not a theatrical or musical or similar per-

---

[4] [1893] 1 Ch. 424.
[5] *Bourne* v. *Norwich Crematorium, Ltd.*, [1967] 2 All E.R. 576, at p. 578.
[6] *On the Interpretation of Statutes*, pp. 289–91.
[7] (1875), L.R. 10 Q.B. 594.
[8] [1964] 2 All E.R. 945.

formance, but "something connected with the enjoyment of refreshment rooms". In *Pengelly's* case the word "floors" in s. 28 (1) of the Factories Act 1961 was held not to extend to parts of the factory floor properly used for the purpose of storage. The Act deals with "floors, steps, stairs, passages and gangways". They are to be kept free from obstruction, and DIPLOCK, L.J., said: "It will be observed that the last four are places used for the purpose of passage. The expression 'floors' in this context and in the light of the word 'obstruction', which means 'blocking or being blocked; making or becoming more or less impassable', is, in my view, limited to those parts of the factory floor upon which workmen are intended or likely to pass and repass."[9] No useful purpose would be served by multiplying examples beyond stressing the point that, as the context with its reference to exceptions precluded the construction of a genus in *Allen* v. *Emmerson*,[10] the context may prevent words from being coloured by their associates. Inclusions had this effect in *Letang* v. *Cooper*[11] where an action for damages for trespass to the person was held to be an action for "breach of duty" within the meaning of the Law Reform (Limitation of Actions) Act 1954. The relevant words were "negligence, nuisance or breach of duty", and it was argued that, since actual damage was an essential prerequisite of an action for negligence or nuisance, "breach of duty" should be similarly restricted. The argument was refuted by the fact that the word "duty" was immediately followed by the parenthetic words "whether the duty exists by virtue of a contract or ... independently of any contract ..."; a breach of contract is of course actionable without proof of actual damage.

The rule of rank

The rule of rank is the second of the rules for the construction of statutes mentioned by Blackstone at the end of the third section of his *Introduction to the Commentaries* where it is formulated as follows:[12]

> "A statute, which treats of things or persons of an inferior rank, cannot by any *general* words be extended to those of a superior. So a statute, treating of deans, prebendaries, parsons, vicars, *and* others having spiritual promotion, is held not to extend to bishops, though they have spiritual promotion; deans being the highest persons named, and bishops being of a still higher order."

The rule is treated with contempt by Bentham: "and who can be sure in such an assemblage what is a superior and what inferior? Suppose deans had been omitted, and prebendaries had been the first

---

[9] *Ibid.*, at p. 947.
[10] P. 116 *supra*.
[11] [1965] 1 Q.B. 232; [1964] 2 All E.R. 929.
[12] *Commentaries*, 1813 edition, vol. 1, p. 104.

word, would canons have been to stand included or excluded?"[13] Yet there are cases where, as a matter of ordinary language, an omission is so striking that one would pause to treat it as included in general words although there is no question of the specific words constituting a relevant genus to which the general words might be limited. Surely most people would hesitate before including the Thames in a prohibition on salmon fishing in "the waters of the Humber, Ouse, Trent ... and all other waters wherein salmons be taken"?[14] If this type of problem can be solved by a rule of language, the *expressio unius* maxim is at least a safer guide than the uncertain rule of rank; but can the *expressio unius* maxim be applied to exclude the literal sense of general words?

Expressio unius

The effect of the Latin maxim *expressio unius est exclusio alterius*, sometimes stated in the form *expressum facit cessare tacitum* (that which is expressed puts an end to that which is silent) is that mention of one or more things of a particular class may be regarded as silently excluding all other members of the class. An example is provided by *R.* v. *Caledonian Railway*. A railway company was authorised to build bridges of the heights and spans shown on a plan. A road was carried on a bridge of the requisite height and span, but with a different inclination from that shown on the plan. It was held that the company was under no obligation to alter the inclination: "We are clearly of opinion that there is no obligation beyond the heights and spans of the bridges as delineated on the plan. These are mentioned in the enactment, and nothing is said as to the rates of inclination of the road. *Expressio unius est exclusio alterius.*"[15] The word "land" is usually apt to include all kinds of mine, but a reference to "lands, houses and coalmines" may mean that no mines are included in the word "lands".[16] When a statute says that, if a purchaser to whom Crown lands have been sold on certain conditions fails to comply with the conditions, the lands shall revert to the crown and be "liable to be sold by auction", it is reasonable to hold that the Crown had not got a choice between another conditional sale by private treaty and a sale by auction.[17]

Yet, although it would be possible to multiply the above examples considerably, it is doubtful whether the maxim does any more than draw attention to a fairly obvious linguistic point, viz. that in many

---

[13] *A Comment on the Commentaries*, p. 140.
[14] 2 Inst. 478.
[15] (1850), 16 Q.B. 19, at p. 30, *per* Lord CAMPBELL.
[16] *R.* v. *Sedgley Inhabitants* (1831), 2 B. and Ad. 65.
[17] *Blackburn* v. *Flavelle* (1881), 6 App. Cas. 628.

contexts the mention of some matters warrants an inference that other cognate matters were intentionally excluded. Allowance must always be made for the fact that the "*exclusio*" may have been accidental, still more for the fact that there may have been good reason for it. This last point is well illustrated by *Dean* v. *Wiesengrund*.[18] Section 14 of the Rent and Mortgage Interest (Restriction) Act 1920 provided that excess rent should be recoverable by the tenant by whom it was paid from the landlord or his personal representative. It was held that the exclusion of the tenant's personal representative did not prevent him from suing. The excess rent was made recoverable retrospectively, and the intention may have been to prevent the personal representatives of tenants who died before the Act came into force from suing. JENKINS, L.J., said:[19]

> "The argument for the landlord is summed up in the maxim *expressio unius est exclusio alterius* which, applied to the present case, is said to compel the conclusion that the express reference to the legal personal representative of one of the parties excludes any implied reference to the legal personal representative of the other. But this maxim is after all no more than an aid to construction and has little, if any, weight where it is possible, as I think it is in the present case, to account for the *inclusio unius* on grounds other than an intention to effect the *exclusio alterius*."

---

[18] [1955] 2 Q.B. 120.
[19] *Ibid.*, at p. 130.

VI

External Aids to Construction

To repeat a passage from one of Lord DENNING's speeches:[1]

> "In this country we do not refer to the legislative history of an enactment as they do in the United States of America. We do not look at the explanatory memoranda which preface the Bills before Parliament. We do not have recourse to the pages of Hansard. All that the courts can do is to take judicial notice of the previous state of the law and of other matters generally known to well informed people."

In the first section of this chapter a little is said about the process of taking judicial notice of matters generally known to "well informed people", a phrase for which "learned lawyers" should perhaps be substituted, and the extent to which these matters, when judicially noticed, may be used as aids to statutory interpretation. The vexed question of legislative history is briefly tackled in Section B. Nothing need be said about the process of taking judicial notice of the previous state of the law. It is simply a matter of consulting the relevant statutes, decisions and textbooks.

A. MISCELLANEOUS

Something must be said about the use, as aids to interpretation, of the historical setting of a statute, dictionaries and other literary sources, the practices of classes of the community to which the statute applies, *contemporanea expositio* and other statutes *in pari materia*. The last three of these items come mainly within the cognisance of lawyers and the aid to be derived from dictionaries tends to be subordinated to that to be gained from judicial statements concerning the meaning of words. It is for these reasons that it was suggested that "learned lawyers" might be substituted for "well informed people" in the quotation from Lord DENNING.

[1] *Escoigne Properties, Ltd.* v. *Inland Revenue Commissioners*, [1958] A.C. 549, at p. 565.

Historical setting. The historical setting of the statute has been invoked as an aid to its construction in several cases which have already been mentioned. The following remark was made by Lord REID in *Chandler* v. *Director of Public Prosecutions*[2] in support of the conclusion that members of the Committee of One Hundred who obstructed an airfield acted for a "purpose prejudicial to the safety or interests of the State" within the meaning of s. 1 of the Official Secrets Act 1911, although they believed that nuclear disarmament would be beneficial to this country:

> "The 1911 Act was passed at a time of grave misgiving about the German menace, and it would be surprising and hardly credible that Parliament of that date intended that a person who deliberately interfered with vital dispositions of the armed forces should be entitled to submit to a jury that government policy was wrong and that what he did was really in the best interests of the country, and then perhaps to escape conviction because a unanimous verdict on the question could not be obtained."

The fact that, in 1870, many Englishmen sympathised with insurgents against continental governments contributed to the construction of the words "an offence of a political character" in s. 1 of the Extradition Act 1870 adopted by a majority of the House of Lords in *R.* v. *Governor of Pentonville Prison, ex parte Cheng.*[3] The offence must be of a political character *vis-à-vis* the State requesting extradition, and not the assassination within the jurisdiction of that State of a public figure from another country.

The examination of the historical setting of a statutory provision sometimes produces a conflict between the literal and mischief rules. For example, s. 83 of the West India Dock Act 1831 exempted lighters from dues or rates if they entered the dock to discharge or receive ballast or goods to or from "any ship or vessel lying therein" so long as such lighter shall be "*bona fide* engaged in discharging or receiving such ballast or goods as aforesaid". In *London and India Docks* v. *Thames Steam and Lighterage Co., Ltd.*[4] two lighters entered the dock with goods intended to be discharged into a steamship then lying therein. Through no fault of the lighters the ship was unable to receive the goods, and they therefore left the dock. The issue was whether the owners of the lighters were liable to dues or rates or whether they came within the exemption provided by s. 83. By a majority of 3 to 2, the House of Lords held that they were liable. Lord LOREBURN, who delivered the majority judgment, first placed s. 83 in its historical setting. When the dock was built, the owners were authorised to charge dues in respect of ships entering it, but it was necessary to pro-

[2] [1964] A.C. 763, at p. 791.
[3] [1973] A.C. 931, [1973] 2 All E.R. 204.
[4] [1909] A.C. 7.

vide an exemption for lighters entering in order to receive or discharge cargo because ships had previously been loaded and unloaded by them in midstream and they had not been liable to any charge. It was also necessary to provide against abuse of the exemption by lighters entering the dock in the hope of getting unloading work, or remaining there after they had discharged their cargo in the hope of getting such work, for, in either event, the dock would become overcrowded. Hence the restriction of the exemption to lighters *bona fide* engaged in discharging or receiving goods. Lord LOREBURN conceded that, if a lighter went into a dock to discharge goods into a ship lying there and came out after doing so, she would be engaged all the time in the business of discharging goods. He also conceded that if only one ton had been taken out of the lighter in such a case she would have been engaged all the time in discharging goods; but he could not bring himself to say that when nothing was taken out she was engaged in discharging goods either "such goods" or any other; "for whatever else goods may be, they are at all events something".[5] The conclusion is quite inconsistent with the object of s. 83 as portrayed in its historical setting, and rendered all the more surprising by the concession that the words "shall be *bona fide* engaged in discharging ... such ... goods" included by necessary implication entering the dock for the purpose of discharging and coming out after that purpose had been accomplished. Why shouldn't the section have been read as if the words "*bona fide* engaged in discharging or in preparing or endeavouring to discharge" were used, as the dissentients suggested?

Dictionaries and other literary sources. Reference has already been made to the use of dictionaries and other literary sources in aid of interpretation.[6] The example given of the use of a dictionary was *R.* v. *Peters*[7] in which case some reliance was placed on Dr. Johnson's definition of "credit". Dr. Johnson was also mentioned by Lord HERSCHELL in *Midland Rail Co. and Kettering, Thrapston and Huntingdon Rail Co.* v. *Robinson*[8] in support of the majority conclusion of the House of Lords that the word "mines" when used in s. 77 of the Railway Clauses Act 1845 was to be broadly construed. The section mentioned "mines of coal, iron ore, slate and other minerals". The question was whether in addition to beds or seams worked underground, places from which minerals were obtained by surface operation were included. Dr. Johnson's definition of a "quarry" as a "stone mine" was held to lend support to an affirmative answer but, in his dissenting speech, Lord MACNAUGHTEN said: "It seems to me that on such a

[5] [1909] A.C. 7, at p. 18.
[6] P. 54 *supra*.
[7] (1886), 16 Q.B.D. 636.
[8] (1890), 15 App. Cas. 19, at p. 31.

point the opinions of such judges as KINDERSLEY, V.-C., TURNER, L.J. and Sir GEORGE JESSEL are probably a safer guide than any definitions or illustrations to be found in dictionaries."[9] It has also been pointed out that dictionaries must be used with caution in certain situations; when, for example, the court is concerned with the meaning of a word at a particular date[10] or the construction of a two word phrase like "unfair competition".[11]

The opinions of writers such as Coke are, when relevant, treated with as much respect in relation to statutory interpretation as in other cases. Further frequently cited examples of the use of literary sources are the consultation of works by John Stuart Mill and Sir James Stephen on the meaning of the phrase "political crime"[12] and the consultation of works on political economy in aid of the interpretation of the expression "direct taxation" used in the British North America Act 1867.[13]

Practice. As long ago as 1744 Lord HARDWICKE said: "The uniform opinion and practice of eminent conveyancers has always had great regard paid to it by all courts of justice,"[14] and nothing has occurred during the intervening years to suggest a change of attitude on the part of the Courts. The practice of conveyancers is of assistance in cases calling for the application of a technical meaning, and it may, presumably, be the subject either of evidence or of judicial notice. In *Jenkins* v. *Inland Revenue Commissioners* the meaning of the phrase "irrevocable settlement", used in s. 21 (10) of the Finance Act 1938 was in issue. It was suggested that the phrase extended to a case in which, although the settlement itself was irrevocable, it would have been terminated in effect if the settlor had gone through a variety of processes such as putting various companies into liquidation. Lord GREENE said: "It seems to me quite illegitimate to take a word which has a technical and precise meaning in conveyancing and then to argue that it has some extended meaning. If the legislature wished to give to the word 'irrevocable' some unusual and extended meaning of this sort, I ask myself why in the world did it not do so."[15] The situations contemplated in the last paragraph are those in which a word used in a statute had acquired a technical meaning by virtue

[9] (1890), 15 App. Cas. 19, at pp. 34–5.

[10] *Hardwick Game Farm* v. *Suffolk Agricultural and Poultry Producers Association, Ltd.*, [1966] 1 All E.R. 309, at p. 323, *per* DAVIES, L.J.

[11] *Lee* v. *Showman's Guild of Great Britain*, [1952] 2 Q.B. 329, at p. 338, *per* SOMERVELL, L.J.

[12] Re *Castioni*, [1891] 1 Q.B. 149.

[13] *Bank of Toronto* v. *Lambe* (1887), 12 App. Cas. 575, at p. 581, *per* Lord HOBHOUSE.

[14] *Bassett* v. *Bassett* (1744), 3 Atk. 203, at p. 208.

[15] [1944] 2 All E.R. 491, at p. 495.

of the previous practice of conveyancers. These situations must be distinguished from those in which the practice of an official body with regard to a statute which concerns it is drawn to the Courts attention as a possible aid to the interpretation of that statute. In *London County Council* v. *Central Land Board*[16] the judge had allowed counsel for the plaintiff to read as part of his argument practice notes provided by the Board for the guidance of its staff in the administration of the Town & Country Planning Act 1947. In the Court of Appeal JENKINS, L.J., roundly condemned the course adopted by the judge in the following terms:[17]

> "Such notes were wholly inadmissible for the purpose of construing the Act, and the judge should have declined to consider them. It was not a desirable practice to allow such inadmissible matter to be read as part of Counsel's argument in a case involving the construction of statutory provisions. Such notes inevitably derived persuasive force from the fact that they represented the views of the persons charged with the administration of the Act and, therefore, possessing special knowledge of its provisions, and however much Counsel might disclaim reliance on them otherwise than as part of his argument, their use might well result in the court being influenced by official opinion, albeit unconsciously, on questions of construction, the decision on which properly rested on the court alone."

Conveyancers are not of course the only class of specialists whose practice may, in appropriate cases, be an aid to statutory interpretation. Commercial usage is, and for a long time has been, at least as important. For example, in *United Dominions Trust, Ltd.* v. *Kirkwood*, the Court of Appeal had to construe the phrase "any person *bona fide* carrying on the business of banking" used in s. 6 (*d*) of the Moneylenders Act 1900. Lord DENNING said: "In such a matter as this, when Parliament has given no guidance, we cannot do better than look at the reputation of the concern amongst intelligent men of commerce".[18]

Contemporanea expositio. The following extract from Maxwell[19] was cited in the judgment of the Court of Criminal Appeal in *R.* v. *Casement*:[20]

> "It is said that the best exposition of a statute or any other document is that which it has received from contemporary authority ... where this has been given by enactment or judicial decision, it is of course to be accepted as conclusive. But, further, the meaning publicly given by contemporary or long professional usage is presumed to be the true one, even where the language has etymologically or popularly a different meaning. It is obvious

[16] [1958] 3 All E.R. 676.
[17] *Ibid.*, at p. 678.
[18] [1966] 2 Q.B. 431, at p. 454.
[19] The passage is now on p. 264 of the 12th edition.
[20] [1917] 1 K.B. 98.

that the language of a statute must be understood in the sense in which it was understood when it was passed, and those who lived at or near the time when it was passed may reasonably be supposed to be better acquainted than their descendants with the circumstances to which it had relation, as well as with the sense they attached to legislative expressions. Moreover, the long acquiescence of the legislature in the interpretation put upon its enactment by notorious practice may, perhaps, be regarded as some sanction of approval of it."

There is little that calls for special mention in relation to the high sounding phrase "*contemporanea expositio*". Even courts that are not bound by them pay respect to a series of decisions on the interpretation of a particular statute and, although they may consider the decisions to have been questionable, they may follow them because of the undesirability of disturbing past transactions. In the absence of such a danger, decisions on the interpretation of a statute do not appear to be any more immune from the liability to be overruled than decisions on the common law. Similarly, great respect is paid to the opinion of writers such as Coke and Hale with regard to the construction of a statute, but no more so than is the case with regard to their opinions concerning the common law. It is true that there are decisions, concerned mainly with ecclesiastical matters, in which the Courts have acted on the construction of a statute adopted and acted upon by those to whom it applied,[1] but the House of Lords has made it plain that reliance can only be placed on *contemporanea expositio* in this sense as an aid to the interpretation of ambiguous language in very old statutes.[2]

The title, marginal notes and punctuation are sometimes spoken of as "*contemporanea expositio*", "which, though useful as a guide to a hasty enquirer, ought not to be relied on in construing an Act of Parliament".[3] This does not seem to mean anything more than that they cannot control the meaning of the words under construction in the sense that, if they are the only cause of doubt, they must be ignored. In the case of a modern statute, the title, marginal notes and punctuation are an indication of the meaning attached to the words under construction by the draftsman, a kind of *contemporanea expositio* which may at least assist the judge to a decision that the statutory words are unambiguous.

Other statutes in pari materia. A later statute may expressly state that it is to be read as one with earlier legislation. In that event the court

[1] *Hebbert* v. *Purchas* (1871), L.R. 3 P.C. 605; for a non-ecclesiastical example see *Alleson* v. *Marsh* (1690), 2 Vent. 181.

[2] *Campbell College, Belfast (Governors)* v. *Valuation Commissioners for Northern Ireland*, [1964] 2 All E.R. 705.

[3] *Per* WILLES, J., in *Claydon* v. *Green* (1868), L.R. 3 C.P. 511, at p. 522.

must construe all the statutes directed to be read together as though they were one act. The result can sometimes be a surprising one. In *Phillips* v. *Parnaby*[4] a conviction under s. 21 of the Weights and Measures Act 1889 for delivering less coal than that shown on the weight ticket had to be quashed because the defendant had not been served with notice of prosecution. No such notice was required by the Act, but notice of prosecution had to be given under s. 12 (6) of the Sale of Food (Weights and Measures) Act 1926, s. 15 of which expressly provided that it was to be read as one with former Weights and Measures Acts, including that of 1889. Judges and commentators frequently allude to the difficulties caused by referential legislation but the subject is beyond the scope of this book.

In *R.* v. *Loxdale*[5] Lord MANSFIELD said: "Where there are different statutes in *pari materia* though made at different times, or even expired, and not referring to each other, they shall be taken and construed together, as one system, and as explanatory of each other". Lord MANSFIELD was construing one of the poor law statutes of Elizabeth I and he treated later statutes as *in pari materia* with it.

It is unlikely that Lord MANSFIELD meant by "taking and construing statutes together as one system" the same thing as "reading them as one" with the possibility of consequences like those of *Phillips* v. *Parnaby*. However that may be, it seems that the present position is that, when an earlier statute is *in pari materia* with a later one, it is simply part of its context to be considered by the judge in deciding whether the meaning of a provision in the later statute is plain.[6] Like the preamble and long title, it may not be allowed to raise an ambiguity, although it may help to resolve an ambiguity raised by other considerations.[7] Earlier statutes are *in pari materia* with later statutes consolidating them, but there is no authoritative definition of the expression. It is said to be not enough that they should deal with the same subject matter, but a lot depends on how narrowly the latter term is defined. It is not very helpful to say that the statutes must form part of a "system", and, with respect, it is difficult to believe that any greater assistance is to be derived from the oft quoted statement of an American judge, made as long ago as 1829, that statutes are *in pari materia* if they relate to the same person or thing, or to the same class of person or thing.[8]

However much an earlier and later statute may be *in pari materia*, the later one cannot be treated as part of the context of the earlier;

[4] [1934] 2 K.B. 299.

[5] (1758), 1 Burr. 445, at p. 447.

[6] Lord SIMONDS referred to statutes *in pari materia* in this way in *A.-G.* v. *Prince Ernest Augustus of Hanover*, [1957] A.C. 436, at p. 461.

[7] Lord RUSSELL OF KILLOWEN in *R.* v. *Titterton*, [1895] 2 Q.B. 61, at p. 65, is to be understood in this sense.

[8] HOSMER, J., in *United Society* v. *Eagle Bank*, 7 Conn. 457, at p. 470.

but it may be used as an aid to the construction of the earlier statute if the two of them can be described as "laws on the same subject" and if the part of the earlier Act which it is sought to construe may be "fairly and equally open to different meanings". The mere fact that a particular construction of the earlier provision would mean that the later one is surplusage is of no great significance, for it might have been enacted out of an abundance of caution. These points were made by Lord RADCLIFFE when giving the advice of the Judicial Committee of the Privy Council in *Re MacManaway*,[9] a case which was concerned with the construction of s. 1 of the House of Commons (Clergy Qualification) Act 1801 according to which "no person having been ordained to the office of priest or deacon, or minister of the Church of Scotland, is or shall be capable of being elected as a member of the House". The question was whether someone who had been ordained by a bishop of the Church of Ireland was within the prohibition. Later Acts concerning the clergy were cited, but they did not have much bearing on the meaning of the Act of 1801, and s. 1 of this Act was not ambiguous in the strict sense, the question being whether the context, which could not be affected by the later Acts, required an implied limitation to episcopal ordination in the Church of England.

The foregoing discussion of statutes *in pari materia* as aids to interpretation has of course been solely concerned with the assistance to be derived in the construction of one statutory provision from the terms of another. Guidance by contrast or analogy may sometimes be derived from a provision of a statute other than that under construction although there is no question of the two of them being *in pari materia*, but there is no obligation on the judge to consider such statutes as there is in the case of those *in pari materia*.[10]. So far as judicial decisions are concerned, although those with regard to the meaning of words of one statute are not binding so far as words of another statute are concerned (unless it consolidates the other statute), they often have great persuasive force.

B. LEGISLATIVE HISTORY

"Legislative history" means (i) the legislative antecedents of the statutory provision under construction, i.e. corresponding sections in previous enactments since repealed and re-enacted with or without modification;[11] (ii) pre-parliamentary material relating to the pro-

[9] [1951] A.C. 161.

[10] For guidance by contrast see *R.* v. *Westminster Betting Licensing Committee, ex parte Peabody Donation Fund*, [1963] 2 Q.B. 750, [1963] 2 All E.R. 544.

[11] This is not the same thing as statutes *in pari materia*. They are considered as forming part of a legislative scheme. Legislative history is considered in order to see how a particular provision got where it is.

vision or statute in which it is contained, e.g. reports of committees and commissions reviewing the existing law and recommending changes; and (iii) Parliamentary materials, i.e. the successive drafts of a Bill, explanatory memoranda, proceedings in committees and Parliamentary debates. All three of these items have claims to be regarded as part of the context of a statute but special rules, which are none too easy to state with confidence, apply to the use which a judge may make of them when giving reasons for his decision. In the first place, reference to legislative history is only permissible when he is in doubt about the meaning of the provision under construction after considering it in its general context as defined by Lord SIMONDS in *A.-G.* v. *Prince Ernest Augustus of Hanover*;[12] secondly it is questionable whether it is strictly correct for him to cite Parliamentary materials in any circumstances; thirdly, reference may only be made to the pre-parliamentary materials listed under head (ii) above in order to ascertain the mischief which the statute, or the relevant part of it, was designed to remedy as distinct from the meaning of the particular provisions by which it was proposed to remedy that mischief. The practice in the United States and Western Europe differs from the English in all three respects.

It will be convenient to illustrate the English approach by reference to *Beswick* v. *Beswick* and then to comment on the three special matters which have just been mentioned. After that has been done, something will be said about statutes designed to implement treaties and international conventions. It may be as well to insist at the outset that the language of the last paragraph was chosen with care. It is often said, not without some justification provided by incautious judicial remarks, that the effect of the English rules is that the judge may not "look at" Parliamentary and pre-Parliamentary materials, subject to the distinction between the mischief and the remedy in the case of the latter. Bad jokes are then made about the fact that the judges often do gaze into the prohibited areas and say that they have come to their conclusion without being influenced by what they saw there. Of course the prohibition is not one against all references to certain materials, it is against the utilisation of such materials as a ground for a decision. This point is vividly illustrated by *Black-Clawson International, Ltd.* v. *Papierwerke Waldhof-Aschaffenburg A.G.*,[13] a case which will be discussed shortly, in which a report of a committee with a draft Bill and commentary annexed was thoroughly discussed in the House of Lords although the majority took the view that no significance could be attached to the commentary on the Bill as an indication of the intention of Parliament, even though that body had

[12] [1957] A.C. 436, at p. 461.
[13] [1975] 1 All E.R. 810.

adopted it without any material alteration. It is only fair to those who made the bad jokes to say that they did so before the *Black-Clawson* case and that, after that case, one is left with a nagging question concerning the extent to which it is possible to consider a report for the purpose of ascertaining the mischief to be remedied without being influenced by its recommendations concerning the remedy. Sceptical remarks of JENKINS, L.J., with regard to this kind of problem have already been cited.[14]

The question in *Beswick* v. *Beswick*[15] was whether a nephew who purchased his uncle's business and undertook to pay his aunt (the uncle's widow) £5 per week was liable in an action for specific performance brought by the aunt as the uncle's administratrix. For reasons with which we are not concerned the House of Lords answered this question in the affirmative but, contrary to the view taken by the majority of the Court of Appeal, not on account of s. 56 of the Law of Property Act 1925 which reads:

> "A person may take an immediate or other interest in land or *other property*, or the benefit of any condition, right of entry, covenant or agreement over or respecting land or *other property* although he may not be named as a party to the conveyance or other instrument."

The background consisted of the common law doctrine of privity of contract, s. 5 of the Real Property Act 1844 (confined to deeds and repealed by the Law of Property Act 1845), s. 5 of the Law of Property Act 1845 (confined to "lands, tenements and hereditaments" and repealed by the Law of Property Act 1925), the real property legislation of 1922–24, consolidated in 1925, and a report of a joint committee of both Houses of Parliament on consolidating Bills relating to the Law of Property Act 1925. The issue was whether the reference to "other property" means that the section applies to personalty. Three law lords held that it does not because, although the definition clause provides in s. 205 (20) that "property" includes "any thing in action and any real or *personal* property", the whole clause is governed by the words "unless the context otherwise requires". It was said that the context does require otherwise because the 1925 Act was a consolidating statute and there is a presumption that consolidating statutes are not intended to change the law. The other two law lords also held that s. 56 did not apply to personalty because it is confined to deeds containing a grant to and covenant with a third party. Lord REID who was one of the three favouring the first view said:[16]

> "In construing any Act of Parliament we are seeking the intention of Parliament, and it is quite true that we must deduce that intention from the

[14] P. 126 *supra*.
[15] [1968] A.C. 58.
[16] *Ibid.*, at pp. 73–4.

words of the Act. If the words of the Act are only capable of one meaning we must give them that meaning, no matter how they got there. But if they are capable of having more than one meaning we are, in my view, well entitled to see how they got there. For purely practical reasons we do not permit debates in either House to be cited. It would add greatly to the time and expense involved in preparing cases involving the construction of a statute if Counsel were expected to read all the debates in Hansard, and it would often be impracticable for Counsel to get access to at least the older reports of debates in select committees of the House of Commons; moreover, in a very large proportion of cases such a search, even if practicable, would throw no light on the question before the court. But I can see no objection to investigating in the present case the antecedents of s. 56."

The plain meaning rule. It would be possible to place an extremely restrictive interpretation on Lord REID's ban on legislative history because it was in terms confined to cases in which the words of the Act are "only capable of one meaning", cases which, as Lord REID subsequently pointed out, must be comparatively few in number;[17] but it seems more in accordance with judicial practice to extend the ban to cases in which the judge is satisfied that one of two or more possible meanings of statutory words, read in a context bereft of their legislative history, "is the meaning which Parliament must have intended the words to convey".[18] Thus understood, the ban is redolent of the words of TINDAL, C.J., in the *Sussex Peerage* case; [19] "if the words of the statute are in themselves precise and unambiguous, then no more can be necessary than to expound those words in that natural and ordinary sense.... But if any doubt arises from the terms employed by the legislature, it has always been held a safe means of collecting the intention, to call in aid the ground and cause of the making of the statute...." Nowadays we call in aid "the ground and cause of the making of the statute" before deciding whether the statutory words are "precise and unambiguous". Why should we shut our eyes to legislative history which may be useful evidence of the object of a statute now that the object is regarded as part of the statutory context?

It is this apparently arbitrary exclusion of part of the context which distinguishes the practice of the English courts with regard to statutory interpretation from that of the courts of the United States and Western Europe. One of the landmark cases in the United States' Supreme Court was *United States* v. *American Trucking Association*, and the following is an extract from the judgment of REED, J.:[20]

---

[17] *Black-Clawson International, Ltd.* v. *Papierwerke Waldhof-Aschaffenburg A.G.*, [1975] 1 All E.R. 810, at p. 814.

[18] *Per* Lord REID in *Director of Public Prosecutions* v. *Ottewell*, [1970] A.C. 642, at p. 649; p. 77 *supra*.

[19] P. 13 *supra*.

[20] 310 U.S. 534, at pp. 543–4, 1940.

"There is of course no more persuasive evidence of the purpose of a statute than the words by which the legislature undertook to give expression to its wishes. Often these words are sufficient in and of themselves to determine the purpose of the legislation. In such cases we have followed their plain meaning. When that meaning has led to absurd or futile results, however, this court has looked beyond the words to the purpose of the Act. Frequently, however, even when the plain meaning did not produce absurd results but merely an unreasonable one 'plainly at variance with the policy of the legislation as a whole' this court has followed that purpose, rather than the literal words. When aid to construction of the meaning of words, as used in the statute, is available, there can certainly be no 'rule of law' which forbids its use, however clear the words may be on superficial investigation."

REED, J., had legislative history in mind when speaking of "aid to construction", and the last sentence of the above passage certainly reveals a difference between the practice of the Supreme Court and the House of Lords.

Speaking of the contrast between the approaches to the problem of interpretation by the French, German and Scandinavian courts on the one hand, and the English courts on the other, Norman S. MARSH, Q.C., a member of our Law Commission, has said[1] that the English judge:

"does not generally feel himself under the same obligation to search as deeply as possible for the most satisfactory meaning of the statute, if he has to hand an interpretation which accords with the normal usage of language as employed in the text of the statute, and of the more obvious and immediate contextual implications of the text."

The reference to the normal usage of language gives the clue to the justification of the English practice. To quote Lord DIPLOCK:[2]

"The acceptance of the rule of law as a constitutional principle requires that a citizen before committing himself to any course of action, should be able to know in advance what are the legal consequences that will flow from it. Where those consequences are regulated by a statute the source of that knowledge is what the statute says. In construing it the court must give effect to what the words of the statute would be reasonably understood to mean by those whose conduct it regulates."

It is quite right that the courts should take such internal matters as the preamble and long title into account because they would be taken into account by the normal user of the English language, but there are limits to the extent to which he, or (and this is where we approach the realities of the situation) his legal adviser, can be expected to consider non-statutory materials. We have seen that the long title and

---

[1] *Interpretation in a National and International Context*, p. 75. It is to be regretted that these lectures, delivered at the Centre for European Studies in Luxembourg in 1973, and published by U.G.A. in Belgium in 1974, are not better known in this country.

[2] *Black-Clawson International, Ltd.* v. *Papierwerke Waldhof-Aschaffenburg A.G.*, [1975] 1 All E.R. 810, at p. 836.

preamble can only serve in the first instance as pointers to a plain meaning, they cannot be allowed to raise an ambiguity, although they may, at a later stage, resolve ambiguities in the enacting words. No greater force should be accorded to legislative history, hence it would be preposterous to expect those acting on the statute extrajudicially to refer to that history when they consider the meaning of the statutory words to be plain without its aid. This justification of the English practice is unanswerable provided the distinction between plain meaning and ambiguity is as clear cut and workable as the practice assumes it to be.

Parliamentary materials. In 1769 WILLES, J., said: "The sense and meaning of an Act of Parliament must be collected from what it says when cast into law; and not from the history of changes it underwent in the House where it took its rise. That history is not known to the other House, or to the Sovereign."[3] Although the justifications of this statement have lost most if not all of their force, it may well represent the present law; but the subsequent history of this matter is such that any writer can be excused if he is a little cautious in his formulation of that law. COLERIDGE, J., laconically expressed the same view as WILLES, J., when he said in *R.* v. *Hertford College, Oxford*:[4] "The statute is clear, and the Parliamentary history of a statute is wisely inadmissible to explain it, if it is not". But, in *R.* v. *Bishop of Oxford*,[5] BRAMWELL, L.J., took a very different line with regard to the Lord Chancellor's speech on the third reading of the Church Discipline Act 1874:

> "But to reject the opinion of the Head of the law as to what is the law, given to advise the highest court of judicature in this country, sitting indeed in its legislative capacity, and at the same time admit the *obiter dictum* of a judge at *nisi prius* either in our own or an American court seems somewhat strange, more especially as it is certain that if it ought to be excluded, any judge knowing of it and excluding it would as soon as he left the court consult the Hansard he had before rejected".

The House of Lords did not approve of these remarks[6] and thenceforth it has been assumed that Parliamentary materials are inadmissible on questions of interpretation for any purpose whatsoever. Even if he considers that the statute is ambiguous, the judge may not cite such materials in support of his decision, and this is commonly thought to be so whether the materials are cited in support of the judge's views concerning the mischief at which the statute was aimed, or the mean-

---

[3] *Miller* v. *Taylor* (1769), 4 Burr. 2303 at p. 2332.
[4] (1878), 3 Q.B.D. 693, at p. 707.
[5] (1879), 4 Q.B.D. 525, at p. 550.
[6] *South Eastern Rail Co.* v. *Railway Commissioners* (1881), 50 L.J.Q.B. 201, at p. 203.

ing he thinks Parliament intended the words under construction to bear.

There are, however, at least three facts which could be regarded as disconcerting by a seeker after certainty in the law. In *Sagnata Investments, Ltd.* v. *Norwich Corporation*[7] Lord DENNING said that he had read the minister's speech on the second reading in the House of Commons of the Betting Gaming and Lotteries Act 1964 in order to ascertain the mischief aimed at by the gaming legislation and cited it at length in his dissenting judgment. In *Beswick* v. *Beswick*[8] Lord UPJOHN referred to the report of the Joint Committee on Consolidation Bills dealing with what became the Law of Property Act 1925, though only for the purpose of ascertaining that the presumption against change in a consolidation measure was not weakened by anything that had taken place in the Committee's proceedings. Finally, a year or so after *Beswick* v. *Beswick* was decided by the House of Lords, Lord REID, while reaffirming the general rule that the courts could not consult Hansard for the reasons he had already given, suggested in *Warner* v. *Metropolitan Police Commissioner*,[9] that there might be room for an exception "where examining the proceedings in Parliament would almost certainly settle the matter immediately one way or the other". He was speaking with special reference to the presumption that *mens rea* is required in the case of statutory crimes, his point being that members of both Houses are particularly interested in the liberty of the subject, and "if it were intended by those promoting a Bill to extend the old but limited class of cases in which absence of *mens rea* is no defence I would certainly expect Parliament to be informed".

It is possible that, in cases to which the literal or plain meaning rule in its modern form is inapplicable, the ban on Parliamentary materials is not quite as absolute as it is usually supposed to be; nevertheless, the contrast with the practice of the courts in the United States and Western Europe is a striking one. In both instances the judge's access to Parliamentary materials appears to be unlimited in theory, although the use made of them is limited by considerations concerning their weight and, even so, it has its critics. Are Lord REID's justifications of the restrictive English practice with regard to Parliamentary debates adequate so far as all Parliamentary materials are concerned? It is submitted that, as things stand, they are. The successive drafts of a Bill would be of little value without an indication of the Parliamentary reasons for the changes in them, and the explanatory memorandum in its present form would be of no value to the courts.[10]

[7] [1971] 2 Q.B. 614, at p. 624.
[8] [1968] A.C. 58, at p. 105.
[9] [1969] 2 A.C. 256, at p. 279.
[10] It is too brief and it is only published with the first draft. Notes on clauses for the use of the minister responsible for the bill are not generally published.

We are thus left with Hansard and reports of proceedings before committees. Lord REID's justifications were based on the expense that would be involved if counsel were expected to read all the debates in Hansard, the comparative inaccessibility of the older select committee reports, and the limited value of the materials. He reiterated this last point in a subsequent case:[11]

> "The questions which give rise to debate are hardly ever those which later have to be decided by the courts. One might take the views of the promoters of the Bill as an indication, but any view the promoters may have had about questions which later come before the court will not often appear in Hansard and often those questions have never occurred to the promoters."

It is probably true to say that much of the Parliamentary material used in the United States and Western Europe is in more accessible and concise form than Hansard. Whether it may not be possible to supply the courts with relevant Parliamentary material in some more digestible form is a question which will be raised in Chapter VIII.

Pre-parliamentary materials. Although it would be possible to cite a fairly large number of instances in which judges have taken account or refused to take account of reports of advisory committees and the like, the present law on the subject can be adequately stated by means of a reference to three cases, *Eastman Photographic Materials Co., Ltd.* v. *Comptroller General of Patents*, *Assam Railways and Trading Co., Ltd.* v. *Inland Revenue Commissioners* and *Black-Clawson International, Ltd.* v. *Papierwerke Waldhof-Aschaffenburg A.G.*

In *Eastman Photographic Materials Co., Ltd.* v. *Comptroller General of Patents*,[12] the legality of registering the trademark "Solio" was in issue. The statute under consideration had been passed in consequence of a report of a Royal Commission on the use of geographical names. When speaking of that report Lord HALSBURY said "I think no more accurate source of information as to what the evil or defect which the act of Parliament now under consideration was intended to remedy could be imagined than the report of that Commission."

In *Assam Railways and Trading Co., Ltd.* v. *Inland Revenue Commissioners*[13] a section of the Finance Act 1920 was under construction. It dealt with relief from English income tax on income which had already been taxed in India, and was enacted in consequence of a Royal Commission's report. Counsel for the appellants argued that the report should be received as evidence of the intention of the legis-

---

[11] *Black-Clawson International, Ltd.* v. *Papierwerke Waldhof-Aschaffenburg A.G.*, [1975] 1 All E.R. 810, at p. 815.

[12] [1898] A.C. 571, at p. 575.

[13] [1935] A.C. 445.

lature in passing the section. The House of Lords rejected this contention, Lord WRIGHT saying:[14]

> "But on principle no such evidence for the purpose of showing the intention, that is the purpose and object, of an Act is admissible; the intention of the legislature must be ascertained from the words of the statute with such extraneous assistance as is legitimate.... It is clear that the language of a minister of the Crown in proposing in Parliament a measure which eventually becomes law is inadmissible and the report of Commissioners is even more removed from value as evidence of intention, because it does not follow that their recommendations were accepted."

Speaking of Lord HALSBURY's action in the *Eastman* case, Lord WRIGHT said that he "refers to the report not directly to ascertain the intention of the words used in the Act", but "as extraneous matter to show what were the surrounding circumstances with reference to which the words were used".

The distinction between the admissibility of pre-Parliamentary materials as evidence of surrounding circumstances and its inadmissibility as direct evidence of Parliamentary intent has survived the *Black-Clawson* case[15] but only just. The question was whether s. 8 (1) of the Foreign Judgments (Reciprocal Enforcement) Act 1933 applied in favour of the defendant to a claim for money due on bills of exchange bought in England against a German company in whose favour a judgment had been given by a German court on an identical claim because, by German, unlike English law, it was out of time. At common law a foreign judgment obtained in such circumstances is not a bar to English proceedings,[16] but under s. 8 (1) of the 1933 Act a judgment to which Part I applies "shall be recognised in any court in the United Kingdom as *conclusive* between the parties thereto in all proceedings founded on the same course of action, and may be relied on by way of defence or counterclaim in any such proceedings". By a majority of 4 to 1 the House of Lords held that s. 8 (1) had not altered the relevant common law. The Act was the outcome of a report of a committee presided over by GREER, L.J. A draft bill, identical in all material respects with the terms of the Act, was annexed to the report, and there was a difference of opinion among their lordships concerning the admissibility of that report together with the clause by clause commentary accompanying the draft bill as evidence of the meaning attached by Parliament to s. 8 (1) in relation to the facts before the court.

Lord REID held the report to be inadmissible for this purpose, though admissible as evidence of the mischief against which the Act

[14] *Ibid.*, at p. 458.
[15] *Black-Clawson International, Ltd.* v. *Papierwerke Waldhof-Aschaffenburg A.G.*, [1975] 1 All E.R. 810.
[16] *Harris* v. *Quine* (1869), L.R. 4 Q.B. 653.

was directed. Lords WILBERFORCE and DIPLOCK agreed with Lord REID, but Lord DIPLOCK's speech was the dissentient one; he considered that the terms of s. 8 (1) were plain and unambiguous. Lord DILHORNE considered that the report was admissible both as evidence of surrounding circumstances and as direct evidence of intention. He was disposed to question the validity of the distinction in general, and in particular when applied to the commentary on a draft bill adopted by Parliament without relevant alteration. As "at present advised" Lord SIMON OF GLAISDALE would have admitted the report as evidence of intent. Accordingly there was a majority of 3 to 2 in favour of maintaining the distinction drawn by Lord WRIGHT in the *Assam Railways* case provided the observations in the dissenting speech are allowed to count, and, as they had nothing to do with the reasons underlying the dissent, there can presumably be no objection to counting them.

The distinction between admitting Parliamentary materials as evidence of the mischief against which statutory words are aimed and admitting them as evidence of the meaning of the words in their application to the case before the court is, it is believed, unheard of in the law of the United States and Western Europe. Can it be justified? Lord REID justified it on the ground that, if pre-parliamentary materials were accepted as evidence of what Parliament intended in relation to the case before the Court, it would be necessary to abandon the prohibition of the citation of Hansard: "If we are to refrain from considering expressions of intention in Parliament it appears to me that *a fortiori* we should disregard expressions of intention by committees or other commissions which reported before the bill was introduced."[17] This is similar to the earlier reasoning of Lord WRIGHT according to which the report of commissioners is "even more removed from value as evidence of intention" than the language of a minister of the Crown. There is of course much force in this reasoning, but it loses some of its strength when it is remembered that one of the grounds for rejecting Parliamentary debates is their inaccessibility. This does not apply to pre-Parliamentary materials.

After making the point that, if a clause by clause commentary on a draft bill subsequently enacted by Parliament were admitted as evidence of the meaning of a particular provision, there would be two documents to construe instead of one, Lord WILBERFORCE said in the *Black-Clawson* case:[18]

> "Legislation in England is passed by Parliament, and put in the form of written words. This legislation is given legal effect upon subjects by virtue

[17] [1975] 1 All E.R. at p. 815.
[18] *Ibid.*, at p. 828.

of judicial decisions, and it is the function of courts to say what the application of the words used to particular cases or individuals is to be. This power which has devolved on the judges from the earliest times is an essential part of the constitutional process by which subjects are brought under the rule of law—as distinct from the rule of the king or of Parliament; and it would be a degradation of that process if the courts were to be merely a reflecting mirror of what some other interpretation agency might say."

It would indeed. But, if a judge who is *ex hypothesi* in doubt about the meaning of a statutory provision takes note of what its author thought it meant it is a little tendentious to describe him as a "reflecting mirror". He is not obliged to act on the author's meaning and there are famous instances in which French courts have not acted on the intentions revealed in the *travaux preparatoires* which they have consulted. It is difficult not to have some sympathy with the point made by Lord SIMON OF GLAISDALE (with acknowledgment to Aneurin Bevan) that rejecting the commentary as evidence of the intended meaning of a particular clause was like gazing in the crystal ball when you can read the book.[19] The distinction between using pre-parliamentary materials as a means of ascertaining the general objectives of a statute and using them as evidence of the intended meaning of a particular provision in its application to the case before the court is not so difficult a law as is sometimes suggested; but, although it is occasionally necessary, any rule according to which evidence is admissible for one purpose but not for another requires to be justified, and, in spite of the undoubted strength of the reasons urged in favour of this particular rule, it is submitted that they do not justify it.

Treaties and International Conventions. In *Ellerman Lines* v. *Murray*,[20] a majority of 4 to 1 in the House of Lords held the words of s. 1 (1) of the Merchant Shipping (International Labour Conventions) Act 1925 were plain and unambiguous. They therefore refused to give the words the meaning which they were intended to bear by an international convention mentioned in the long as well as the short title, referred to in the preamble and partially set out in the schedule. The object of the Act was to give effect to a convention about the wages of shipwrecked mariners engaged on contracts for a single voyage. At common law they got nothing because the voyage had not been completed. Under s. 158 of the Merchant Shipping Act 1894 they got their wages up to the date of the wreck. Under the convention they were to receive wages for the unexpired portion of their contracts of service up to a maximum of two months. Section 1 (1) of the Act read:

"Where by reason of the wreck or loss of a ship on which a seaman is

[19] *Ibid.*, at p. 847.
[20] [1931] A.C. 126.

> employed his service terminates before the date contemplated by the agreement he shall . . . be entitled, in respect of each day on which he is in fact unemployed during a period of two months from the date of the termination of the service, to receive *wages* at the rate at which he was entitled at that date."

In cases in which the remaining period of the voyage would have been less than two months, this appears to mean that the employer was under a heavier liability to pay wages than he would have been if the ship had not been wrecked. Murray's ship was wrecked on 27th February, his contract would have ended when the ship reached Middlesborough on 11th March at the latest, nevertheless the majority held that he was entitled to wages for two months after 27th February. Although very little was said about the general rules of statutory interpretation, the decision of the majority was in exact accordance with those rules as stated in this book provided s. 1 (1), read without reference to the long title, etc., could be said to have been unambiguous. If, after reading the statute as a whole, the judge found that the only reason for having doubts about the meaning of the provision under construction were the terms of the long title and preamble, he was not entitled to act on those doubts. The dissentient view of Lord BLANESBOROUGH was based on a specialised meaning of the word "wages" as "remuneration for service which, but for the wreck, would have continued to be due". There being an ambiguity in his opinion, he was entitled to rely on the convention but did not do so to any great extent.

The lesson to be learnt from *Ellerman Lines* v. *Murray* is that there should be a special rule concerning statutes which are expressed, or even commonly known, to be implementations of treaties or international conventions. In these cases the judge should be able to place such reliance as he sees fit on the treaty or convention, due regard being had to the fact that:[1]

> "there is a *prima facie* presumption that Parliament does not intend to act in breach of international law, including therein specific treaty obligations; and if one of the meanings that can reasonably be attributed to the legislation is consonant with the treaty obligations and another or others are not, the meaning which is so consonant is to be preferred."

These remarks were made by DIPLOCK, L.J., in a case in which he distinguished *Ellerman Lines* v. *Murray* because there was an ambiguity in the statute which he was construing. The reversal of *Ellerman Lines* v. *Murray*, with the result that treaties and international conventions would have to be considered by the judge, even in the case of an otherwise clear statutory provision, would not be inconsistent with the jus-

---

[1] *Salomon* v. *Commissioners of Customs and Excise*, [1967] 2 Q.B. 116, at p. 143.

tification favoured in this book of the general rule that legislative history is only admissible where the statute is unclear. That justification is based on the paramount importance of not adding unduly to the burdens of those who have to act or advise on the statute without reference to the courts. In this instance, the statute would refer to the convention, or it would be common knowledge among those to whom the statute was addressed that it was intended to give effect to the convention, and the terms of the latter would or should be known to such people.

Summary. It may not be out of place to conclude this account of the use made by the courts of legislative history with a concise statement of the author's views concerning the need for a change of practice: (i) the existing rule that there can be no reference to legislative history when the meaning of the statute is plain without recourse to it should be retained; (ii) the existing ban on the citation of Parliamentary materials should be retained unless and until some means of presenting them in a short and simple form is evolved; (iii) the judge's existing power to refer to pre-parliamentary materials when he has real doubt about the meaning of a statutory provision should be extended so as to enable him to rely on those materials, not merely as evidence of the mischief against which the statute was directed (part of the circumstances in which it was passed), but also as a pointer to the meaning which he should attach to the particular provision under construction; (iv) *Ellerman Lines* v. *Murray* should be overruled by the House of Lords or reversed by statute. It must be recognised, however, that there is much to be said for two other views, namely (*a*) that no change of any kind in the existing practice is called for and, at the other extreme, (*b*) that the judge should have an unrestricted power to cite legislative history for any purpose whenever he considers it to be relevant, and whether or not he has any doubt about the meaning of the statute without recourse to such history.

VII

Presumptions

A. PRESUMPTIONS GENERALLY

Although the word "presumption" is used with different shades of meaning in different branches of the law, its use always relates in some way to the burden of proof. The implication is that a particular conclusion is likely to be drawn by the court in the absence of good reason for reaching a different one. In the law of statutory interpretation there are two kinds of presumption which merge into each other and the sovereignty of Parliament gives the clue to the nature of the first kind.

For the purpose of the present discussion let it be assumed that the courts will give effect to any law Parliament sees fit to pass provided it is expressed in clear terms. Allowance must be made for the fact that statutes are not enacted in a vacuum. A great deal inevitably remains unsaid. It is assumed that the courts will continue to act in accordance with well recognised rules:[1]

> "The mental element of most crimes is marked by one of the words 'maliciously', 'fraudulently', 'negligently' or 'knowingly', but it is the general—I might, I think, say, the invariable—practice of the legislature to leave unexpressed some of the mental elements of crime. In all cases whatever, competent age, sanity and some degree of freedom from some kinds of coercion are assumed to be essential to criminality, but I do not believe they are ever introduced into any statute by which any particular crime is defined."

Long-standing principles of constitutional and administrative law are likewise taken for granted, or assumed by the courts to have been taken for granted, by Parliament. Examples are the principles that discretionary powers conferred in apparently absolute terms will be exercised reasonably, and that the jurisdiction conferred on administrative tribunals will be exercised in accordance with the principles of natural justice. One function of the word "presumption" in the

[1] *Per* STEPHEN, J., in *R.* v. *Tolson* (1889), 23 Q.B.D. 168, at p. 187.

context of statutory interpretation is to state the result of this legislative reliance (real or assumed) on firmly established legal principles. There is a "presumption" that *mens rea* is required in the case of statutory crimes, and a "presumption" that statutory powers must be exercised reasonably. These presumptions apply although there is no question of linguistic ambiguity in the statutory wording under construction, and they may be described as "presumptions of general application". At the level of interpretation, their function is the promotion of brevity on the part of the draftsman. Statutes make dreary enough reading as it is, and it would be ridiculous to insist in each instance upon an enumeration of the general principles taken for granted.

But these presumptions also operate at a higher level for they are expressions of fundamental principles governing the relations between Parliament, the executive and the courts. As such they are beyond the scope of this book. It is, however, necessary to say something about the means by which they may be rebutted. Although the point lacks clear authority, it is probably true to say that some of them can only be rebutted by express words; nothing in the nature of implication, even necessary implication, will suffice. On the other hand, it is tolerably clear that some presumptions of general application are rebuttable by implication which need not always be particularly necessary. The requirement of *mens rea* in the sense of guilty knowledge may be excluded by implication from the purpose and background of criminal statutes; more may well be required to exclude defences such as insanity or duress. The principle that no-one shall be allowed to gain an advantage from his own wrong is of general application for it undoubtedly applies so as to qualify the effects of statutory words which are wholly unambiguous.[2] But it is somewhat easily refuted by the statutory context.[3]

To be contrasted with presumptions of general application are "presumptions for use in doubtful cases". An example of such a presumption was mentioned at the end of the last chapter. The "*prima facie* presumption that Parliament does not intend to act in breach of international law" was said to apply where one of the meanings which can reasonably be attributed to the legislation is consonant with treaty obligations and the other is not. This example is on the borderline between the two kinds of presumption, for there are those who would say that the presumption in favour of a construction complying with international law can only be excluded by clear words and is

[2] *Re Sigsworth*, [1935] Ch. 89; p. 28 *supra*.

[3] See e.g., *Workington Harbour and Dock Board* v. *S.S. Towerfield (Owners)*, [1951] A.C. 112, at p. 160, *per* Lord Radcliffe; and *Smith* v. *East Elloe*, [1956] A.C. 736; [1956] 1 All E.R. 855.

not one which is merely brought into play in cases of ambiguity; but *Ellerman Lines* v. *Murray*[4] is against this view. The rules of language mentioned at the end of Chapter V are sometimes stated in the form of presumptions, and other linguistic presumptions, such as that to the effect that the same word bears the same meaning throughout the same statute, have also been mentioned elsewhere in this book. We have seen how the object of a statute, in addition to forming part of its context which may assist the judge to the conclusion that the meaning is clear, may be taken into consideration at a later stage in order to assist in the resolution of an ambiguity. There is then a presumption that if, of two meanings reasonably attributable to the legislature, one would give effect to the object more than the other, that meaning is to be preferred. This presumption may conflict with others, notably that in favour of a strict construction of penal statutes. If, after applying the first two of the basic rules set out on p. 43, *supra*, the judge is still in doubt concerning the interpretation of a statutory provision, rule 2 may come into play again, but this time as a presumption for use in doubtful cases. If, of two meanings which might reasonably be attributed to the legislature, one would and the other would not lead to an absurd result, the latter meaning is to be preferred. A broad meaning was given to the word "absurdity" in the illustrations of rule 2 in Chapter IV, and the presumption which has just been mentioned is often subdivided into presumptions against inconvenience, injustice or absurdity. Here too conflicts with other presumptions are conceivable, but, if we exclude the presumption concerning penal statutes, it is open to question whether the possibility of conflicting presumptions for use in doubtful cases presents great practical difficulties. At any rate it is certain that they could not be arranged in any kind of hierarchy because their strength is so largely dependent on the particular facts. They are pointers to a certain conclusion, not rules obliging the judge to reach it.

Presumptions are often said to express "policies of clear statement". Whether this is the right way to regard the presumptions, other than the linguistic one concerning words bearing the same meaning throughout a statute, which have been mentioned so far is open to question, but it is certainly an excellent way of describing those to be discussed in the next section. They can all be looked upon as warnings to the draftsman: "If you do not express yourself clearly, there is a risk that the courts will hold that your words will not have effected the changes in the law intended by your instructors." They are all presumptions for use by the courts in cases in which there is an ambiguity in the draftsman's words.

---

[4] P. 139 *supra*.

B. PRESUMPTIONS AGAINST UNCLEAR CHANGES IN THE LAW

The main presumption against unclear changes in the law goes back to the days when by far the greater proportion of law was common law and statutes were, for the most part, thought of as minor emendations of that law. In modern times it is possible to make a travesty of the presumption by stating it in some such form as that "it is to be presumed that a statute alters the common law as little as possible". So stated the presumption is of course ridiculous when applied to such matters as social welfare legislation concerning subjects on which there is not and never has been any common law. Sensibly stated, the presumption can be of undoubted assistance in resolving ambiguities. To quote Lord REID in *Black-Clawson International, Ltd* v. *Papierwerke Waldhof-Aschaffenburg A.G.*:[5]

> "There is a presumption which can be stated in various ways. One is that in the absence of any clear indication to the contrary Parliament can be presumed not to have altered the common law farther than was necessary to remedy the 'mischief'. Of course it may and quite often does go farther. But the principle is that if the enactment is ambiguous, that meaning which relates the scope of the act to the mischief should be taken rather than a different or wider meaning which the contemporary situation did not call for."

The presumption was one of Lord REID's grounds for holding, contrary to the view of some other members of the House, in the *Black-Clawson* case that s. 8 of the Foreign Judgments (Reciprocal Enforcement) Act 1933 did not apply to judgments given in favour of a defendant simply dismissing a claim made by the plaintiff. In the earlier case of *Maunsell* v. *Olins*[6] Lord REID had relied on this presumption in support of his conclusion that the word "premises" in s. 18 (5) of the Rent Act 1968 did not extend to farm land. The provision under construction being, in his opinion, ambiguous, he was entitled to consider how it came to be where it was, and he traced it back to s. 41 of the Housing Rents and Repairs Act 1954 the object of which was to get rid of the decision in *Cow* v. *Casey*[7] which was not concerned with agricultural leases. The restriction of the scope of a statute to the immediate mischief it was designed to remedy was described by Lord SIMON OF GLAISDALE in his dissenting speech as a misuse of the mischief rule, but Lord REID was after all only speaking of a presumption to be called in aid in a case of ambiguity. The real difference between the majority and the dissentients in *Maunsell* v. *Olins* was over the question whether there was an ambiguity.

---

[5] [1975] 1 All E.R. 810, at p. 815.
[6] [1975] A.C. 373, [1975] 1 All E.R. 16.
[7] [1949] 1 K.B. 474, [1949] 1 All E.R. 197.

An earlier instance of the presumption against unclear changes in the law in the form stated by Lord REID is *Leach* v. *R.*[8] Section 4 (1) of the Criminal Evidence Act 1898 provides that the spouse of a person charged with an offence under any enactment mentioned in the schedule *may* be called as a witness either for the prosecution or for the defence. Subject to irrelevant exceptions, a wife could not be called to give evidence against her husband at common law, and it was held by the House of Lords that s. 4 (1) had only made her a competent witness for the prosecution in the scheduled cases; she was not compellable: "the principle that a wife is not to be compelled to give evidence against her husband is deep seated in the common law of this country, and I think if it is to be overturned it must be overturned by a clear, definite and positive enactment, not by an ambiguous one such as the section relied upon in this case".[9] No useful purpose would be served by multiplying examples, but it should be pointed out that the presumption applies to changes in statute law. Thus, in *Bennett* v. *Chappell*,[10] it was held that a provision in one of the schedules to the Local Government Act 1933 under which a poll might be demanded before the conclusion of a parish meeting "on any question arising thereat" had not altered the law laid down in a schedule to the Local Government Act 1894 which provided for a poll on any "resolution". The 1933 wording was said not to be "sufficiently plain to indicate an intention to depart entirely from the basic conception of the Act of 1894, that only resolutions were liable to a poll demand".[11] A change of language on re-enactment will, however, fairly readily be held to indicate a change of law, although this is much less so when the re-enactment is a consolidating statute for there is a well recognised presumption that consolidating statutes do not change the law.

Ex parte Campbell. When a statutory provision is re-enacted in the same words, and those words have been the subject of a judicial decision, it is natural to assume that the draftsman was aware of that decision, and it is not unreasonable to say that there is a presumption that Parliament intended to endorse that decision. This is how the matter was put by SALMON, L.J., in *R.* v. *Bow Road Justices (Domestic Proceedings Court), ex parte Adedigba*,[12] but JAMES, L.J., used much stronger language in *Re Cathcart, ex parte Campbell*:[13]

---

[8] [1912] A.C. 305.
[9] *Ibid.*, at p. 311.
[10] [1966] Ch. 391; [1965] 3 All E.R. 130
[11] *per* HARMAN, L.J., *ibid.*, at p. 399.
[12] [1968] 2 Q.B. 572, at p. 583.
[13] (1869), 5 Ch. App. 603, at p. 706.

> "Where once certain words in an Act of Parliament have received a judicial construction in one of the Superior Courts, and the legislature has repeated them without alteration in a subsequent statute, I conceive that the legislature must be taken to have used them according to the meaning which a court of competent jurisdiction has given to them."

If this is the statement of an absolute rule the consequences could be somewhat striking. If a high court judge of first instance were to construe a section of a statute in a particular way, and that section were to be re-enacted in the same form, neither the Court of Appeal nor the House of Lords could construe it in a different way. Lord BUCKMASTER did not hesitate to draw this conclusion from the rule laid down by JAMES, L.J., which he described as "a salutary rule and one necessary to confer upon Acts of Parliament that certainty which, though it is often lacking, is always to be desired".[14] More recently, however, DENNING, L.J., said he did not believe that whenever Parliament re-enacts a statute, it thereby gives statutory authority to every erroneous interpretation which has been put upon it,[15] and in *R.* v. *Bow Road Justices*, the Court of Appeal overruled a decision of 1849 on a statutory provision which was re-enacted in 1872 and again in 1957. No doubt the position is simply that the fact that a former decision concerned a statutory provision which has been re-enacted is a reason why courts with power to overrule that decision should be more than ordinarily cautious before doing so. Whether it is correct to talk in terms of a presumption is perhaps debatable, but it is common practice, and the language of presumptions is occasionally used in relation to cases of statutory interpretation when the fact that Parliament had the opportunity to reverse the effect of a decision but did not do so is urged as a reason for following it.

Special examples of the presumption against unclear alteration of the law are the presumption against ousting the jurisdiction of the courts, the presumption against interference with vested rights and the presumption in favour of a strict construction of penal statutes. They can all be subsumed under the notion of policies of clear statement, but they also raise issues connected with the relations between the Courts, Parliament and the executive which will not be investigated.

Ouster of jurisdiction. It is only necessary to mention *Pyx Granite Co., Ltd.* v. *Minister of Housing and Local Government*[16] as an illustration of the presumption against ousting the jurisdiction of the courts. Section 17 of the Town and Country Planning Act 1947 provided a

---

[14] *Barras* v. *Aberdeen Fishing and Steam Trawling Co., Ltd.*, [1933] A.C. 402, at p. 412. See also Lord WIDGERY, C.J., in *Zimmerman* v. *Grossman*, [1972] 1 Q.B. 167, at p. 177.

[15] *Royal Crown Derby Porcelain, Ltd.* v. *Raymond Russell*, [1949] 2 K.B. 417, at p. 429.

[16] [1960] A.C. 260; [1959] 3 All E.R. 1.

special procedure by way of application to the Local Planning Authority to determine the question whether planning permission was necessary for any operations on land. There was a right of appeal to the minister and his decision was to be final. The House of Lords held that the company might nevertheless seek a declaration from the courts that planning permission was unnecessary for the proposed operations. Lord SIMONDS spoke of what lawyers like to call "the inalienable remedy of Her Majesty's subjects to seek redress in Her courts"; whatever the true implication of the word "inalienable" may be, it is obvious that the clearest exclusionary words are required to oust jurisdiction. Quite apart from any question of their constitutional position, the courts take the view that they are the only tribunals really fitted for the task of settling legal disputes,[17] and who is to say them Nay?

Vested rights. "The well established presumption is that the legislature does not intend to limit vested rights further than clearly appears from the enactment."[18] One striking modern illustration will suffice. *Allen* v. *Thorn Electrical Industries, Ltd.*[19] was concerned with the Prices and Incomes Act 1966 under which the Secretary of State was empowered to make orders imposing a "wages freeze". Section 29 (4) provided that "an employer shall not pay remuneration to which this section applies for work for any period while the order is in force at a rate which exceeds the *rate of remuneration paid* by him for the same kind of work before July 20th 1966". Did "paid" mean actually paid or contracted to be paid? The Court of Appeal unanimously came to the latter conclusion with the result that, where immediately effective pay increases had been agreed but not paid before July 20th, the increased rate was the rate of remuneration paid before that date. Lord DENNING had no doubt but added:[20]

> "If I were wrong in this view, I am clear that, at any rate, the requirement in the statute is ambiguous and uncertain, in which case the rights under the contract must prevail. No man's contractual rights are to be taken away on an ambiguity in a statute, nor is an employer to be penalised on an ambiguity."

WINN, L.J., used language which, though less common among modern judges, is surely no less significant:[1]

[17] *Lee* v. *Showman's Guild of Great Britain*, [1952] 2 Q.B. 329, at p. 354, *per* ROMER, L.J.

[18] *Re Metropolitan Film Studios, Ltd* v. *Twickenham Film Studios, Ltd.* (Intended action), [1962] 3 All E.R. 508, at p. 517, *per* UNGOED-THOMAS, J.

[19] [1968] 1 Q.B. 487, [1967] 2 All E.R. 1137.

[20] *Ibid.*, at p. 503. The statute penalised employers who did not comply with it.

[1] *Ibid.*, at p. 508.

"I must reject as quite untenable any submission . . . that if in any case one finds (a) that a statute is worded ambiguously in any particular respect, and (b) finds also clear indications *aliunde* that Parliament intended that they should have the strictest and most stringent meaning possible, therefore the court is then compelled to construe the section in the sense in which Parliament would have desired it to take effect, by giving the words their most stringent possible meaning. On the contrary, I think the right view is, and as I understand it always has been, that in such a case of ambiguity, it is resolved in such a way as to make the statute less onerous for the general public and so as to cause less interference, than the more stringent sense would, with such rights and liabilities as existing contractual obligations."

There is more to interpretation in general than the discovery of the meaning attached by the author to his words. Even if, in a particular case, that meaning is discoverable with a high degree of certitude from external sources, the question whether it has been adequately expressed remains. This question has to be raised in the interests of those who have to act and advise on the words under construction. In the case of statutory interpretation, there is the further question of the role of the courts when they have doubts about the meaning which the ordinary, or, where appropriate, the specialist, reader would attach to the provision with which they are concerned. When they have notice *aliunde* of Parliamentary intent, who is to have the benefit of those doubts, Parliament or the holder of the right? The orthodox answer is "the holder of the right" although, as we shall see, this may require some qualification in the case of certain taxing statutes. The issue is primarily a constitutional one. From the point of view of interpretation pure and simple, it could be argued that, on facts such as those of *Allen* v. *Thorn Electrical Industries, Ltd.*, those who have to act or even advise on the statute would not be prejudiced if the benefit of the doubt were given to Parliament, for Parliamentary intent in such a case is a matter of common knowledge for which all those concerned should make allowance. Against such an argument it could very properly be urged that the descent of the Gadarene slope into confusion would indeed have started if those who are concerned extrajudicially with statutory construction had to assess Parliamentary intent by criteria other than those which have been dealt with in this book. It only remains to add that, although they undoubtedly represent current legal opinion, the observations of Lord DENNING and WINN, L.J., in *Allen* v. *Thorn Electrical Industries, Ltd.*, were technically *obiter* because no member of the Court of Appeal thought there was any ambiguity in the wording of s. 29 (4) of the Prices and Incomes Act 1966.

Strict construction of penal statutes. The phrase "penal statute" is used to cover both statutes creating a crime and those providing for the recovery of a penalty in civil proceedings. In either case the present position is that if, to use the words of Lord Reid in *Director of Public Prosecutions* v. *Ottewell*,[2] "after full inquiry and consideration, one is left in real doubt", the accused or person from whom the penalty is claimed must be given the benefit of that doubt. Lord Reid proceeded to stress the point that it is not enough for the provision under construction to be ambiguous in the sense that it is capable of having two meanings, and the same point is embodied in the following frequently quoted passage from one of Lord Esher's judgments:[3]

> "If there is a reasonable interpretation which will avoid the penalty in any particular case, we must adopt that construction. If there are two reasonable constructions we must give the more lenient one. That is the settled rule for construction of penal sections."

So understood, the presumption in favour of a strict construction of penal statutes is simply an example of the presumption against unclear changes in the law. For instance, in *Sales-matic Ltd.* v. *Hinchliffe*,[4] the Divisional Court held that the declaration in s. 21 of the Betting and Lotteries Act 1934 that "all lotteries are unlawful" did not create a criminal offence because it did not refer to specific conduct in connection with lotteries such as promoting them or participating in them; this kind of conduct was dealt with in detail in subsequent sections, but it was questionable whether what the defendants did was covered, hence the prosecution under s. 21. Allowance must of course be made for the fact that the presumption operates against the Crown with the result that it requires a liberal interpretation of sections which provide the accused with a defence. This was the ground of the decision of the Court of Criminal Appeal in *R.* v. *Chapman*.[5] Section 2 of the Criminal Law Amendment Act 1922 deprived men charged with unlawful intercourse with a girl between the ages of 13 and 16 of the defence of reasonable cause to believe that she was over 16, but there was a proviso under which in the case of a man "of 23 years of age or under, the presence of reasonable cause to believe that the girl was over 16 years shall be a valid defence on the first occasion on which he is charged".[6] The defence was held to be available to a man over 23 but under 24.

In earlier times the presumption was a good deal more than an example of the presumption against unclear changes in the law. This was especially true in the case of criminal statutes. If they were

---

[2] [1970] A.C. 642, at p. 649. See also *per* Lord Denning, M.R., in *Farrell* v. *Alexander*, [1975] 3 W.L.R. 642, at p. 650–1.

[3] *Tuck & Sons* v. *Priester* (1887), 19 Q.B.D. 629, at p. 638.

[4] [1959] 3 All E.R. 401.

[5] [1931] 2 K.B. 606.

[6] See now Sexual Offences Act 1956, s. 6 (3).

capable of two meanings, however unreasonable one of those meanings might be, it was applied if favourable to the accused. Examples are *R.* v. *Harris*,[7] in which case someone who bit off the end of his victim's nose was held not guilty of "wounding" and the case mentioned by Blackstone[8] in which doubts were raised concerning the application of a statute of Edward VI which deprived those convicted of stealing horses of benefit of clergy to a man who stole but one horse. Decisions of this sort were amply justified on humanitarian grounds but they have been rendered unnecessary by the mitigation of the rigours of the criminal law and the modern rule, under which all that is required is that persons liable to a penalty should have the benefit of a genuine doubt about meaning, but not of a spurious one created by excessive literalism, is surely the correct one. But the spirit engendered by the old humane decisions lives on and it is difficult to escape the conclusion that it has animated some decisions since the establishment of the modern rule. A stock example is *Whiteley* v. *Chappell*.[9] Under s. 3 of the Poor Law Amendment Act 1851 it was an offence for any person, pending or after the election of any guardian of the poor to "personate any person *entitled to vote at such election*". The defendant signed and handed in a voting paper in the name of a deceased person who was entitled to vote as a ratepayer duly entered on the rate-book. He was convicted by a magistrate but his conviction was quashed by a Divisional Court because the legislature had not used words wide enough to make the personation of a dead person an offence. This decision owes its notoriety among those on statutory interpretation to the penetrating discussion it receives in a collection of materials by two American professors. The culminating point is reached when we are told that "the opinion is linguistically, philosophically, legally, and generally ignorant. It is deserving of nothing but contempt."[10] One can entertain doubts about the correctness of the decision without going to these extremes, and there are others open to the same criticism of an unduly literal approach.[11] In order to ensure that the presumption in favour of a strict construction of penal statutes should not be treated as anything more than the expression of a policy of clear statement which it is nowadays, it might be

---

[7] P. 10 *supra*.

[8] P. 19 *supra*.

[9] (1868), L.R. 4 Q.B. 147.

[10] Hart and Sacks, *The Legal Process*, tentative edition 1958, at p. 1157. This unpublished collection is available in some libraries.

[11] The choice of a decision manifesting an excessively literal approach is rather a subjective matter, but candidates for the kind of criticism which *Whiteley* v. *Chappell* has received, mentioned in this book, are *Fisher* v. *Bell*, p. 11 *supra*, *R.* v. *Munks*, p. 10 *supra* and *London and North Eastern Rail. Co.* v. *Berriman*, p. 63 *supra*. Other examples of excessive literalism have been mentioned, but they have nothing to do with penal statutes.

as well to provide, for the avoidance of doubt, that penal statutes are subject to the same canons of construction as any other statute.

Revenue statutes. This is usually assumed to be the present position with regard to revenue statutes. If they are clearly worded they must be applied even though they operate against the subject in a manner that may appear to have been unintended by Parliament, but "... if the provision is capable of two alternative meanings, courts will prefer that meaning more favourable to the subject".[12] There is, however, a complicating factor due to the legitimate state of war which exists between the subject and his advisers on the one hand and the Inland Revenue on the other hand. The former are bent on avoiding payments to the latter so far as they legally can, and the latter are bent on procuring statutory provisions which will, so far as possible, be foolproof. Lord REID recognised this problem when he said: "The draftsman of provisions for the prevention of tax evasion is often faced with this difficulty: if he uses narrow language the ingenuity of tax-payers' advisers will find a way to circumvent it, while if he uses wider language it will catch cases which do not really involve any element of evasion".[13] This remark was made in a case in which the House of Lords applied a wide but clearly worded provision against the tax-payer. In a later case Lord REID emphasised the danger of stretching the words of a revenue statute against the subject:[14]

> "Counsel for the respondent said, no doubt truly, that if this appeal were allowed the door would be open for wholesale evasion of stamp duty. But this consideration has never prevailed over the rule that the words of a taxing act must never be stretched against a taxpayer. And there is a very good reason for that rule. So long as one adheres to the natural meaning of the charging words the law is certain, or at least as certain as it is possible to make it. But if courts are to give to charging words what is sometimes called a liberal construction, who can say just how far this will go? It is much better that evasion should be met by amending legislation."

By 1972, however, Lord REID's attitude had changed somewhat. Speaking in a case in which a broad construction was placed on legislation aimed at dividend stripping he said:[15]

> "We seem to have moved a long way from the general and salutary rule that the subject is not to be taxed except by plain words. But we must recognise that plain words are seldom adequate to anticipate and forestall the multiplicity of ingenious schemes which are constantly being devised

---

[12] *Per* Lord THANKERTON in *Inland Revenue Commissioners* v. *Ross and Coulter*, [1948] 1 All E.R. 616, at p. 625.

[13] *Jamieson* v. *Inland Revenue Commissioners*, [1964] A.C. 1445, at p. 1461.

[14] *Cory & Sons, Ltd.* v. *Inland Revenue Commissioners*, [1965] A.C. 1088, at p. 1107.

[15] *Greenberg* v. *Inland Revenue Commissioners*, [1972] A.C. 109, at p. 137.

to evade taxation. Parliament is very properly determined to prevent this kind of tax evasion and, if the courts find it impossible to give very wide meanings to general phrases, the only alternative may be for Parliament to do as some other countries have done, and introduce legislation of a more sweeping character which would put the ordinary well intentioned person at much greater risk than is created by a wide interpretation of such provisions as those which we are now considering."

These are ominous words and they contrast strikingly with those of WINN, L.J., in *Allen* v. *Thorn Electrical Industries Ltd.*,[16] but they seem to have been confined to statutes aimed at tax evasion. Let us hope they will not be extended beyond this sphere too readily.

C. PRESUMPTION AGAINST RETROSPECTIVE OPERATION

The presumption against the retrospective operation of statutes concerned with the substantive law could perhaps be treated as a facet of the presumption against interference with vested rights, but it is more convenient to give a separate account of the subject. One of the best known judicial statements is that of R. S. Wright, J., in *Re Athlumney*:[17]

"Perhaps no rule of construction is more firmly established than this—that a retrospective operation is not to be given to a statute so as to impair an existing right or obligation, otherwise than as regards matter of procedure, unless that effect cannot be avoided without doing violence to the language of the enactment. If the enactment is expressed in language which is fairly capable of either interpretation, it ought to be construed as prospective only."

In order that the presumption should apply, the statute must be genuinely retrospective in its operation. It is not enough that the offence on which the operation of the statute depends should have occurred before it came into force. The statute must take away some vested right or impose a penalty for past acts which were not penalised when they were committed. To cite an old example, s. 2 of the Poor Removal Act 1846 provided that "no woman residing in any parish with her husband at the time of his death shall be removed ... from such parish, for twelve calendar months next after his death, if she so long continue a widow." It was held in *R.* v. *St. Mary, Whitechapel*,[18] that the section operated to prevent the removal of a widow whose husband had died before it came into force. It was argued that the right to remove was vested in the appropriate authority on the husband's death, but the court held that the statute was not retrospective

[16] P. 149 *supra*.
[17] [1898] 2 Q.B. 547.
[18] (1848), 12 Q.B. 120.

because it related to future removals: "...it is not properly called a retrospective statute because a part of the requisites of its action is drawn from time antecedent to its passing".[19] The statute would have been genuinely retrospective if it had set aside past removals of widows made within twelve months of their husband's death.

Commissioners of Customs and Excise v. *Thorn Electrical Industries Ltd.*[20] is a modern illustration of the same point as that made in *R.* v. *St. Mary Whitechapel.* The Commissioners claimed value added tax on payments made to the company in and after April 1973 under an agreement for the hire of a television set executed on 20th July 1972. The Finance Act 1972 received the royal assent on 27th July, and s. 7, dealing with value added tax, together with regulations made under it, came into force on 1st April 1973. According to one of the regulations:

> "...where goods are or have been supplied under an agreement to hire they shall be treated as being successively supplied on hire for successive parts of the period of the agreement and each of the successive supplies shall be treated as taking place when a payment under the agreement is received...."

The House of Lords held that the supply of goods under a hire agreement was a continuing process, so there could be no question of the regulation operating retrospectively. But Lord MORRIS OF BORTH-Y-GEST said: "The fact that as from a future date tax is charged on a source of income which has been arranged or provided for before the date of the imposition of the tax does not mean that a tax is retrospectively imposed".[1] The case is also of some interest because both Lord MORRIS and Lord FRASER OF TULLYBELTON[2] used language indicating agreement with the following remark in the judgment of the Divisional Court: "If the meaning of words in an enactment is clear, there is no presumption against them having a retrospective effect if that is indeed the result they produce".[3]

In *Carson* v. *Carson*[4] SCARMAN, J., had to construe s. 3 of the Matrimonial Causes Act 1963 according to which "adultery which has been condoned shall not be capable of being revived". He held that this changed the substantive law according to which condoned adultery could be revived by subsequent desertion, and since Parliament had neither expressly, nor by necessary implication, made the provision retrospective, adultery was revived by a desertion which took

---

[19] *Per* Lord DENMAN, *ibid.*, at p. 127.
[20] [1975] 3 All E.R. 881.
[1] *Ibid.*, at p. 890.
[2] *Ibid.*, at p. 896.
[3] [1975] 1 All E.R. 439, at p. 447, *per* THOMPSON, J.
[4] [1964] 1 All E.R. 681.

place before the Act came into force. *Carson* v. *Carson* may be contrasted with *Blyth* v. *Blyth*[5] which turned on s. 1 of the Matrimonial Causes Act 1963 under which a husband was permitted for the first time to give evidence in rebuttal of the presumption that adultery was condoned by subsequent matrimonial intercourse. It was held by the Court of Appeal whose decision on this point was approved by the House of Lords that s. 1 operated retrospectively. The presumption was treated as procedural and, to quote Lord DENNING: "the rule that an act of Parliament is not to be given retrospective effect only applies to statutes which affect vested rights. It does not apply to statutes which only alter the form of procedure, or the admissibility of evidence or the effect which the courts give to evidence."[6]

Enough has been said in this brief account of the presumption against retrospective operation to show that the law on the subject is difficult because the distinction between statutes which operate retrospectively for the purpose of the presumption and those which do not is hard to draw. It also seems that there may be some inconsistency in judicial views concerning the nature of the presumption. Is it of general application in the sense that it applies unless rebutted by clear words or necessary implication, or is it a presumption which only comes into play when there is an ambiguity? The preponderance of authority undoubtedly favours the former view,[7] but the statement of R. S. WRIGHT, J., with which the section began and the remark quoted from the judgment of the Court of Appeal in *Customs and Excise Commissioners* v. *Thorn Electrical Industries Ltd.* certainly suggest the contrary. Finally, the distinction between substantive law and procedure can be as difficult to draw in this context as elsewhere.

---

[5] [1966] A.C. 643.

[6] *Ibid.*, at p. 666.

[7] The following sentence, now on p. 215 of the 12th edition of Maxwell, *On the Interpretation of Statutes*, has frequently been cited with judicial approval: "It is a fundamental rule of English law that no statute shall be construed to have retrospective operation unless such a construction appears very clearly in the terms of the act, or arises by necessary and distinct implication".

VIII

Legislative Proposals and Concluding Questions

The English and Scottish Law Commissions' paper published in 1969[1] contains a draft of some modest legislative proposals on the subject of statutory interpretation. They are set out in Section A of this chapter, together with a brief commentary which incorporates the observations of the Renton Committee whose report on the preparation on legislation was published in 1975.[2] A few other legislative proposals are also mentioned in Section A, and some questions of a critical nature are raised in Section B.

A LEGISLATIVE PROPOSALS

The first of the draft clauses set out in Appendix A of the Law Commissions' paper deals with aids to interpretation and reads:

> 1. (1) "In ascertaining the meaning of any provision of an Act, the matters which may be considered shall, in addition to those which may be considered for that purpose apart from this section, include the following, that is to say—
>
> (*a*) all indications provided by the Act as printed by authority, including punctuation and side-notes, and the short title of the Act;
>
> (*b*) any relevant report of a royal commission, committee or other body which had been presented or made to or laid before Parliament or either house before the time when the Act was passed;
>
> (*c*) any relevant treaty or other international agreement which is referred to in the Act or of which copies had been presented to Parliament by command of Her Majesty before that time;

---

[1] *The Interpretation of Statutes* (Law Comm. 21; Scott. Law Comm. 11); for commentary see 33 *Modern Law Review* 197, and J. H. Farrar, *Law Reform and the Law Commission*, pp. 47 *et seq*.

[2] Cmnd. 6953; for commentary see 38 *Modern Law Review* 593. Chapter 19 deals with the interpretation of statutes and in general no reference is made to paragraphs of that chapter in the following footnotes.

(*d*) any other document bearing upon the subject-matter of the legislation which had been presented to Parliament by command of Her Majesty before that time;

(*e*) any document (whether falling within the foregoing paragraphs or not) which is declared by the Act to be a relevant document for the purposes of this section."

(2) "The weight to be given for the purposes of this section to any such matter as is mentioned in subsection (1) shall be no more than is appropriate in the circumstances."

(3) "Nothing in this section shall be construed as authorising the consideration of reports of proceedings in Parliament for any purpose for which they could not be considered apart from this section."

It is recognised that, even in countries with the most highly codified systems, the principles of interpretation largely rest on a body of flexible doctrine developed by legal writers and by the practice of the courts. Accordingly the Commissions do not propose any comprehensive statutory enumeration of the factors to be taken into account by the courts in the interpretation of legislation; but the italicised words in the following extract from para. 81 show that, from the theoretical point of view at least, a change of approach is contemplated by clause 1 (1):

> "We think, however, that a limited degree of statutory intervention is required ... to clarify, and in some respects to relax the strictness of, the rules which, in the determination by our courts of the proper context of a provision, exclude altogether or exclude *when the meaning is otherwise unambiguous*, certain material from consideration."

It is, for example, a mistake to suppose that the sole effect of clause 1 (1) (*a*) would be to place punctuation, side-notes and the short title on a par with the preamble, if any, long title and cross-headings. In that event, all six of the items could merely resolve, but not raise, an ambiguity. If the subclause were to become law "all indications provided by the Act as printed by authority" might be considered in ascertaining the meaning of the provision in dispute. The weight to be attached to a particular "indication" would of course vary from case to case, a matter for which allowance is expressly made by clause 1 (2); but in theory any one "indication" could control the meaning of otherwise unambiguous enacting words. The precise form of reasoning underlying some past decisions would no longer be applicable. If facts like those of *Ward* v. *Holman*[3] were to recur when clause 1 (1) (*a*) was in force, no court could hold that s. 5 of the Public Order Act 1936 applies to the use of threatening, abusive or insulting words in a street in furtherance of a private quarrel simply because it is "impossible to look at" the preamble or long title when the operative

---

[3] P. 110 *supra*.

words of an enactment are unambiguous. The case might well be decided in the same way because, having taken due account of the long title, the court could easily conclude that it was of insufficient weight to restrict the clear words of s. 5 since it is by no means uncommon for the enacting words to go beyond the matters mentioned in the long title. A concatenation of non-enacting words might, however, displace the clear meaning of enacting words as if, in the case put, the short title had been "The Public Meetings Act", the side-note to s. 5 had referred to public meetings and that phrase had occurred in a relevant cross-heading.

Clause 1 (1) (*a*) has the strong support of a dictum of Lord REID in *Director of Public Prosecutions* v. *Schildcamp*,[4] although it was made without reference to the question whether the non-enacting parts of a statute should ever control the plain meaning of enacting words. The subclause also has the blessing of the Renton Committee, but without consideration of the point which has just been mentioned.[5] It certainly seems to be desirable that, as a matter of law, it should be made clear that the punctuation, side-notes and short title can be considered where appropriate, although it is perhaps more debatable whether they, any more than other non-enacting parts, should ever be able to displace an otherwise clear meaning.

We saw in Section B of Chapter VI that, as things stand, a judge may only make use of relevant reports of royal commissions and the like as a ground for his decision when he considers that the statutory words are ambiguous, and then only in order to ascertain the mischief which the provision before him was designed to remedy. Neither of these restrictions would apply if clause 1 (1) (*b*) were enacted. The Renton report disapproves of the subclause in spite of the approval of most of the judicial witnesses who gave evidence to the Committee. The basic reason for the disapproval was the supposedly time-consuming nature of the proposal. It was thought that its adoption would lead to discussions in court of the extent to which Parliament intended to adopt the report, place too great a burden on those conducting litigation and complicate the giving of advice before any controversy had arisen. These objections would be more convincing if it were not the present practice of the courts to consult the reports in question for the purpose of ascertaining the mischief to be remedied. The danger of unduly protracted discussion concerning the extent to which Parliament intended to stick to the report is probably exag-

[4] P. 114 *supra*.

[5] The Renton Committee does not appear to have appreciated that it was the intention of the Law Commissions to alter the law with regard to the use that may be made of preambles. Para. 19.33 of its report seems to be inconsistent with the welcome accorded to clause 1 (1) (*a*).

gerated, and the supposedly unhappy predicament of those who give advice before a controversy has arisen would largely cease to exist if it were made clear that pre-parliamentary material could only be utilised by the courts when they considered that the enacted words were ambiguous.

The Renton report approves of clause 1 (1) (*c*). The subclause should be read together with clause 2 (*b*) according to which a construction which is consistent with the international obligations of the United Kingdom is to be preferred to one which is not. The combined effect of the two subclauses should be sufficient to get rid of *Ellerman Lines* v. *Murray*.[6]

The Renton report objects to clause 1 (1) (*d*) for the same reasons as those underlying its objections to clause 1 (1) (*b*) with the addition of the greater breadth of the material comprised in the subclause. A white paper which did no more than set out the tentative thoughts of the government would be included.

Clause 1 (1) (*e*) is, as the Renton report points out, superfluous because Parliament can declare that any document it chooses to mention should be regarded as relevant to the construction of a particular statute. The Committee was therefore doubtful about the value of the subclause although, in discarding clauses 1 (1) (*b*) and 1 (1) (*d*), its report does say that it would be preferable to leave it to Parliament if it saw fit to declare in an act that specified material outside that act (and not admitted by the Law Commissions' clause 1 (1) (*c*)) should be admissible for the purpose of interpreting it. Clauses in the Matrimonial Proceedings and Property Bill 1970 and the Animals Bill 1970 provided that, in ascertaining the meaning of any of their provisions, regard might be had to specified reports of the Law Commission. Although they were supported in the House of Lords by Lords DENNING, MORRIS OF BORTH Y GEST and WILBERFORCE, they met with a storm of opposition in the House of Commons and neither clause became law. The ground of the opposition was that the effect of the clauses would be to reduce the authority of Parliament and inflate that of the Law Commission.[7] This is not very encouraging for those who believe in even a modest extension of the notion of the context of a statute. For them the best course would be the adoption of clause 1 (1) (*b*) coupled, it may be, with the abandonment of clause 1 (1) (*d*) because it is too wide and of clause 1 (1) (*e*) because it is superfluous. Reasons were given in Section B of Chapter VI in favour of the restriction of the utilisation of material such as that mentioned in clause 1 (1) (*b*) to cases in which the judge is in real doubt about

---

[6] P. 139 *supra*.

[7] See for example Sir David Renton's speech in 794 H.C. Debates, col. 1566–7.

the meaning of the words under construction; if the subclause were so restricted the change in the law which it would effect would be confined to the purposes for which the pre-legislative material might be used. It would become available for the ascertainment of the meaning of the statutory words as well as for the ascertainment of the mischief at which the statute was aimed.

Clause 1 (2), approved by the Renton Committee, does not call for comment.

Clause 1 (3) is strongly indorsed by the Renton Committee. It was recommended by the Law Commissions in spite of the fact that their paper cites examples of cases in which the specific point at issue appears to have been in the mind of some of the participants in the parliamentary debates which preceded the statute in question. Though they are probably comparatively rare, such cases do undoubtedly occur from time to time, and there are instances in which the ministerial answer to the question subsequently before the court differs from that which it gives.[8] A suggestion made by Lord SIMON OF GLAISDALE since the publication of the Law Commissions' paper is that:[9]

> "Where the promoter of a bill, or a minister supporting it, is asked whether the Act has a specified operation in particular circumstances, and expresses an opinion, it might well be made a constitutional convention that such contingency should ordinarily be the subject-matter of specific statutory enactment—unless, indeed, it were too obvious to need expression."

The Renton Committee was mildly fearful lest such a practice would increase the amount of specific detail mentioned in statutes, but suggested that it might be fitted in with the "general principle" approach to statutory drafting recommended in its report.[10] The specified circumstances covered by the minister's opinion would become an example in a schedule to the Act.

The main reason for the Law Commissions' decision not to recommend any change in the law with regard to the reference by the Courts to reports of parliamentary proceedings was the inaccessibility of such material. Influential considerations were the difficulty of isolating information which would assist the courts, the difficulty of providing such information as could be given in an accessible form and the possibility that the function of legislative material in the interpretative process could be better performed by specially prepared explanatory

---

[8] For an instance occurring after the publication of the Law Commissions' paper see *Santos* v. *Santos*, [1972] Fam. 247; [1972] 2 All E.R. 246 as contrasted with 303 H.L. Debates, col. 1334–60, and 304 *ibid.*, col. 1082–1128.

[9] *Dockers' Labour Club and Institute, Ltd.* v. *Race Relations Board*, [1974] 3 All E.R. 592, at p. 601; see also *McMillan* v. *Crouch*, [1972] 3 All E.R. 61, at p. 76.

[10] Paras. 10.4 and 10.13.

material. What the Commissions had in mind was a document prepared by the promoters of a bill and altered as the bill passed through Parliament so as to make allowance for amendments. Various methods of obtaining parliamentary approval of such a document were discussed, but no recommendation apart from that contained in clause 1 (1) (*e*) was made. The difficulty about all proposals relating to specially prepared explanatory materials is that their implementation would tend, in the end, to leave the courts with two documents to construe. This danger is spoken of as that of the "split level" statute. No doubt it is a real one and it accounts for the Renton Committee's objections to specially prepared explanatory material, but there is something to be said for an occasional experimental provision under which the courts are authorised to refer to explanatory material specifically mentioned in a particular enactment.[11]

The second of the Law Commissions' draft clauses deals with principles of interpretation and reads as follows:

> 2. "The following shall be included among the principles to be applied in the interpretation of Acts, namely—
>
> (*a*) that a construction which would promote the general legislative purpose underlying the provision in question is to be preferred to a construction which would not; and
>
> (*b*) that a construction which is consistent with the international obligations of Her Majesty's Government in the United Kingdom is to be preferred to a construction which is not."

Both limbs of the clause are approved by the Renton report. They probably represent the current practice of the courts, but no harm could be occasioned by their enactment, and clause 2 (*a*) has the merit of serving as a succinct reminder of the desirability of a purposive approach to statutory interpretation.

Section 5 (*j*) of the New Zealand Acts Interpretation Act 1924, mentioned in the introduction to this book, is set out in para. 33 of the Law Commissions' paper. The subsection reads:

> "Every Act, and every provision or enactment thereof, shall be deemed remedial, whether its immediate purpose is to direct the doing of anything parliament deems to be for the public good, or to prevent or punish the doing of anything it deems contrary to the public good, and shall accordingly receive such fair, large and liberal construction, and interpretation as will best insure the attainment of the object of the Act and of such provision or enactment according to its true intent, meaning, and spirit."

It is said that little attention is paid to this provision by the New Zealand courts, and the Commissions think that this may be because exhortations to the courts to adopt "large and liberal" interpretations

---

[11] The Law Commissions' object in recommending clause 1 (1) (*e*) was to encourage such experiments.

beg the question as to what is the real intention of the legislature, which may require in the circumstances either a broad or a narrow construction of language. It does seem, however, that the New Zealand provision has at least had the effect of displacing any special presumption in favour of a strict construction of penal statutes.[12] It is not suggested that this is a reason for enacting a provision in anything like the the same words as s. 5 (*j*) of the New Zealand Act, but there is something to be said for a provision that penal statutes are subject to the same canons of construction as any other statute, even if the only purpose it would achieve under the modern law is the avoidance of doubt.[13]

Paragraph 19.32 of the Renton report recommends the following provision: "In the absence of any express indication to the contrary, a construction that would exclude retrospective effect is to be preferred to one that would not." We saw in the last chapter that there are some uncertainties with regard to the presumption against the retrospective operation of a statute, and a provision such as that which has just been quoted would prevent their future occurrence, but it is to be hoped that the provision itself would not be retrospective in the sense that it would apply to statutes passed before its enactment. If it were retrospective in that sense, the construction of procedural statutes, such as that on which *Blyth* v. *Blyth*[14] turned, would be problematic.

So far as any future enactment is concerned there is a great deal to be said for a general statutory presumption in favour of a particular construction of provisions which give rise to frequently recurring problems. Clause 4 of the Law Commissions' legislative recommendations is therefore to be welcomed. It reads:[15]

> "Where any Act passed after this Act imposes or authorises the imposition of a duty, whether positive or negative and whether with or without a special remedy for its enforcement, it shall be presumed, unless express provision to the contrary is made, that a breach of the duty is intended to be actionable (subject to the defences and other incidents applying to actions for breach of statutory duty) at the suit of any person who sustains damages in consequence of the breach."

---

[12] See the article by Professor Burrows in 3 New Zealand Universities Law Review 253.

[13] P. 151 *supra*.

[14] P. 155 *supra*.

[15] Clause 3 is not set out in the text because it is concerned with subordinate legislation. It reads: "Sections 1 and 2 above shall apply with the necessary modifications in relation to orders in council (whether made by virtue of any act or by virtue of Her Majesty's prerogative) and to orders, rules, regulations and other legislative instruments made by virtue of any act (whether passed before or after this Act), as they apply in relation to actions."

The need for such a clause is made plain by the following remarks of Lord DU PARCQ:[16]

> "To a person untutored in the science or art of legislation it may well seem strange that Parliament has not by now made it a rule to state explicitly what its intention is in a matter which is often of no little importance, instead of leaving it to the courts to discover, by a careful examination and analysis of what is expressly said, what that intention may be supposed probably to be."

The question whether a statute imposing a duty entitles someone injured by its breach to sue in tort is a notoriously difficult one. What is needed is a recognised presumption one way or the other. The Law Commissions' paper says they considered which way round the presumption should operate but gives no reason for its conclusion in favour of an action for damages.

Another field of legislation in which a statutory presumption one way or the other would be highly desirable is that of the criminal law. Even though most recent cases make it tolerably plain that there is a presumption that *mens rea* in the sense of guilty knowledge is required in spite of the absence of any indication one way or the other in the statutory definition of a crime, there is something to be said for an express provision to that effect on the lines of clause 4 of the Law Commissions' draft, but this was not proposed because it was thought that the matter was best left to be dealt with by those working on the proposed codification of the criminal law.

There is general agreement that the Interpretation Act 1889 should be updated. Use might well be made of parts of the Interpretation (Northern Ireland) Act 1954 which contains helpful provisions, such as s. 7, under which future statutes would not bind the Crown unless it was named therein.[17] In recommending a new interpretation Act, the Renton Committee suggested that such of the Law Commissions' clauses of which it approved might be incorporated in that statute.

The foregoing paragraphs show that no-one has suggested anything in the nature of revolutionary or comprehensive general legislation on the subject of statutory interpretation. The adoption of the Law Commissions' proposals might do a little good and could do little harm, but it is doubtful whether it would have much practical effect on the action of the courts. An updated Interpretation Act would merely tend to shorten future legislation and facilitate its drafting by rendering definitions of a variety of expressions unnecessary and by

---

[16] *Cutler* v. *Wandsworth Stadium, Ltd.*, [1949] A.C. 398, at p. 410.

[17] See the articles by W. A. Leitch and A. H. Donaldson in 11 *N.I.L.Q.* 43, and by W. A. Leitch, 16 *ibid.* 215. The doctrine that the Crown may be bound by necessary implication as well as express reference has given rise to much difficulty. See the cases cited in 11 *N.I.L.Q.* at pp. 72–5.

enacting some helpful presumptions. At the more exalted level of general principles the subject does not lend itself to legislation. This fact enhances rather than diminishes the role of the academic writer and it will be submitted in the next section that the challenge has, in England at any rate, hardly been acknowledged, let alone accepted.

B CONCLUDING QUESTIONS

A few questions will now be raised about the role of the courts and academic lawyers in relation to statutory interpretation and the possible effect of the entry of the United Kingdom into the European Economic Community.

The courts

It is unnecessary to spend much time on the first and third questions raised in the introduction about the part played by the courts because the answers are obvious. Do the courts interpret statutes too narrowly without adequate regard to the social purpose of the legislation? Is their approach to the interpretation of statutes designed to effect social change too conservative? In each instance the answer is "at times yes, but not to such an extent as to merit wholesale condemnation, and there have often been important countervailing considerations".

To begin with the first question, the Law Commissions' paper concludes that:[18]

> "There is a tendency in our systems, less evident in some recent decisions of the courts but still perceptible, to over-emphasise the literal meaning of a provision (i.e. the meaning in the light of its immediate and obvious context) at the expense of the meaning to be derived from other possible contexts; the latter include 'the mischief', or general legislative purpose, as well as any international obligation of the United Kingdom ..."

Of course a literal approach need not be a particularly narrow one. An unrestrictive construction of general words may be excessively literal and insufficiently purposive, but the usual charge under this head is one of narrow literalism. The Law Commissions' paper refers to three cases which have been mentioned in this book: *Whiteley* v. *Chappell* (impersonation of a dead voter);[19] *Fisher* v. *Bell* (flick-knife in shop window not offered for sale);[20] and *Bourne* v. *Norwich Crematorium, Ltd.* (cremation not "subjection of goods or materials to any process").[1] The most difficult to defend is the construction adopted

[18] Para. 80 (*c*).
[19] P. 151 *supra*.
[20] P. 11 *supra*.
[1] P. 64 *supra*.

in the third of these cases. It was entirely non-purposive and, to say the least, highly debatable as an application of the plain meaning rule. The constructions adopted in the first two cases were certainly not purposive, but penal statutes were involved. Even if it is accepted that there is no special presumption in favour of a strict construction of such statutes (a point which was far from clear when *Whiteley* v. *Chappell* was decided), it is questionable whether the exposure of goods in a shop window should be treated as an offer for sale within the meaning of a statute addressed to shopkeepers. Many examples of what appears to be an excessively literal approach could be cited, but it would be wrong to treat them as typical. Although it is a pity that he did not give instances, there is no doubt much truth in the following extract from Lord DIPLOCK's speech in the House of Lords in *Carter* v. *Bradbeer*:[2]

> "If one looks back to the actual decisions of this House on questions of statutory construction over the last 30 years one cannot fail to be struck by the evidence of a trend away from the purely literal towards the purposive construction of statutory provisions."

As to the question whether the courts' approach to statutes designed to effect social change is too conservative, it is of course possible to cite numerous instances for and against such an hypothesis. The construction of housing legislation is an example cited by protagonists on both sides.[3] A body of case-law has come into being concerning the construction of the provision in successive enactments that, in the case of lettings of property of low value, the landlord impliedly undertakes to keep the premises reasonably fit for human habitation. It must be admitted that the Acts have not always been construed strictly in accordance with the view expressed by a recent writer:[4]

> "Social legislation involves the 'sacrifice of liability based on individual fault so as to place loss in accordance with social justice and economic expediency'. The guilt of an individual landlord is quite irrelevant in this context."

At the same time there are, as the writer concedes, important exceptions.[5] In any event, when statutory language has to be construed

---

[2] [1975] 3 All E.R. 158, at p. 161. An example of purposive construction by the House given in this book is *Luke* v. *Inland Revenue Commissioners*, p. 79 *supra*.

[3] See the article by J. F. Reynolds in 37 *Modern Law Review* 377. The rejoinder by M. J. Robinson in 39 *Modern Law Review* 43 suggests that the divination of social purpose is a challenge to the sovereignty of parliament.

[4] J. F. Reynolds, 37 *Modern Law Review*, at p. 397, quoting the late Professor Ungar, 5 *Modern Law Review* 266.

[5] *E. G. Summers* v. *Salford Corporation*, [1943] A.C. 283 (house not reasonably fit for human habitation when, owing to a broken sash cord, the bedroom window could

against the common law background of the absence of liability on the part of a landlord to keep demised premises fit for human habitation, it would be completely wrong to ignore that background. If the intention of the legislature had been to eliminate all reference to the common law, the legislature should have used very different language.

So far as each of the two questions which have just been discussed is concerned, if the choice is between the plain meaning, ascertained with due regard to the purpose of the statute, and something other than the plain meaning which appears to give greater effect to the statutory purpose, it is to be hoped that the courts will always opt in favour of the former. The fact that words do not always have a plain meaning, even after due allowance has been made for the context, and the fact that ordinary people, as well as lawyers, sometimes take different views about the plain meaning of words does not mean that there is no such thing. Most statutory provisions do have a plain meaning when fairly read in their context, and fair-minded readers will usually be in agreement with regard to that meaning.

But what about the case in which there is no plain meaning, or, if there is one, it produces absurd results? This raises the second question mentioned in the introduction. Are the courts too timorous when confronted with an obvious mistake or omission? The answer is a resounding "yes" if they really are, in Lord HALSBURY's words, "to proceed upon the assumption that the legislature is an ideal person that does not make mistakes".[6] But we have seen that there are cases decided both before[7] and after[8] those words were spoken which show that this is not the invariable attitude of the courts, especially when the assumption which has to be made is that a provision was erroneously included in a statute. It is easy to see why the courts act with greater caution when the apparent legislative error is one of omission because the reading in of words which are not in a statute, even if it can be said that they are there by necessary implication, looks more like legislating than does the ignoring of statutory words; but the distinction is of doubtful validity. It might be thought to have gained some currency by the reference to the filling in of gaps

---

not be opened without personal danger): "The section must, I think, be construed with due regard to its apparent object, and to the character of the legislation to which it belongs. The provision was to reduce the evils of bad housing accommodation and to protect working people by a compulsory provision out of which they cannot contract, against accepting improper conditions. . . . It is a measure aimed at social amelioration, no doubt in a small and limited way. It must be construed so as to give proper effect to that object" (*per* Lord WRIGHT, at p. 293).

[6] P. 96 *supra*.

[7] *Salmon* v. *Duncombe*, p. 90 *supra*.

[8] Re *Lockwood*, p. 91 *supra*.

in a statute as "a naked usurpation of the legislative function under the thin disguise of interpretation". These were the words of Lord SIMONDS in *Magor and St Mellons Rural District Council* v. *Newport Corporation*,[9] and they are certainly not to be numbered among the most helpful of his observations on the subject of statutory interpretation. What was Lord PARKER doing but filling in gaps when, in *Adler* v. *George*,[10] he read the words "in the vicinity of" in s. 3 of the Official Secrets Act 1920 as meaning "in or in the vicinity of"? What was Lord LYNDHURST doing but filling in gaps when, in *Re Wainewright*,[11] he added the italicised words in the following extract from s. 33 of the Fines and Recoveries Act 1833 in order to make good an obvious omission?

> "If any person, protector of a settlement, shall be convicted of treason or felony; or if any person not being the owner of a prior estate under a settlement shall be the protector of such settlement and shall be an infant, ... His Majesty's High Court of Chancery shall be the protector of such settlement *in lieu of the person who shall be convicted and* in lieu of the person who shall be an infant. ..."

We saw in Section 5 of Chapter IV that Lord PARKER could be said to have been merely stating expressly words which were already in the statute by necessary implication, but we also saw how thin is the line between that process and adding words in order to correct an obvious error. The course adopted by Lord LYNDHURST comes on the latter side of the line.

Surely it would be better for all judges to recognise that they possess a limited power to add to, alter or ignore statutory words in the circumstances mentioned by Lord REID in his speech in *Federal Steam Navigation Co., Ltd.* v. *Department of Trade and Industry*.[12] The existence of such a power seems to be established by the authorities, and the advantage of frankly recognising it would be the development of rules concerning its limits. Such a development is unlikely as long as it is thought that *all* fillings in of gaps are naked usurpations of the legislative function. A case in point is *Fisher* v. *Bell*[13] in which Lord PARKER refused to remedy the omission of some such words as "has in his possession for sale" from s. 1 (1) of the Restriction of Offensive Weapons Act 1959. Lord PARKER was evidently not convinced that there was a *casus omissus*, but he would not have supplied the omission even if there were. Was this because the intention to include the case

---

[9] [1952] A.C. 189, at p. 191, p. 37 *supra*. The ensuing criticism of these words must not be taken as necessarily implying disapproval of the actual decision in this case.

[10] P. 32 *supra*.

[11] P. 86 *supra*.

[12] P. 94 *supra*.

[13] P. 11 *supra*.

of possession for sale had to be inferred from the language of the enactment, just as, in the case of will construction, the testator's intention to include omitted words must appear "within the four corners of the will"? Such a requirement could account for the difference between the courses adopted by Lord PARKER in *Fisher* v. *Bell* and by Lord LYNDHURST in *Re Wainewright*, but we will never know the answer to such questions as long as the implementation of an obvious, though erroneously expressed, legislative intention is thought of as a usurpation of the legislative power.

The curious reluctance of some judges to recognise what amounts to a power to rectify a statute when construing it, however limited that power may be, is almost as great an obstruction to the development of a jurisprudence of statutory interpretation as the equally curious reluctance of other judges and some writers to recognise that the plain ordinary meaning of statutory words must yield to a secondary meaning when the application of the ordinary meaning would lead to a result which "cannot reasonably be supposed to have been the intention of the legislature".[14]

Academic lawyers

Why is it that, in the field of the general principles of statutory interpretation, the English academic lawyer does not perform his ordinary function of synthesising and criticising the case-law, and, where appropriate, making proposals for reform? The answer depends partly on the conflicting statements of principle which have been made from time to time by the courts, partly on the necessarily narrow operation of the doctrine of precedent in relation to statutory interpretation and partly on the effect of one landmark law review article.

Reference has already been made to the paucity of rules and confusion of principles which justify Lord WILBERFORCE's description of statutory interpretation as a non-subject, at least so far as law reform is concerned.[15] The point has also been made that a decision on the interpretation of one statute generally cannot constitute a binding precedent with regard to the interpretation of another statute with the result that a general rule of interpretation, unlike other common law rules, can never be rendered more specific by the *rationes decidendi* of later cases.[16] The subject is dependent upon *dicta* and academics like to work with decisions. Even at the level of the meaning to be attached to particular words:[17]

[14] See *per* Lord REID in *Pinner* v. *Everett*, [1969] 3 All E.R. 257, at p. 258, p. 29 *supra*. See also p. 81 *supra*.
[15] P. 29 *supra*.
[16] P. 42 *supra*.
[17] *Per* Lord DIPLOCK in *Carter* v. *Bradbeer*, [1975] 3 All E.R. 158, at p. 161.

"A question of statutory construction is one in which the strict doctrine of precedent can only be of narrow application. The *ratio decidendi* of a judgment as to the meaning of particular words or combination of words used in a particular statutory provision can have no more than a persuasive influence on a court which is called on to interpret the same word or combination of words appearing in some other statutory provision."

The matters which have just been mentioned are certainly inimical to syntheses of case-law, but it is open to question whether more attempts in that direction would not have been made but for the article entitled *Statutory Interpretation in a Nutshell* contributed by Professor J. Willis to the *Canadian Bar Review* for 1938.[18] After warning his readers that it is a mistake to suppose that there is only one rule of statutory interpretation because there are three—the literal, golden and mischief rules—Professor Willis maintains that a court invokes "whichever of the rules produces a result which satisfies its sense of justice in the case before it".[19] No doubt the warning had its point in 1938 when practitioners' books tended to state the literal or plain meaning rule without any embellishments referring to the context, including the object, of the statute. The thesis was maintained so persuasively that the tendency of subsequent English academic discussion has been to do no more than treat the cases as illustrations of one or more of the three rules;[20] but it is submitted that the most cursory consideration of a collection of decisions and *dicta*, such as that made in this book, reveals that the thesis is not supported by the authorities. If a three rule approach, such as that canvassed by Professor Willis, is to be adopted, allowance must be made for the primacy of the literal rule, but it is surely better to recognise that the three rules have been fused. This point, derived from Mr E. A. Driedger's book, was made at the end of Chapter I, but its acceptance does not involve the acceptance of the reformulation of Lord WENSLEYDALE's golden rule canvassed by Mr Driedger.[1]

The position maintained in this book can best be summarised by a further reference to Lord WENSLEYDALE's words: "[T]he grammatical and ordinary sense of the words is to be adhered to, unless that would lead to some absurdity, or some repugnance or inconsistency

---

[18] 16 *Canadian Bar Review* 1.

[19] *Ibid.*, at p. 16.

[20] See for example the interesting final chapter of the current edition of Odgers's *Construction of Deeds and Statutes*. The complaint I am making is of course confined to English academics; the literature mentioned in Appendix C of the Law Commissions' paper is proof of the interest of academics from other countries in the subject. To this may be added the further Canadian contribution of Mr E. A. Driedger's *The Construction of Statutes*, and the contribution from Australia of Mr D. C. Pearce's *Statutory Interpretation in Australia*. This came my way too late for use in this book. My complaint is of course also confined to the general principles of interpretation. There is a large number of excellent English works on the construction of particular statutes.

[1] P. 82 *supra*.

with the rest of the instrument, in which case the grammatical and ordinary sense of the words may be modified, so as to avoid the absurdity and inconsistency, but no farther". If this is to be treated as a succinct statement of the present law, allowance must be made for the now accepted fact that the "grammatical and ordinary sense of the words" means those senses after due allowance has been made for the context. The "context" includes the object of the statute. The "mischief" rule has insinuated itself into the literal rule. "Some absurdity" is broader than "some repugnance or inconsistency with the rest of the instrument"; it includes a construction which leads to "quite unreasonable results".[2] The golden rule is a gloss upon the literal rule, not, as the Law Commissions' paper suggests, a "less explicit form of the mischief rule".[3] Even if it were legitimate to do so in 1938, it is wrong to cite JARVIS, C.J.'s words in *Abley* v. *Dale*,[4] as Professor Willis does, as a modern statement of the literal rule.

Whatever the cause may be, it is greatly to be regretted that English academic lawyers have not performed their usual functions with regard to the general principles of statutory interpretation. This book has been written in the hope of making good the deficiency, albeit in a very minor way.

The European influence

Two crucially important matters relevant to statutory interpretation are drafting and the possible repercussions on interpretation of our membership of the EEC. We saw in Chapter I how drafting and interpretation are mutually dependent and how an excessively literal approach to interpretation can lead to excessively detailed drafting.

In his evidence to the Renton Committee Lord DENNING went so far as to say:[5]

> "It is because the judges have not felt it right to fill in the gaps and have been giving a literal interpretation for many years that the draftsman has felt that he has to try and think of every conceivable thing and put it in as far as he can so that even the person unwilling to understand will follow it. I think the rules of interpretation which the judges have applied have been one of the primary causes why draftsmen have felt that they must have a system of over-detail, over-long sentences, and obscurity."

The Committee recognised that the demand for detail would continue in the case of statutes with a substantial political or administrative

[2] See *per* Lord REID in *Richard Thomas and Baldwins, Ltd.* v. *Cummings*, p. 81 *supra*; in *Luke* v. *Inland Revenue Commissioners*, p. 80 *supra*; and in *Pinner* v. *Everett*, p. 29 *supra*.

[3] Para. 32 *ad fin.*

[4] "If the precise words used are plain and unambiguous ... we are bound to construe them in their ordinary sense, even though it leads ... to an absurdity or a manifest injustice": 11 C.B. 378, at p. 391 (1851).

[5] *The Preparation of Legislation*, para. 19.1.

content, but suggested that, in the case of statutes dealing with private law, there might be a statement of general principle in the body of the Act, leaving details to be filled in in a schedule.

The adoption of this course would tend to bring the drafting of English statutes more into line with that of western European statutes, for, to quote from the Renton report: "The European legislative tradition has been to express the law in general principles; in this country the tradition has been to specify in detail the application of the law in particular circumstances."[6] The alignment would be far from complete because the details would simply be concealed, no doubt with much stylistic advantage, in a schedule. It is a moot point which of the two techniques is to be preferred. A judge in a state of justifiable exasperation with the minutiae of an English finance Act may well feel inclined to long for the adoption of the European technique,[7] but a solicitor or barrister charged with the duty of giving advice which is unlikely to be tested in court would benefit from a considerable amount of detail.

Whichever of the two drafting methods is to be preferred, there can be little doubt that English judges and draftsmen will be affected at certain points by our accession to the Treaty of Rome. "Community Instruments" have to be interpreted according to the decisions of the European Court, and they tend to be drafted in accordance with the European legislative tradition. Such questions as the length of time which will elapse before that tradition becomes influential, or the likely extent of the influence, are beyond the scope of this book; but it is certainly right that Lord DENNING, the butt of Lord SIMONDS's hyperbole in the *Magor and St Mellons* case, and a critic of our drafting technique as well as of our rules of interpretation, should have the last word. After making some observations similar to those which have just been quoted from his evidence to the Renton Committee, he said in *H. P. Bulmer, Ltd.* v. *J. Bollinger S.A.*:[8]

> "How different is this treaty. It lays down general principles. It expresses its aims and purposes. All in sentences of moderate length and commendable style. But it lacks precision. It uses words and phrases without defining what they mean. An English lawyer would look for an interpretation clause; but he would look in vain. There is none. All the way through the treaty there are gaps and lacunae. These have to be filled in by the judges or by regulations or directives. It is the European way."

---

[6] *Ibid.*, Chapter 20 (Conclusion) (7).

[7] Although some French and German fiscal legislation appears to be elaborate enough.

[8] [1974] 2 All E.R. 1226, at p. 1237.

Index

ABSURDITY
construction of section leading to, in others, 102, 103
extended meaning avoiding, 79, 80
golden rule, application in case of, 14, 15, 43, 74, 75, 81
in relation to rest of statute, 82, 83
ordinary meaning producing, 14, 15, 43, 74, 75
repugnancy or inconsistency, whether synonymous with, 75, 81–83, 170
restrictive interpretation avoiding, 80, 81
secondary meaning avoiding, 14, 15, 43, 74, 75, 101

ACCIDENT
meaning, 58, 59, 62, 70

ACTS OF PARLIAMENT. *See* STATUTES

ADDITION
words to statute, of, 33, 43, 86, 88, 92, 93, 94

ADMIRALTY COURT
Act of 1861—
interpretation of remedial statute, 6
statutes overlapping, effect of, 3, 4, 69
action in, 45

AGE OF MARRIAGE ACT, 1929
territorial extent, 4

ALTERATION
statutes, of, 43, 84, 88–90, 92, 94

AMBIGUITY
meaning, 76
Parliamentary materials not admissible, 134, 135
preamble and long title and, 109–111, 133, 134, 140
statute *in pari materia* and, 128

AMENDMENT
interpretation contrasted, 32, 33

"AND" AND "OR"
meaning, 89, 90

ANOMALY
absurdity, whether synonymous with, 75, 81, 82

ATTEMPTING TO DRIVE
driving or, meaning, 27, 59, 71, 72
fringe meaning, example of, 71, 72

A.-G. v. *PRINCE ERNEST AUGUSTUS OF HANOVER*,
absurdity of ordinary meaning, 42, 43, 47, 48
construction, relevance of date of statute in, 47, 48
context defined, 130
preamble, use of, 47, 48, 109, 110

AUSTIN
interpretation "*ex ratione legis*", 23, 24, 25
statutory interpretation, on, 23–25

BAR
meaning (intoxicating liquor), 55, 104

BENTHAM
A Comment on the Commentaries, 20, 23
criticism of Blackstone, 20
extensive and restrictive interpretation, 22, 23
Of Laws in General, 22, 23
rule of rank, on, 119
statutory interpretation, on, 20–23
strict and liberal interpretation, 22, 23

BICYCLE
carriage, whether, 57, 68

BLACKSTONE
Bentham's criticisms of, 20

BLACKSTONE—*contd.*
Introduction to the Commentaries, 17
penal statutes, construction of, 19, 21
rule of rank, on, 119
statutory interpretation, on, 17–20, 65

CANONS OF INTERPRETATION. *See* INTERPRETATION

CARRIAGE
whether bicycle a, 57, 68

CASUS OMISSUS
draftsman and problems of interpretation, 11–13, 170
Gray on, 26
history, 10–12, 23
meaning, 10

COKE
opinions, as aid to construction, 125, 127

COMMERCIAL USAGE
construction, as aid to, 126

COMMON LAW
presumption against unnecessary change in, 26, 28, 31, 145

CONSTRUCTION. *See also* STATUTORY INTERPRETATION
commercial usage as aid to, 126
contemporanea expositio, 122, 126, 127
cross-headings, 107, 108, 112
dictionaries, 54, 124
ejusdem generis, rule of, 99, 115–118
enabling parts of same statute, 99 *et seq.*
change of language, effect of, 99–101
interpretation clauses, 103, 104
other parts distinguished, 107
other sections, resulting in absurdity in, 102, 103
proviso, relationship to main clause, 104–107
repugnancy, 101
avoidance of, 101, 102
expressio unius, maxim of, 115, 120
external aids to, 50, 54, 55, 122 *et seq.*
headings, 107, 108, 112
historical setting as aid to, 45–47, 123, 124
internal aids to, 99 *et seq.*
language, rules of, 115 *et seq.*
Law Commission on aids to, 156 *et seq.*
legislative history as aid to, 129 *et seq.*
plain meaning rule, 132–134
long title, 107, 108–111
contemporanea expositio, as, 127
marginal notes, 107, 108, 113
contemporanea expositio, as, 127
noscitur a sociis, maxim of, 115, 118

CONSTRUCTION—*contd.*
other parts of same statute, 99, 107 *et seq.*
enacting parts distinguished, 107
respective weight attached to, 107, 108
other statutes—
as guide to, 30, 129, 168
in pari materia, 18, 50, 127–129
practice of conveyancers, 125
preamble, 19, 47, 48, 50, 107, 108–111
ambiguity, in case of, 109–111, 133, 134, 140
punctuation, 107, 114, 115
contemporanea expositio, as, 127
rule of rank, 115, 119
short title, 107, 108, 111
side-notes, 107, 108, 113
statutory interpretation, possible distinctions, 18. *See also* STATUTORY INTERPRETATION

CONTEMPORANEA EXPOSITIO
construction, as aid to, 122, 126, 127
long title as, 127
marginal notes as, 127
punctuation as, 127

CONTEXT
statutes, of, 44–52. *See also* STATUTES

CONTRADICTION
absurdity, whether synonymous with, 75, 81, 82

CONVEYANCERS
practice as aid to construction, 125

CREDIT
obtaining of, meaning, 54, 124

CREMATION
meaning, 64, 164

CROSS-HEADINGS
construction, as aids to, 107, 108, 112

DICTIONARIES
construction, as aids to, 54, 124

DRAFTING
problems of interpretation and, 11–13, 170

DRIEDGER, MR. E. A.
ejusdem generis rule, on, 115
golden rule, on, 82, 83, 169

DRIVING
attempting to drive, or, meaning, 27, 59, 71, 72
fringe meaning, example of, 71, 72

DWORKIN, PROF. R. M.
canons of interpretation, on, 27–29

EJUSDEM GENERIS RULE
construction, rule of, 99, 115–118
Driedger, Mr. E. A., on, 115
meaning, 58, 116
mischief rule overrides, 117, 118
two word phrase, application to, 116, 117

ENGINE
meaning, 10, 11, 52

ERRORS. *See* MISTAKES

EUROPEAN COMMUNITY
drafting and statutory interpretation, effect on, 170, 171

EVIDENCE
construction, aids to. *See* CONSTRUCTION
statutory interpretation, in, 52–56

EXPRESSIO UNIUS
maxim of construction, 115, 120
meaning, 120

FAMILY
member of, meaning, 46, 99, 100

FLOORS
meaning (factories), 119

FRINGE MEANING
examples of, 57, 67, 71

GENERAL WORDS
extension of, 69–71
extent of, with reference to context, 43, 57, 58, 61, 67, 68–74
limits on, 57, 58, 68, 69
meaning, 68
tests for determining meaning, defects of, 71–74

GENERALIA SPECIALIBUS NON DEROGANT
statute, repeal of, 3, 69

GOLDEN RULE
absurdity, application in case of, 14, 15, 43, 74, 75, 81
canon of interpretation, 29–31, 169, 170
Driedger, Mr. E. A., on, 82, 83, 169
history, 14–16
meaning, 14, 15, 74

GRAY
casus omissus, on, 26
interpretation defined, 25, 40
statutory interpretation, on, 25–27

GYPSY
meaning (highway obstruction), 62

HANOVER CASE. *See A.-G.* v. *PRINCE ERNEST AUGUSTUS OF HANOVER*

HEADINGS
construction, aids to, 107, 108, 112

HEYDON'S CASE
mischief rule, illustration of, 9, 10, 11, 13, 16, 19

HIRE OR REWARD
meaning, 100

HISTORICAL WORKS
construction, as aids to, 55, 125

HOSPITAL
meaning, 66

IGNORING
words in statute, 43, 84, 90–92

IN MOTION
meaning (machinery), 81

IN PARI MATERIA
statute—
ambiguity and, 128
construction, as aid to, 18, 50, 127–129
context of statute includes, 18, 50, 128

IN THE VICINITY OF
meaning (airfield), 32, 84, 167

INCLUDES
meaning, 103

INCONSISTENCY
absurdity, whether synonymous with, 75, 81–83, 170

INDECENT
meaning (disturbance in church), 61, 62

INDUSTRIAL BUILDING
meaning (income tax), 64

INSULTING BEHAVIOUR
meaning, 53, 55, 110, 157

INTENTION OF PARLIAMENT
analysis of meanings, 34–40
judicial statements as to, 36–40
prevention of injustice, whether consideration relevant, 36
principal situations involving, 35, 36
statutory words, derived from meaning of, 36, 38, 39, 40, 41

INTERNATIONAL CONVENTIONS
statutes implementing, construction of, 130, 139–141

INTERNATIONAL LAW
presumption that Parliament acts in accordance with, 28, 140, 143

INTERPRETATION
Act of 1889 . . . 6, 42
suggested revision, 163
amendment contrasted, 32, 33
canons of, 27–33
Lord Reid, *dicta* of, 29–31
mischief rule, 51
Prof. R. M. Dworkin, views of, 27–29
rules and principles contrasted, 27–29
clauses as aids to construction, 103, 104
draftsman, problems of, 11–13, 170
meaning, 40, 41
different kinds of, 56–60
Gray on, 25, 40
rectification contrasted, 32, 33
statutory, generally. *See* STATUTORY INTERPRETATION
subordinate legislation, 7
Law Commission, on, 162*n*.

JUDICIAL NOTICE
matters known to "well-informed people", 56, 122
ordinary meaning of statutory words, of, 54, 57
decisions as to, binding precedents, 55
previous state of law, as to, 56, 122
public Acts, of, 5

LAND
meaning, 120

LAW COMMISSION
Courts, role of, 164–168
legislative proposals, 2, 156–164

LEGISLATIVE HISTORY. *See also* PARLIAMENT
construction, as aid to, 129 *et seq.*
foreign courts, practice of, 132, 133, 138
suggested changes, 141
international conventions, statutes implementing, 130, 139–141
meaning, 129
Parliamentary materials, 50, 130, 134–136
plain meaning rule and, 132–134
pre-parliamentary materials, 129, 136–139
general objectives, admissibility as to, 137–139
meaning of particular provision, inadmissibility as to, 137–139
treaties, statutes implementing, 130, 139–141

LITERAL MEANING. *See also* LITERAL RULE
construction of statutes, use in, 59, 60
natural or ordinary meaning, as, 59

LITERAL RULE
Blackstone on, 19, 20
historical setting as aid, conflict with, 123
history, 8, 13, 14–16
mischief rule, relationship with, 13, 164, 169, 170
social legislation and, 164, 165

LITERARY SOURCES
construction, as aids to, 55, 125

LONG TITLE
statute, of. *See* TITLE

MARGINAL NOTES
construction, as aids to, 107, 108, 113
contemporanea expositio, as, 127

MARRY
meaning, 100

MAXWELL
contemporanea expositio, on, 126
noscitur a sociis, on, 118
punctuation, omission of, on, 114
repugnancy of sections, on, 101
retrospective operation, on, 155*n*.
statutory interpretation, on, 20, 42

MEANS
meaning, 103

MECHANICALLY PROPELLED VEHICLE
meaning, 67

MENS REA
presumption that statutory crime requires, 58, 135, 143, 163

MINES
meaning, 124

MISCHIEF RULE
Blackstone on, 19, 21
canon of interpretation, as, 51
classic statement of, 9
context, account to be taken of general, 18, 48–52
ejusdem generis rule, overrides, 117, 118
Heydon's case, 9, 10, 11, 13, 16, 19
historical setting as aid, conflict with, 123
history, 9, 13, 14, 16
literal rule, relationship with, 13, 164, 169, 170
strict construction of penal statute, conflict with, 63

MISTAKES. *See also* CASUS OMISSUS
additions, not rectifiable by, 92, 93
Courts, attitude to, 166
drafting errors, whether rectifiable, 86–88, 167
generally, 43, 84, *et seq.*

NATIONAL ORIGINS
meaning, 62, 63

NATURAL MEANING. *See* ORDINARY MEANING; ORDINARY MEANING RULE

NOSCITUR A SOCIIS
construction, maxim of, 115, 118
meaning, 118

OBJECT OF STATUTE. *See also* MISCHIEF RULE
context, account to be taken of general, 18, 48–52
Hanover case, 48
Sussex Peerage case, 13, 14, 44, 132

OBSTRUCTION
meaning (highways), 66

OFFENCE
any, meaning, 52
committing an, meaning, 78, 84
political character, of, meaning, 56, 57, 123

OFFENDER
meaning, 78, 79, 84

OFFERS FOR SALE
meaning, 11, 65, 164, 167

OMISSION. *See* CASUS OMISSUS

"OR" AND "AND"
meaning, 89, 90

ORDINARY MEANING
rule. *See* ORDINARY MEANING RULE
secondary meaning—
absurdity, avoiding, 14, 15, 43, 74–84, 101. *See also* ABSURDITY; GOLDEN RULE
choice between, 43, 74–84
distinguished, 58, 59
words, of, 1, 56
absurdity, producing, 14, 15, 43, 74, 75
choice between—
ordinary and technical meaning, 43, 61, 64–67
ordinary meanings, 61–64
secondary meaning and, 74–84
context, in, 43, 44, 45, 61 *et seq.* *See also* STATUTES
evidence as to, admissibility, 53
judicial notice of, 54, 55, 57
question of fact, 52, 57

ORDINARY MEANING RULE. *See also* LITERAL RULE; ORDINARY MEANING
application of, 1, 13, 43, 53, 61
canon of interpretation, 29

OUSTER OF JURISDICTION
presumption against, 147

PARLIAMENT
absurdity not intended by. *See* ABSURDITY
Acts of. *See* STATUTES
committee reports, 50, 136
debates inadmissible, 50, 55, 135
drafts of Bill, 135
draftsman and problems of interpretation, 11–13, 170
Hansard, 136
intention of. *See* INTENTION OF PARLIAMENT
international law, acts in conformity with, 28, 140, 143
legislative history as aid to construction, 129 *et seq.* *See also* LEGISLATIVE HISTORY
Parliamentary materials as aids to construction, 50, 130, 134, 136
pre-parliamentary materials as aids to construction, 129, 136–139

PENAL STATUTE
presumption of strict construction, 2, 10, 19, 52, 63, 77, 144, 150–152, 162

PLAIN MEANING RULE. *See also* ORDINARY MEANING; ORDINARY MEANING RULE
legislative history and, 132–134

PREAMBLE
construction of, 19, 107, 108–111
ambiguity, in Case of, 109–111, 133, 134, 140
context, in, 47, 48, 50
meaning, 109

PRECEDENT
binding, whether applicable to statutory interpretation, 30, 42, 168

PREMISES
meaning, 66, 67, 100, 145

PRESUMPTIONS
absurdity, against, 2, 15, 144
accused not to be deprived of general defences, 58, 150
advancement of statutory purpose, of, 52, 144
burden of proof, 142
consolidating statute does not change law, 131, 135, 146

PRESUMPTIONS—*contd.*
general application, of, 143
generally, 142–144
linguistic, 144
mens rea required for statutory crime, 58, 135, 143, 163
no-one should profit from own wrong, 28, 143
ouster of jurisdiction, against, 147
policies of clear statement, expressed as, 144
re-enactment, effect on judicial construction, 146, 147
retrospective operation of statutes, against, 153, 162
revenue statutes, as to, 152
same word bears same meaning in same statute, 144
statutory powers exercised reasonably, that, 143
strict construction of penal statutes, 2, 10, 19, 52, 63, 77, 144, 150–152, 162
unclear changes in law, against, 26, 28, 31, 145–153
unjust or inconvenient result, against, 2, 15, 144
unnecessary change in common law, against, 26, 28, 31, 145
use in doubtful cases, for, 143
vested rights, against interference with, 147, 148, 149, 153

PROPERTY
meaning, 33, 69, 86

PROVISO
main clause, relationship to, 104–107

PUBLIC
section of, meaning, 72–74

PUNCTUATION
construction, as aid to, 107, 114, 115
contemporanea expositio, as, 127

RECTIFICATION
interpretation contrasted, 32, 33
statutes, of, 43, 94–98, 168

RENTON COMMITTEE
drafting, on, 170, 171
report on the preparation of legislation, 2, 156, 158 *et seq.*

REPAIRING
meaning (railways), 55, 63

REPRESENTATION
meaning (will), 44, 45, 58, 84

REPUGNANCY
absurdity, whether synonymous with, 75, 81–83, 170

REPUGNANCY—*contd.*
enacting parts of same statute, in, 101
avoidance of, 101, 102

REVENUE STATUTES
presumptions as to, 152

ROYAL MARRIAGE ACT, 1772
interpretation of, 44
territorial extent, 4, 13, 14

RULE OF RANK
construction, as aid to, 115, 119

SECONDARY MEANING
absurdity, avoiding, 14, 15, 43, 74, 75, 101
ordinary meaning—
distinguished, 58, 59
words of, choice between, 74–84
reading in of statutory words and, 85

"SHALL"
meaning, 45

SHORT TITLE
statute, of. *See* TITLE

SIDE-NOTES
construction, as aid to, 107, 108, 113

SINGLE WOMAN
meaning, 70

STATUTES
"always speaking", deemed to be, 45–47
change of meaning with time, etc., 45–47
codifying, 5
commencement, 3
consolidating, 5
earlier statutes *in pari materia*, 128, 129
presumption that law not changed by, 131, 135, 146
construction. *See* CONSTRUCTION
context, 44–52, 170
A.-G. v. *Prince Ernest Augustus of Hanover*, 42, 43, 47, 48, 51
date of statute, relevance of, 45–47, 123
general words, extent of, 43, 57, 58, 61, 67, 68–74
meaning of word in, 44, 45
object of statute, 48–52
ordinary meaning, in—
ascertainment of, 44, 45, 51
choice between meanings, 61–64
place of provision in statute, 49
preamble, 47, 48, 50
enacting parts of same, 99 *et seq.*
in pari materia, 18, 50, 127–129
interpretation act, 6, 42, 163

STATUTES—*contd.*
judicial notice, 5
mistakes, 43, 84 *et seq.*
object of. *See* MISCHIEF RULE; OBJECT OF STATUTE
obsolete, 3
other parts of same, construction of, 99, 107 *et seq.*
other statutes—
construction, as guide to, 30, 129, 168
in pari materia, 18, 50, 127–129
penal, presumption of strict construction, 2, 10, 19, 52, 63, 77, 144, 150–152, 162
private, 4, 5
public, 4, 5
Queen's Printer's copy, proof by, 5
reading words in and out of, 43, 84 *et seq.*
rectification, 43, 94–98, 168
remedial, 5, 6
repeal, 3
express, 3
generalia specialibus non derogant, 3, 69
implied, 3
repealing enactment, of, 4
revenue, presumptions as to, 152
territorial extent, 3, 4
words—
addition of, 33, 43, 86, 88, 92, 94
express provisions excluding, 93 94
mistake not rectifiable by, 92, 93
alteration, 43, 84, 88–90, 92, 94
"and" and "or," 89, 90, 94
ignoring, 43, 84, 90–92
necessarily implied in, 32, 84–86, 88, 90
reading in and out of, 43, 84 *et seq.*

STATUTORY INTERPRETATION. *See also* CONSTRUCTION
academic lawyers, role of, 164, 168–170
Austin on, 23–25
Bentham on, 20–23
binding precedents not applicable generally, 30, 42, 168
Blackstone on, 17–20, 65
canons of interpretation, 27–33
construction, possible distinctions, 18
Courts, role of, comments on, 164–168
European influence, 170, 171
evidence, 52–56
fringe meaning, 57, 67, 71
generality of words, limits on, 43, 57, 58, 61, 67, 68–74
Gray on, 25–27
history, 8–16
introduction, 1–7

STATUTORY INTERPRETATION—*contd.*
jurists, views of, 17–27
Law Commission, proposals as to, 2, 156–164
Maxwell on, 20, 42
meaning of interpretation, 40, 41
different kinds of, 56–60
"problems of the penumbra," 57
rules of, 43, 61 *et seq.*

STRADLING v. *MORGAN*
general words, interpretation of, 68
restrictive interpretation, example of, 8, 9, 11, 50

SUBORDINATE LEGISLATION
interpretation, 7
Law Commission on, 162*n.*

SUSSEX PEERAGE CASE
object of statute, 13, 14, 44, 132

TECHNICAL MEANING
rule. *See* TECHNICAL MEANING RULE
words, of—
admissibility of evidence, 53, 54
choice between ordinary meaning and, 43, 61, 64–67
practice of conveyancers, 125, 126

TECHNICAL MEANING RULE. *See also* TECHNICAL MEANING
application of, 1, 13, 43
statute dealing with particular trade or business, 1, 53, 65

TERMS OF ART. *See also* TECHNICAL MEANING; TECHNICAL MEANING RULE
Blackstone on, 65

TEXTBOOKS
construction, as aids to, 54, 122

TITLE
long—
ambiguity and, 109–111, 133, 134, 140
construction of, 107, 108–111
contemporanea expositio, as, 127
meaning, 108
short, construction of, 107, 108, 111

TREATIES
statutes implementing, 130, 139–141

UNREASONABLE
absurd, whether synonymous with, 83

UT RES MAGIS VALEAT QUAM PEREAT
canon of construction, 19, 20

VISCOUNTESS RHONDDA'S CLAIM
general words, limits on, 68

WILLIS, PROF. J.
statutory interpretation, on, 169, 170

WINDING-UP
in the course of, meaning, 49, 112

WORDS AND PHRASES
accident, 58, 59, 62, 70
action in Admiralty Court, 45
"and" and "or", 89, 90
bar (intoxicating liquor), 55, 104
crawling boards, 65
cremation, 64, 164
driving or attempting to drive, 27, 59, 71, 72
engine, 10, 11, 52
estate and interest for lives (1584), 9
fettling, 65
floors (factories), 119
gypsy, 62
hire or reward, 100
hospital, 66
in motion (machinery), 81
in the vicinity of (airfield), 32, 84, 167
includes, 103
indecent (disturbance in church), 61, 62
industrial building (income tax), 64
insulting behaviour, 53, 55, 110, 157
irrevocable settlement, 125

WORDS AND PHRASES—*contd.*
land, 120
marry, 100
means, 103
mechanically propelled vehicle, 67
member of family, 46, 99, 100
mines, 124
national origins, 62, 63
obstruction (highways), 66
offence—
any, 52
committing an, 78, 84
political character, of, 56, 57, 123
offender, 78, 79, 84
offers for sale, 11, 65, 164, 167
"or" and "and", 89, 90
premises, 66, 67, 100, 145
property, 33, 69, 86
pruned or lopped, 54
raising materials, 69
receivers and treasurers (1560), 8
repairing (railways), 55, 63
representation (will), 44, 45, 58, 84
section of the public, 72–74
shall, 45
single woman (affiliation), 70
unsworn evidence of children, proviso as to, 59, 60, 85
winding-up, in the course of, 49, 112
wounding, 10, 151

WOUNDING
meaning, 10, 151